Kyle Oliver
The Next Horizon

Kyle became intrigued when he read of the trek Lewis and Clark made two decades before, and desires to experience what they had, while seeing his new homeland from east to west.

James Oliver Virmala

FORWARD

Native foods that helped feed the Lewis and Clark expedition

Jerusalem Artichoke

When leaving the Mandan village Sacagawea showed the expedition how to find the Jerusalem artichoke by digging them with a sharp stick. Its roots have tubers that resemble ginger root. The tubers have a slightly sweet flavor and can be eaten raw, cooked, or pickled.

They are in the sunflower family, have large leaves and grow from four to nine feet-high. The tubers were taken back to Europe by early explorers and planted. They have no connection to artichokes, nor Jerusalem.

Camas

Camas were one of the root plants that the expedition ate during their trek. They can be good or poisonous. The good ones have blue flowers and leaves that look somewhat like an onion. The tubers that grow on the roots are edible and have a taste similar to sweet potatoes. Another version with white flowers is poisonous, therefore it is best to pick them while they're still in bloom to ensure getting the good camas.

The hungry expedition of Lewis and Clark were fed the good ones by the Shoshone and suffered from stomach pain and flatulence from overeating.

ACKNOWLEDGMENTS

The pioneers that faced the rigors and dangers while traveling west looking for a better life for their families. The only reward for many was seeing the unspoiled land they traveled through.

CONTENTS

BOOKS BY THE AUTHOR

Oli's Gold Book One
Search For Oli's Gold Book Two
Return To Oli's Gold Book Three
To Be A Mountain Man
Trouble On The Kansas Plains
Frontier Justice
Return Of The Mountain Man
The Tall Man
The Prospector
The Green Valley
Twilight Of The Mountain Man
The Mother Lode
Quest Of The Mountain Man
Journey's End
Rufus Pike
Rufus And The Pup
The Winding Trail Home
Rufus The Lost Years
The Kankakee Kid
Bogus Island
Tyler Tomas The Brothers War
War of 1812 The Choice

CHAPTER ONE

The slim man hardly dared to breathe as he stalked his prey. Kyle Oliver had spotted the white tail deer grazing on the fall grass at the edge of an opening. The 20 year-old man raised his French-made Charleville long gun and slowly pulled the hammer to full cock. As he breathed out, Kyle squeezed the trigger. There was a flash of the prime, which ignited the powder behind the .69 caliber ball sending it streaking between the trees, toward the animal.

Blinded by the smoke, he did not see the deer leap and bound into the trees. Kyle's blond, shoulder-length hair caught in the branches as he ran forward, ducking between the trees. Pulling his British flintlock pistol from his waistband, he searched for signs of the animal. As he reached the place where he'd seen the deer, he found the small clearing empty.

Then the slim man spotted blood on the mature fall grass. There were deep hoof marks where the deer had leaped ahead, drops of blood marking the direction it had run. Confident that he had a good hit, Kyle put the pistol back into his waist band and took time to reload the Charleville.

Moving into the trees, he spotted the downed deer only 25 paces from where it was grazing. Prodding it with the barrel of the muzzle loader confirmed that the animal was dead. Kyle breathed a sigh of relief. Lying in the fall leaves was enough meat to last him a few weeks. The cold nights would help preserve the venison that he didn't make into jerky.

Dragging the deer to the edge of the trees, Kyle headed back beyond the place where he'd fired to get his dapple-gray horse. It was pulling at the grass, uninterested in the returning hunter. "We have work to do," Kyle told the horse. "I have been living off nuts and cattail roots for days."

Kyle was in a valley south of the Blue Ridge Mountains of Virginia. Since leaving Vergennes, Vermont after the war of 1812 ended, he had changed his plans about going east to Boston, where his good friend Christopher was located. Instead, he'd chosen to search for a woman who had lived in a small cabin.

Karen Green was her name. While hunting close to the logging camp he'd been working at, he'd come across the place while tracking some deer. She'd been there alone while her husband was with the Vermont militia.

While attracted to her, Kyle had realized she was off limits. It had been obvious that Mrs. Green was having a tough time getting by and this gave him the excuse to return a couple of times, and each visit he'd had supplies she might use.

The last time he'd seen her, Karen had just received notice that her husband was ill. Illness was a common occurrence due to crowded conditions in the militia winter quarters. Helpless to do anything more than be a sympathetic ear, Kyle had listened and then left the cabin.

Shortly after, Kyle had signed onto the *Eagle*, a ship built in the Vermont shipyard and commissioned to join the fleet tasked with keeping the British out of Lake Champlain. This was done after some soul searching due to the slim man being from England.

Shortly after signing up, the *Eagle* engaged in the Battle of Plattsburgh where the American fleet fought and won against the superior British fleet. Surviving the carnage of the battle with only a couple of wounds, the slim man was discharged after the decommissioning of most of the American ships on Lake Champlain.

Unable to get the lone woman out of his mind, Kyle had made one final visit to the cabin in the woods and found Mrs. Green gone and a note on the table addressed to him. It said that her husband had died and that she had gone to Virginia to be with family. It did not say where in Virginia she'd gone.

The feeling of loss was severe in the slim man, and he'd then left a note to anyone who might know where Karen had gone, to send the information to Boston, in care of Christopher at The Raven. It would be a long shot, but it was an act of a desperate man. So much so that it had brought Kyle to the mountains and valleys of Virginia.

After spending the summer unsuccessfully searching from town to town, he'd run out of money and hope of finding her, and was returning to Boston to find solace from his longtime friend Chrisopher.

The friendship had begun in the small fishing village in England where Kyle had grown up with Christopher, or Kit as he was called then. As they got older their goals changed. The slim man had had his whole life planned, fishing in the channel and building a life with a pretty, strawberry blond girl named Rebecca.

Kit had lived a life of charming the local girls and earning what was needed at a fish market. He dreamt of bigger things and was forever sharing his dreams with Kyle. Finally, Kit shared a scheme where the two of them would partner up with two men who Kit had met. The two men had claimed that they knew of ships that the four of them could join and become privateers. Soon they would be rich from the sale of the cargo from captured ships.

Kyle had had the boat they'd needed to get to France, and during a night of too much ale they'd finally broke down the slim man's resistance. Unknown to the two young men, they sailed away from the village with stolen items aboard Kyle's yoal, making any return to the village impossible. Once they landed in France, the two strangers stole the yoal and left the two exhausted young men sleeping on the beach.

Needing work and unable to return to the village they eventually ended up working on a ship bound for America carrying brandy. Kyle had chosen to work making additional transits to France while Kit, now called Chrisopher, met and married a woman whose father had money from interests he had on the Boston wharf.

Now after a summer of searching for Karen Green, Kyle was out of money and was forced to give up. His only option was to head back to Boston. There he could get work on another ship, and with the war being over the chances of it being taken prize by a Royal warship would not be a concern. Pirates would be, but a ship with a few cannons could defend themselves.

Expertly, Kyle slit and gutted the deer. Placing the liver and heart onto a windfall, he returned to the task of skinning the animal. Giving the twelve-inch blade a couple of swipes on a whetstone, he dropped the stone back into his shooting bag and knelt to start.

Shards from the bark on the tree next to him hit his beard-covered cheek as he knelt, and then there was the sound of a shot! Dropping his knife, the slim man leaped forward and rolled, coming up next to his Charleville.

With his long gun at the ready, Kyle looked for the shooter. "What the hell are you doing shooting deer in our valley?" the unseen assailant shouted.

Searching for the source of the voice, Kyle replied, "Ain't nobody owns the deer!"

"You a damn Brit?" the shooter snarled. "That gives me two reasons to shoot you."

Through the trees, Kyle caught a slight movement and fired. There was a yelp. Lying alongside the windfall, the slim man reloaded the Charleville. Hoping to prevent the shooter from rushing him, he snarled, "Come at me you bastard! I got a pistol aching to put a ball in you!"

The sounds reaching Kyle were of the

shooter running away. Then the man shouted, "I'm getting my brother, and we will hunt you down and kill you, you son-of-a-bitch!"

"I will be long gone when you get back," Kyle whispered.

Within a couple of minutes the slim man had the deer tied across the back of the saddle, the Charleville and his knife in their places with the reins in one hand and the liver in the other, he was putting distance between himself and the angry shooter.

Since getting to America, Kyle had liked the idea that nobody owned the wildlife, and anyone could hunt them. Evidently, he had just met someone who didn't agree with that. All the slim man knew was that he needed the meat.

The fall days were shorter, and it was almost dark when he finally stopped near a small stream flowing through a stand of cedar. It was off the main trail, and it would be unlikely that any pursuers would spot him through the dense branches.

Kyle hadn't dared to stopped anywhere to clean up and finish skinning the deer. Kneeling next to the stream, he washed the dried blood off his hands. The horse came up beside him and drank thirstily. Shaking the water from his hands, the slim man took the reins, led the dapple gray near some sparse grass and, dropped the reins.

As he pulled the deer and other gear off the animal, Kyle said, "This will have to do for you. I got no grain, and I know you don't like venison."

The night air was quickly getting cold as the slim man finished skinning the deer. His stomach ached with hunger, but the venison hadn't had a chance to cool, and he wanted to get the night air to the meat.

Hanging the quartered animal in the tree branches, he dragged the head and other waste downstream, well away from his camp. By the time he got back it was full dark. He had left the liver in the folds of the hide. It would make a fine meal.

The horse had worked its way down the stream in search of grass. Throughout the summer, he'd found out that the dapple-gray would stay close to the camp. Most often he'd put it on picket just before going to sleep. Tonight, the sparse grass had forced it to graze a little farther away.

Collecting wood as he walked to get the horse, Kyle led it back to camp. Tying it to a cedar branch, he dumped the wood and dug the flint and steel from his shooting bag. Shortly, he had the fire going and Kyle had saved a stick to broil the liver.

The feeble light from the fire lit up the hide and Kyle dug through to get the liver. His mouth began to water as he anticipated the tasty meal. Feeling between the folds of the hide, he didn't find the liver. Cussing to himself, the slim man slowly unfolded the hide and then exclaimed, "What the hell!" The liver was gone!

Frustrated, Kyle shook out the hide and found nothing. A fox or some other varmint had visited the camp while he was hauling the head and stuff away and stole the liver. Looking at the horse he snapped, "Weren't you watching?"

The animal ignored him and stood half-dozing in the chilly night air. Tears of anger stinging his eyes, Kyle went to the quarters hanging in the cedars and removed a tenderloin. Returning to the fire, he sat broiling it and muttering.

If it had been a coyote or wolf, the horse would have alerted him. Something small like a fox, fisher, or even racoon would not have startled the animal. The meat was tender and satisfied him. It had barely gotten hot clean through before he began to tear at it ravenously and gulped down the poorly chewed venison.

With the meal finished, Kyle allowed the fire to burn down as he rolled out his blanket on the ground cloth. The air continued to get cooler, which would help preserve the meat. As a precaution, the slim man hung the quarters a little higher in the trees.

With only a few coals still smoldering

in the fire, he lay under his blanket. The Charleville lay under the edge of the blanket, his pistol within easy reach under the saddle which he used for a pillow.

Kyle lay staring into the dark. He realized it was time to give up the search for Karen. It had been a foolish thing to attempt to begin with, but the desire to find her and make sure she was okay had been strong. And then there were the other hopes of something more.

When he'd left Vergennes, he had over a hundred dollars, plenty of supplies, and a degree of confidence that he would find her. The slim man had talked to the folks at the trading post where she had purchased supplies and was disappointed at how little they knew about her. All they knew was that there was a sister-in-law named Ann, and that when they left they'd joined another family and had gone south.

The money hadn't lasted nearly as long as he'd hoped. Kyle had even discontinued having the dapple gray shoed and gave up coffee and tobacco. Finally, down to the bare staples, he had made the decision to return to Boston. There, with the help of his friend Christopher, he hoped to earn enough money to board his horse and feed himself over the winter. The pleasures of drink and ladies would have to be avoided.

One thing Kyle would not do was accept

charity from his friend. If he could not afford something, he would rather do without. Maybe a night or two when he got there could be considered as Christopher being hospitable, but after that he'd sleep in the livery if he had to and clean stalls to pay his way.

Sometime in the night, the slim man fell asleep. He dreamt he was back in England, working on his yoal and waiting for the tide to come in. The seagulls were flying overhead, then the sounds of their cries changed to almost a snorting sound. Then he was awake.

The eastern sky was just showing the first signs of coming morning. In the scant light, Kyle saw the horse stomping and snorting while looking into the trees at something near the meat. "What the hell," he breathed, reaching for the pistol under his saddle.

Then he saw it, the dark body of a raccoon up in the cedars, chewing on one of the front quarters. Cocking the .75 caliber British flintlock pistol, he took his time aiming at the animal and pulled the trigger.

The flintlock recoiled in his hand, the smoke and fire from the barrel obscuring the target, causing him to lose sight of it. There was a thump and the sound of leaves rustling. "I might have missed you, you bugger, but you'll not be coming back to my camp for a meal."

The flash of the burning powder still left spots in front of his eyes as the slim man tossed off his blankets and picked up the long gun. There was frost on the leaves, and he could see his breath. Pulling on his boots, Kyle hurried over to the cedars with the quarters hanging.

The dapple gray snorted, and the slim man replied, "I agree. We had an intruder."

Then to his surprise he saw the raccoon lying about 20 feet away from the cedars with the meat. He had managed to get a ball into it and the animal had gone only a few yards before dying. Prodding the raccoon with the Charleville barrel, he found that the ball had done its job. Kyle knew that a wounded raccoon could be vicious, and he didn't need any wounds from their filthy teeth.

Lifting it by the tail, Kyle headed back to his camp. Holding it up for the horse to see, he said, "It may have gotten the liver, but now I'll have a fine meal from its carcass and a skin to sell."

Dropping the animal near the cold fire, the slim man took the horse off the picket so it could wander and find grass. He then headed into the cedars to relieve himself. On the way back, Kyle collected some dead branches for his fire. Breaking them up, he got the fire going.

His morning drink for some time had

been hot water. Taking a pot to the stream, he drank and then filled it. Placing the pot near the small fire, he picked up the raccoon and walked a short distance out from his camp and skinned the animal.

The ball had struck the raccoon behind the ribcage and had ripped through the intestines. It was a smelly job preparing the animal for roasting. Choosing to remove the meat from the raccoon to make a quicker meal, the slim man got out the frying pan.

Using fat from the deer, Kyle fried the raccoon in his blackened pan. The gamey meat was satisfying as he tore at the chunks. He used the salt sparingly to season it. Most of what he had left was used to preserve the hides.

It was midmorning when the meal was eaten, and the horse was packed with his gear. The deer and raccoon hides were folded behind the saddle, with the venison quarters wrapped in his flytarp and hung on each side.

He worked his way back to the main trail leading the horse. There were no fresh tracks of two or more riders, and Kyle was confident that other than taking a shot at him and shouting threats, those he'd fought with the day before had given up.

Swinging into the saddle, the slim man continued toward the Blue Ridge Mountains. He hoped to run across a trading post or mercantile where he could do some dickering for supplies. Wrapped in a small piece of canvas was the last of the raccoon meat and, if necessary, it would be his supper.

The smell of smoke let him know that he was getting close to folks. Shortly he came by a small farm with the house built of logs. There were also outbuildings made of rough-cut boards. There was a man in the pumpkin patch with a hoe chopping at the weeds.

Stopping the horse, Kyle tied it to a split rail fence and called to the man, "You folk have some kind of a store near here?"

Pulling a hanky from his pocket, the man mopped his brow as he walked toward the slim man. Leaning on the hoe on the other side of the fence, he said, "I didn't hear you. The cannons left me near deaf from the war."

Smiling, Kyle said, "I understand. Mine still ring from the noise."

The man's brow furled, and he asked, "Were you on the British or American side?"

"The American," the slim man told him. "I was on the *Eagle* in the battle of Plattsburgh."

"Now what is it that you wanted to know?" the man asked.

"I'm looking for some kind of store," Kyle told him. "I have some hides and venison I want to trade."

"Venison?" the man asked.

"I got a whole deer less the backstraps," the slim man replied.

"Backstraps is the best part," the man said, sounding like he had just begun to dicker.

"It was shot yesterday and cooled overnight," Kyle told him. "Now, about the store?"

"Just hold on there," the man replied. "You wouldn't be interested in some side meat?"

"That I would," Kyle said. "I am hoping to trade for a few necessaries and side meat would be one of them."

"You are a half-day's ride to the nearest trading post," the man told him. "That venison will be two days-old by that time."

Rubbing his face to hide his smile, the slim man replied, "It should be aged just about right by then."

"Why don't you take your horse over to the house and tell ma to give it a bit of grain after you water it," the man said. "I got to finish the hoeing and I'll be right along." Then before turning he said, "My name is George."

"You got another hoe?" Kyle asked.

"Ma's hoe is near the front door," the man replied.

Ma was a pleasant woman and immediately went around to one of the sheds to get some grain. There was a pump near the cabin, and using a wooden bucket the slim man watered his horse. When the woman came back, he said, "My names Kyle."

"Mine's Rose," she told him.

"Rose, I am going to borrow your hoe and help George in the garden," he told her.

The woman just smiled and nodded as she started to feed the grain to the horse. Taking the hoe, Kyle joined the man and together they worked up and down the rows of pumpkins. "What we don't eat goes to the hogs," George told him.

"They look ready to pick," the slim man said.

"This is the last hoeing," the man replied. "I start picking in a couple of days. No sense in leaving the weeds to fight with next year."

In nearby fields Kyle could see turnips, cabbage, carrots, and some beets. They would do a good job filling his root cellar for hearty winter soups. Two hours later they were finished, and George mopped his face again.

"Ma's got supper on," the man said. "Put venison in the shed behind the house and your horse in the barn. There's hay in the loft."

In the barn he saw two milk cows, a team of horses, and some young stock. After stripping the gear off the animal, Kyle gave them all hay along with his horse. When he'd put the venison in the shed, the slim man had seen a lot of smoked meat hanging in the rafters. As he stepped out of the barn he could hear and smell other hogs in a pen a short distance away.

Supper was a soup made with new potatoes and ham in a milk broth. Slices of graham bread and a dish of butter were in the middle of the table to be eaten with the soup. After a short prayer, the three of them dug into the meal.

"The soup is very good," Kyle told Rose. She just smiled and nodded.

Apparently eating was a serious business for the old couple. Not a word was spoken until the final drop of soup was eaten and the final bite of bread was swallowed. Then using his hanky, George wiped his mouth and sat back. Rose began to collect the dishes.

"Well now," the old man began. "Your venison would save me having to go hunting and I could get right to harvesting my gardens."

"I will need it for my meals," Kyle told him. "I'm headed for Boston and that will keep me on the road for at least another month, maybe a bit more."

"Every September we get the false summer with some mighty warm weather," George replied. "That venison won't hold through that. Also, I noticed that your horse is about done in. You got mountains to go over, and the extra weight might just do it."

Kyle fought to hide any reaction, but

the condition of his horse was one of his worries. Poor feed and carrying all his gear while being ridden was taking its toll. Not being shoed also could be dangerous while crossing the poor roads over the mountains. A split hoof would be the end of the animal.

Realizing the old man was harboring some kind of offer, the slim man asked. "What do you recommend I do?"

George heaved himself up in his chair and gave the slim man a serious look. "That there deer adds over 100 pounds on your poor horse. It will take you a couple weeks before the smell of it is so strong that you'll be leaving it alongside the trail for varmints to eat."

"If I salt it down, and wrap it in a tarp, it might save longer," Kyle suggested.

"Son, the weight is still on the horse," the old man replied.

"I guess I'll have to lead the animal," the slim man suggested.

"Or," George said, holding up a finger. "You could trade it for side meat. Twenty pounds of smoked and salted side meat will take you to Boston and back."

Now the slim man figured the old man was stretching things a bit, but it would take him most of the way to Boston. "A hundred pounds of fine venison for twenty pounds of side meat," Kyle replied, trying to look doubtful.

"The side meat is for you, and being a caring man, I would throw in a little grain to get your horse over the mountains," George offered.

It just made sense what the old man had pointed out. Also, it would save using the last of his salt. "I keep the deer hide on this deal," Kyle said.

Reaching out the old man shook on the deal and then turned to his wife. "Rose, we got to get the deer salted down tonight."

With the sounds of his wife processing the deer in the shed, George and Kyle sat on the front porch and chewed some of the old man's tobacco. Suddenly the old man asked, "What brought you to being on the *Eagle* during the war? Your accent is pure British."

"Of no fault of mine, I got myself in trouble in England. Unable to go back, I got a berth on an American ship the *Spencer*. After a couple trips between America and France we were seized by two British warships. They were taking us into a British-controlled port in Canada. Being from England and serving on an American ship, I knew I'd be impressed into the Royal navy."

"I heard about that happening," George said. "They also impressed lots of Americans when they seized ships."

"As it happened an American friend and I went over the side while anchored in the St. Lawrence River. Quick as a wink the

British classified us as deserters and put posters all over Canada offering a reward. I kept ahead of them and then ended up trapping for a winter in Canada. With the money I got from the furs I managed to make my way into the United States. One thing led to another, and I ended up fighting for America on the *Eagle*."

It was getting dark, and George stood up. "I am glad you were on our side," he said. "Sounds like Ma's about done. You're welcome to sleep in the barn. I am tuckered out and got to start early tomorrow."

"Thanks for everything," Kyle called after him. The old man just waved and continued into the cabin.

While spreading his blankets in the hay loft, the slim man thought, *I no longer have the deer. I haven't seen any side meat, nor have I gotten any grain.*

With a full belly and a dry place to sleep, it was full light when Kyle woke. He could hear someone moving around below in the barn. Quickly, he rolled up his blanket and climbed down the ladder with it under one arm.

He came face-to-face with the startled Rose. "I am sorry," she said. "I was trying to be as quiet as I could."

She had a bucket of milk in one hand and a milking stool in the other. Tossing the blanket near his gear, Kyle said, "Let me carry the milk."

Handing it over, the slim man followed her to the house. "I got your porridge saving on the back of the stove," she told him.

Kyle could see George out in the field pulling turnips. Rose had bread rising on the sideboard and a place set for the slim man at the table. "Put the milk on the sideboard next to the bread and have a seat. I'll get you your breakfast."

Soon he was sitting with a bowl of porridge slathered with butter and honey. Next to the bowl was a tall mug of fresh milk. By the smell there was also the promise of coffee. Sitting in the kitchen eating, there was the twinge inside as he remembered his own mother treating him the same way as this woman.

As soon as he finished the meal with the last swallow of the fresh warm milk, she took his bowl and said, "I imagine you got to be going. I got your side meat and grain in the shed. George told me to add a couple turnips for you. He appreciated your help yesterday."

As she put the bread into loave pans, he thanked her and headed to get the dapple-gray and his gear. Almost too soon he had everything set and was ready to ride out. He saw the old man look up and Kyle waved to him. In return George gave a quick wave and bent back to his work.

As he rode away, Kyle realized that most unexpectedly he'd been plunged back into the normal life of a family. It had given him a warm, comfortable feeling. It was a feeling he regretted leaving. The slim man wondered if he'd ever have a home like this old couple had.

He rode along the rough road that followed the trail that the tribes had used for hundreds of years. It was midafternoon when he reached a trading post just off the trail. It had a few cabins scattered about and the promise of some kind of town in the future.

It was also a reminder to Kyle that he had no money and would be unable to purchase anything while there. Whatever the owner gave him for the deer and raccoon skin he'd have to keep for later up the trail. The slim man would need money for ferries and such.

The smell of spices, leather, oiled metal traps, and a pot of coffee on the potbelly stove filled his nostrils as he entered. All were out of his reach. The owner looked up and smiled, "What can I get you?"

Getting right down to business, Kyle asked, "What can you give me for a deer hide and a raccoon skin?"

"Depends on the condition," the man said. "Bring them around back."

Going out, the slim man led the horse around to the back of the trading post. The owner was standing near a shed that reeked of the smell of stored hides. Kyle quickly realized why the man asked him to go around back. All the good smells of the trading post would be fouled by the smell of hides.

There was an old table near the shed and the owner pointed to it. "Put them there."

After looking them over, the man weighed them on a fat-covered scale in the shed. Then looking them over a bit more, he folded them on the fur side in and placed them onto piles of like furs. "Meet me inside," the owner said.

Kyle hoped to get $5 or even a bit more. He had taken care skinning the animals and didn't leave fat and meat on them. He also did not poke any holes while skinning. The only other furs he had to compare were the beaver pelts he'd sold in the past.

Tying the dapple-gray to the chewed-up hitching rail in front of the trading post, he went in. The owner was behind the plank counter with a ledger and stubby pencil. "I just reviewing what I've been getting for deer and raccoon this year." Then he smiled and said, "Sure wish you'd have gotten a bear. They are giving top dollar for those hides."

"What can you give me?" the slim man asked as he looked at the tobacco on the shelf behind the counter.

"I'll give you $2 for the deer hide," the man replied. "At that I will more than likely just break even. For the coon all I can give you is store credit. Often times all I get is fifty cents for the tail. They don't even want the fur."

"So, you'll give me $2 for the deer and fifty cents store credit for the raccoon," Kyle said, feeling anger rising inside.

"No, mister," the owner assured him. "I'll give you a dollar credit in the store for the racoon. I know I'll lose on the deal, but it wouldn't feel right if I didn't do it."

Frustrated and feeling in a weak position to dicker, Kyle said, "Throw in a cup of that coffee and we got a deal."

"I got the feeling that you ain't happy with the deal and if there was anything else I could do, I would. Yes, I will throw in the coffee and help yourself to biscuits in that barrel. It won't go against your store credit."

Brooding near the potbelly stove with a mug of coffee and a tooth-dulling biscuit soaking in the brew, Kyle thought about what he should get on his store credit. The owner had moved to the back of the store and busied himself.

With the coffee drank and a few extra biscuits in his shooting bag, the slim man called to the owner. "How about some tobacco, coffee, beans, and salt for the store credit."

"I can do that," the man said. "Have another cup of coffee while I put it together."

The pot was almost down to grounds, but Kyle squeezed out every drop he could into the mug and drank it while he watched the owner put a small bag of flour, coffee beans, navy beans, and a twist of tobacco in the plank counter.

"That ain't very much tobacco," Kyle told him.

"I am kind of over the credit with the other three," the owner whined, wringing his hands.

The slim man just gave him a cold look. It worked. The man put another twist on the counter. After putting all the items in a larger sack, the owner handed it to Kyle.

"If you're this way again with furs bring them here. I always give the best price in the area," the man said, following the slim man out the door.

His voice still cold, Kyle told him, "I will do that. Can you tell me about the best route over the mountain ridge?"

"There is Flower Gap or Old Piper's Gap just to the north or west of here. There is the freight wagon route just to the east. It is steep, but it's another gap through the Blue Ridge Mountains. By the way," the man chuckled, "you might think Flower Gap is named for the flowers growing there, but it ain't. Years ago, a bag of flour got spilt on it and that's how it got its name. Later it was spelt like a flower, but it's the same gap."

Having little interest in the man's lesson on history, Kyle nodded to him and rode off. He did finally break into a smile thinking about all the ways that places got named.

CHAPTER TWO

Choosing the freighters' road over the Blue Ridge Mountains, Kyle found it to be plenty steep and rugged. Shortly after starting up the trail to the ridge line, the slim man dismounted and led the dapple-gray. He regretted not making camp at the bottom, but the ridge was only a few miles to the top and Kyle had figured it was a better place to start tomorrow rather than having to face the climb first thing.

It was dark when the slim man reached the ridge. He was just over 3,000 feet above sea level and the wind was cold. He was blessed with a full moon and clear skies, making the stars and planets stand out. As far as Kyle was concerned, they were all stars and had guided seafaring men for years.

Stripping the gear off the horse, he let it wander to find forge. Just off the trail he built a small fire, and using water from his leather waterbag, he put some in a pot to heat for coffee. Taking out the blackened frying pan he roasted a few coffee beans, taking care not to burn any. While the coffee brewed, he sliced some side meat into the pan and then sat and enjoyed the sound and smell of the meat frying over the fire.

He was glad that lean times were over for a while, and he even had some money in his shooting bag. Not much, but some money. The anger he had felt earlier during the deal had been worked out on the tough climb up to the ridge. He now felt happy and was looking forward to the coming day. After a satisfying meal, he cut a chew off the twist and sat against a pine and enjoyed the night.

Kyle was half-dozing when he felt a cold, wet nose nuzzled him. Waking he realized it was his horse and water was dripping from its nose. "You found water!" he exclaimed. "Way up here you found water."

Rubbing the side of the animal's head, he said, "I bet you'd like some grain."

After giving the horse a bit of grain and tying the animal to a pine limb, Kyle rolled out his blanket and crawled under. The cold wind tugged at his blanket as he snuggled under it to keep warm. The metal of his Charleville felt icy cold as his hand brushed it.

The sun was just breaking in the east when the slim man woke. He was curled up and shivering. The cold was coming right through his blanket and clothes. He debated between staying put or getting colder by climbing out and making a fire. Nature answered the question for him as Kyle threw back the covers and relieved himself on the other side of the pine.

The leather vest that an Ojibwa woman had made from an elk hide was tied to the back of his saddle. He pulled it loose and put it on. It did cut the wind that had been finding its way through the wool shirt. With trembling hands, he got the fire going. Wishing he had more wood, Kyle poured some more water over the used coffee grounds and put it near the flames to heat.

Untying the horse, the slim man said, "Show me where you found the water."

The animal just stood watching him, probably hoping it had more grain coming. Kyle knew it had walked up the ridge to graze, so he headed that way to find the source of water that the dapple-gray had drunk from the night before.

He found a small stream that flowed from an unknown source further up the ridge. It then flowed over the edge, creating a small waterfall. The horse had followed him and drank while Kyle filled his water bag. He then drank from the stream after washing his face and hands. The water was cold and sweet.

After some less than satisfying coffee and the last two hard biscuits, it was time to get the gear onto the horse and leave the ridge. While putting the saddle on the dapple-gray he looked over its back at the distant mountain that rose on the other side of a wide valley. The broad vista was breathtaking in the early morning. "I could live here," he told the horse.

He had the last of his gear on the horse when the sound of swearing came from below the ridge. There was the crack of a whip and the crunch of steel rims over rock. Leading the horse back to the trail, Kyle saw a freight wagon slowly working its way to the top of the ridge pulled by six mules.

The slim man's face broke into a smile as he remembered hauling ore from Monkton to Vergennes before he joined the war. They had no steep grades like this to climb, but what they had had caused the demise of more than one wagon and team.

Impressed at the lone driver working the reins and the whip, Kyle found a seat on a windfall and watched the slow progress. Finally, the team and wagon reached the summit. The teamster had dirty white hair sticking out from under his drooping hat. His beard was tobacco-stained and his face was deeply tanned and wrinkled.

He climbed down and looked at the slim man. "You sure as hell weren't any help coming up the grade. If you wouldn't mind, I could use some help watering these tired beasts."

It took little encouragement as they unhitched the mules. The animals had been here before and headed for the stream. "If we don't turn them back after watering, the stubborn buggers will forget they have a job to do and will continue up the ridge."

It was an hour before the team was watered, fed some grain and back in their harnesses. The teamster was impressed when he realized that Kyle knew that each of the mules had a position pulling the wagon. After they were hitched the teamster let them rest so they wouldn't be pulling on a full belly of water.

"Could you use some coffee?" the teamster asked.

Kyle wanted to get going, but being short on things like extra coffee, he nodded. "I wouldn't mind some. I'll get wood for a fire."

While waiting for the water to heat, introductions were made. The teamster's name was Dutch. After introducing himself, the slim man asked, "Don't you usually have a partner on a run like this?"

"My partner got himself thrown in jail for busting up a tavern," Dutch told him. "I waited half a day for a replacement and finally had to head out on my own."

"Who works the brake on the way down a steep grade?" Kyle asked.

"Hand of God, I guess," the man said, chuckling. "The mules will hold it back some, but when needed I'll have to wrap the reins around something and pull the brake back for all I got."

"How far you headed?" the slim man asked.

"This freight is heading for a boat on the Susquehanna River in Harrisburg," the man said. "I should be there in just under two weeks."

"That's a long way to drive without a swamper," Kyle told him.

"I change mules the day after tomorrow and they should have someone to replace the bum I left behind," Dutch replied.

"Is Harrisburg on the way to Boston?" the slim man asked.

"I have made that run before," the man said. "It's about halfway."

"Do you mind if I was your swamper until you get a replacement?" Kyle asked. A plan was forming in his mind that might save wear and tear on his horse.

"You know the term, but do you know what the job is?" Dutch asked.

Kyle replied, "I have done the job before hauling ore in Vermont."

"Well then, pull your gear off the horse and throw it onto the wagon," the man told him. "Tie the animal to the back."

When the slim man came back from doing so, the man warned him, "If you don't hold your own, I will leave you on the trail."

The first test was coming off the ridge. The grade on the north side was much easier to navigate. It had been a long time since Kyle had worked a brake and he felt some tension as the wagon started with a jolt and headed down.

The slim man tested it a bit and was satisfied that it was properly adjusted. Between the driver using the mules to hold the wagon back and Kyle on the brake, they made a successful descent from the ridge.

Little did the two men know that in fifteen years one of the freighters would notice a cut just a few miles to the west that would provide an easier route, and he would called it a fancy alternative to the present one. The name would stick, and it would become known as Fancy Gap.

As it worked out, Dutch was more than pleased with Kyle's knowledge and never requested a replacement for the drunk. Two weeks later they drove down the dirt streets of Harrisburg to the docks of the Susquehanna River to offload the freight.

Harrisburg had no evidence of any type of industry. The streets were well-laid out and the place had a country village feel. There were two large keelboats tied up to a wharf, with men offloading cargo using a wide gangways.

As it turned out, the slim man's pay for helping on the run was meals, grain for the horse, and his gear on the wagon. Dutch had told him that if he had requested a swamper, the company would have charged Kyle as a passenger, and he'd have had to pay for any grain the horse got.

While putting the gear back onto the horse, the teamster went into the small, shabby office to check in. The dapple-gray was saddled and Kyle was contemplating ways to get across the Susquehanna when Dutch came back to the wagon.

The slim man reached out to shake the man's hand and the teamster pressed something into his palm. It was five $1 coins. "You did a lot of work for me on this trip, and I figured I owed you something to help with the ferry across the river and some chow for your trip."

Kyle felt awkward at the man giving him money out of his own pocket. Just giving him a ride and saving on the horse would have been more than enough. Wanting to remain even with the teamster, the slim man untied the leather vest from his saddle.

There had been several hills they'd gone over with the cold fall wind hitting them and Kyle had worn his vest. Every time Dutch would comment on how he wished he had such a vest. At one time the vest had meant a lot to the slim man, but time had faded the memories of the Ojibwa woman who had made it, and he had nothing else to give.

"I want you to have this vest, Dutch," the slim man said. "You'll have more need for it than I will, and every time you wear it you will remember the swamper that hitched a ride with you."

Kyle had started to walk away when the teamster stopped him. "Wait a minute before you leave."

Dutch hurried into the shabby office and returned with a piece of paper in his hand. "This here is what they call a recommendation. Give it to the freight office on the east side of the river and they might have an opening going toward Boston."

The gesture humbled the slim man. Nobody had ever given him such a thing. "Thank you, Dutch," Kyle told him and then he hurried away toward the ferry dock.

* * *

It was a dollar for the ferry across the Susquehanna River. Standing at the front of the ferry, Kyle looked up and down the river. The view in both directions was impressive. The wide, slow-moving river was lined with trees with branches drooping towards the water. Rocks were visible protruding from the water. Small, tree-covered islands could be seen, which split the water along each side.

The ferry bumped on the east side dock and the slim man waited while they lowered a plank ramp for the passengers and wagons to disembark. Leading the horse off, he looked for a freighting office. The east side had fewer buildings than the west. One of the larger buildings appeared to be a livery.

Leading the dapple-gray, Kyle headed for its large bay doors. The hostler was at a cluttered desk near what appeared to be a tack room. The sound of the horse's hooves on the plank floor caught his attention.

The stocky man looked over his shoulder and said, "I'll be right with you."

Stepping back outside, Kyle let the animal drink from the water trough. As the horse finished drinking the hostler came over. "You looking to put your horse up here?" the man asked.

"I am," the slim man said. "First, can you tell me where the freight office is?"

"It's about half-mile down the river," the hostler replied. "That's near the wharf that the boats come in on this side of the river."

It made no sense to Kyle that the freight offices wouldn't be across the river from each other. "I will be back shortly," he told the hostler.

Swinging into the saddle, he headed downriver. Two weeks of the saddle lying in the wagon had changed the shape a bit and the slim man squirmed as he rode south, trying to make it feel right. Or maybe it was the two weeks of sitting on the wagon bench.

The freight office on the east side was more impressive. Several wagons were being filled with items carted from the wharf. A man with a ledger book was doing his best to keep track of everything. After some effort, Kyle caught his attention.

"Can you tell me who to talk to about signing on with a freighter?" the slim man asked.

"It certainly wouldn't be me," the man snorted. "Freight company offices are inside."

Kyle wanted to point out that he didn't think it would be him, but instead just shook his head and brought the horse over to the rail. The building had a wide, covered porch. Climbing the two steps to the porch, he looked back. This side was much busier the slim man decided.

There were four offices toward the back with the doors closed. Each had a window so whoever was in the office could look out, or vice versa for those coming in. There was a desk in the front which seemed to guard the remaining desks in the large front room.

The slim man decided to check with

this man first. He was young and seemed pleasant. "Who do I talk to about signing on to a Boston-bound freight wagon?"

"Boston," the young man said, smiling. "I have always wanted to go to Boston."

"Yes, it is worth the visit," Kyle agreed. "Now, who do I talk to?"

Then the young man frowned. "None of our wagons go as far as Boston. We have a line going to Albany. That's up in New York, but I don't know if they are short of drivers."

"Albany would be just fine," the slim man told him. "Who do I talk to?"

If Kyle was hoping to get some rest before leaving, that did not happen. The young man directed him to a fat, balding man who continually kept mopping his brow with a dirty hanky. He clenched an unlit cigar on one side of his mouth and was plainly upset.

"You want to join a wagon going to Albany?" the man asked. "I got a spot, but do you know how to drive a mule team?"

The slim man handed over the recommendation to the man, and after glancing at it, he looked up smiling. "Do you got your stuff with you?"

"My gear's on my horse and it is tied up outside," Kyle told him.

"You got a horse, hey," the man grunted. "Well, hell. Have them toss on some extra grain. Your wagon is number three and is behind the building. Jake Campbell in the boss of the run. Check in with him. Your train is already an hour behind."

Campbell was a square-shouldered man with slicked-back salt and pepper hair. He wore some kind of canvas pants, a plaid wool shirt, and low-heeled boots. A flat-brimmed hat was tilted to the back of his head. He squinted as he looked at Kyle. "I sure hope the hell you know how to drive mules. We just grabbed your swamper off the street. I think he was anxious to get out of town."

Kyle managed to get the extra grain for his horse, and as he tied it to the back of the wagon, he apologized to it that they didn't get a little rest in Harrisburg. With his gear tied onto the canvas-covered load, he looked around for his swamper. He saw a sandy-haired, gangly man who wasn't much more than a lad looking over the mules.

There was a shout from Jake. "Climb up, men! It's time to move this damn freight."

The slim man climbed onto the wagon and put his Charleville behind the seat and looked for the sandy-haired lad. He was teasing one of the lead mules. Kyle shouted, "Get up here, young man, or I'll drive these mules right over you."

In a flash the sandy-haired lad climbed onto the wagon. The wagon lurched forward as Kyle called "Get up" and snapped the whip above the mules. The lad damned near fell off. The way out from behind the freight offices was rutted, which caused the wagon to rock. His mules were doing a poor job of pulling together, so it was a rough start for the slim man.

Snapping the whip above those that weren't pulling, and shouting and cussing, Kyle finally got things settled down by the time they reached the main trail. A north wind kept most of the dust off the drivers, drifting it to the south. The freight wagons were soon strung out almost a quarter-mile.

Then the lad said his first words, "I am glad we are out of there."

"Did you have trouble back in town?" Kyle asked, making conversations.

"I owed some men some money," the sandy-haired lad said. "They got me into a game and when I run out of money, one loaned me some. I had a good hand and didn't want to fold, so I took it. I got beat and then things went down from there."

"Did it occur to you that they were ganging up on you?" the slim man asked.

"Maybe they were, but after they won everything but my clothes, I told them I needed to go relieve myself and I didn't stop going," the lad said. "It wasn't long, and I heard shouts. I think they were hunting me. I hid and slept behind the freight building. When the boss man asked if I was the new swamper, I just told him yes."

"So, you got no gear," Kyle said.

"Just what I got on," the lad said. Then he asked, "What's a swamper?"

"The swamper is an important job. You'll be harnessing and unharnessing the mules. They need to be watered and fed grain. That will be your responsibility."

"I don't know much about doing that kind of stuff," the lad told him. "It won't matter, though. I just needed a ride out of town. I'll be gone by tomorrow."

Damn youngsters, Kyle thought. Then he asked, "How are you going to eat and where will you be sleeping?"

"I'll get by," the sandy-haired lad said. "Folks leave stuff out for the taking and maybe I'll find a horse. I want to head south. Maybe the Carolinas."

Kyle was steaming under his flat-brimmed hat. He had been taught the importance of being honest at a young age and had always lived by it. Beside him was a young man who felt he could just take anything he wanted and damn the feelings of those he took from.

"When you signed on to this job, you signed on for the full trip to Albany," the slim man said, choosing his words carefully. "The boss needs every one of us to do our job. Once we finish the trip, you are welcome to go and continue taking things that don't belong to you if you want, but not until then."

The lad chuckled, and said, "Well, it is a good thing I didn't sign nothing. Hell, I don't even know how to write."

"Do you know what giving your word is?" Kyle asked. "You gave your word that you'd do a job when the boss asked if you were the swamper. That is your bond, and if you break it you are in the wrong."

"Damn!" the lad said. "I guess I have broken my bond a bunch of times. It ain't hurt me so far."

Biting his tongue to stop from lashing out at the little bugger, Kyle breathed deep and asked, "What's your name?"

"Josh," the lad said. "Josh Albert. Why do you want to know?"

"I just like to know the name of a person I am going to shoot," the slim man replied.

With a surprised look, young Josh asked, "You would shoot me?"

"Only in the foot," Kyle said. "That way you could still do your job with the mules."

"I am a pretty fast runner," the lad said, a little unsure of himself.

"I am a pretty fast shooter, and I don't miss," the slim man told him. "If you get too far away I'd have to use the long gun and that would take half your foot off. Of course that would make it harder to do your work, but with a little less sleep that would work out."

"What if I go when you're sleeping?"

Josh asked.

"I'm a light sleeper. I learned it in the war," Kyle said. "Though then I would have to use the long gun."

For the next couple of hours, the lad had one eye on Kyle and the other on the side of the road, calculating how far he could get before the man next to him could pull the pistol. At midday they stopped near a stream and the mules had to be watered.

The stream was wide enough for all three teams to drink at once. Kyle had the lad take off his boots and walk alongside the animals. Once across it was time to give them and his horse some grain. "I'll need my boots now," Josh said.

"Just give them the grain. I noticed your boots are about my size and it would be a shame to put a hole through one of them," the slim man told him.

Josh was not a very happy passenger when the freighters were back underway. He decided that he didn't want to talk to Kyle. One might say the barefoot lad was pouting. They passed a lake with high hills on the far side.

"Yonder there reminds me of the cove I grew up near. After my folk died . . . ." Kyle paused for a moment in memory. "I was about your age, maybe a bit younger. Anyway, I got me a yoal. That's a kind of a boat. Well, I worked on it and got it so I could sail out on the channel and fish. That's how I made my living. I was lucky, though. I found an old stone cottage on the bluff and I stayed there. The owner came by one day when I was working on the yoal and he said I could stay and once I had some money from fishing I was able to pay him some rent."

Figuring he had a point to make, Josh said, "So you found a boat and just took it. Then you moved in a man's house without asking him first."

"I did," Kyle replied. "I was able to find odd jobs to keep from starving, but I had no money, and the English coast has severe weather. But when I did find out who owned the house, a deal was made to pay rent. As far as the boat, it had washed in from the channel and should someone have come in and said it was theirs, I would have given it back to them along with the work I had done on it."

"What's a channel?" Josh asked.

"It's the English Channel. It runs all along one side of Britain. Europe is on the other side of the channel. It is 90 miles wide and more in most places," Kyle explained.

It was a simple explanation, but at least Josh knew that the channel was water near the cove, whatever that was, and could be fished in. Then the lad asked, "How did your folks die?"

"An influenza went through our village,

and they got sick and died," the slim man told him.

With concern on his face, the sandy-haired lad asked, "What causes it?"

"Some say the it's the influence of the cold. Others think it is influenced by the planets and stars. I don't think it is planets or stars. We had lots of cold weather, and I think that caused it," Kyle replied.

By their evening stop, the lad knew a lot about Kyle's early years and had endless questions about things the slim man spoke of. Kyle couldn't believe he had so much to say and with a good listener, it felt good to talk about the past. He decided to give the lad his boots back.

They pulled in a small clearing for the night. The wagons were in a half-circle and the mules would be kept within it. "I will show you the way to unhitch the animals this time and how to get them hitch tomorrow, but after that it will be your job."

Kyle didn't know if the lad would start running the minute his feet hit the ground, or if he'd stick around and help. He stayed and seemed to like Kyles company. The slim man pointed out the positions of each animal and what special training they had for it. Each animal had a metal tag on its halter with a position they were trained for stamped onto it. It also had the number of the wagon.

The harnesses and collars were stacked

on the hitch and the animals were given grain before being led to a nearby creek. Each man led three mules. Kyle would water his horse after. Josh seemed to enjoy interacting with the animals until Kyle warned him that they could bite or kick.

"Most often they are nice as can be, and then, bang! They get you," the slim man said.

After grain and watering, the mules were picketed on whatever grass that was available. Due to the popularity of this small clearing, there was not much. The two men walked into the trees to relieve themselves after picketing the mules.

"There's a rabbit!" Josh hissed.

It began to hop away when Kyle drew the pistol from his belt. Needing to fire and reload the weapon anyway, he planned to scare it more than hit it. He fired. Sparks and smoke filled the air, the rabbit did a flip and lay in the leaves kicking.

The sandy-haired lad's eyes were wide. "You are a good shot!"

"Awe, that was easy," Kyle told him. "It was close."

Truth was, the slim man had been ready to tell Josh that a man doesn't just kill things for no reason and that was why he didn't hit it, but instead he looked at the lad and said, "That could have been your foot."

Campbell came running, shouting, "Who the hell is shooting! You'll scare the animals."

"I was just giving the lad a lesson," the slim man said, "and now he'll clean the rabbit, and it can go into the soup pot."

"I ain't got a knife," Josh told him. Kyle handed him his skinning knife and headed back for the wagon. The boss was in hot pursuit behind him.

"What the hell was that all about?" Campbell asked.

"My swamper had every intention to take off running at the first opportunity and I'd warned him that I would shoot him in the foot if he tried," Kyle told him. "As it worked out, I managed to hit the rabbit and now he believes I could hit his foot. Just maybe he'll stay around for the whole trip."

"Well, try and find quieter ways to teach him, like chaining him to the wagon wheel or something," Jake said. "If these damn jugheads start running, we'd never get them back."

The cook made bean soup for everyone and on the side of the fire he roasted the rabbit. Kyle suggested they let Josh eat it since he skinned and cleaned it. The lad received a little razzing from the others as he enjoyed the meat. He seemed to enjoy the attention, and it gave the slim man hope that the lad would last the trip.

They rolled their blankets out under the wagon after tying the mules to a picket line strung between trees. Kyle used his saddle from the wagon for a pillow and put the loaded pistol under it. Alongside his blanket he had the Charleville.

"Why do you do that?" Josh asked.

"Why do I put the pistol and long gun within reach?" Kyle questioned the inquiry. "If trouble comes, or anything else I have to be ready." Then he told the lad about the bear he'd had to shoot in Canada when it came after his side meat.

The slim man slept restlessly that night. It wasn't so much that he was worried about Josh running. It was what would happen when he got to Boston. He would make $25 for driving the wagon to Albany. His clothing was worn, his boots falling apart, the horse needed to be shoed, and he needed supplies for the trip. That would eat up most of the money. Once in Boston, how was he going to pay for anything?

Finally, he did sleep. The sounds of the cook getting the fire going woke Kyle. The slim man looked over and saw that Josh was still there and sound asleep. He put the long gun onto the wagon and tucked the pistol into his belt.

The cook already had the coffee going and was about to get water for the porridge. "I can get that for you," Kyle told him.

Grabbing the pot handle, the slim man walked down to the stream and took a drink and then filled the pot. On the way back, he saw someone coming with three mules. He was pleasantly surprised to see it was Josh.

"I'll get these three first and then the others," the lad said.

"By the time you get them watered, the cook should have coffee done. I'll bring you a cup so you can have some while we're giving the animals grain."

Kyle spent time brushing his horse while waiting for the porridge to get done. "I'm sorry you have to be tied behind the dusty wagon all day." The horse just shook its head and snorted as though to say it was okay.

The morning routine was finished with some missteps on getting the mules hitched up. Kyle was pleased to see that Josh was trying, and again he seemed to like the animals. The sun had been up less than two hours, and the wagons were once again on the road.

The sandy-haired lad, lamented as they bounced along the rough road, "I'm usually hunting for my next meal. Here the cook has it waiting twice a day."

"It is the benefit of having a job that provides meals," Kyle agreed. "I had many hungry days this summer during my search for Karen Green." Then he told the lad about the woman in the cabin.

While at the midday stop, the cook came around with biscuits to tide the men over until supper. The slim man chewed on the slightly burnt fare and drank water to wash it down. They had to haul buckets of water from the small stream for the mules, so Kyle helped the lad.

On the third day, Josh asked, "Can you teach me to drive?"

"Why do you want to learn how to drive?" the slim man asked.

"You're making $25 for driving and I'm making $15 as a swamper," the lad said. "Who knows, I might want to drive mules someday."

Handing the reins to the lad, the slim man said, "You should have picked up the commands of gee, haw, whoa, and get up by just listening to me. The whip is to get their attention, not to punish them. You hit them and then you will lose all control of the team."

"I would never hit them with the whip." Josh said. "I've been whipped before and it ain't good."

"The only time you should even have to raise your voice is if the mules have been in the corral getting fat for a while. Sometimes they forget how to work," Kyle told him.

The lad picked up driving quickly, which relieved the slim man some during the ten-hour days.

On the fifth day the lead wagons stopped out of sight behind an outcrop of rock. The boss came running back to stop the following wagons. "The road is blocked! Stop your wagons!"

Ahead was a rise that, once gone over, would save the wagons almost a day's travel. Someone had rolled rocks and dumped trees across the road. Campbell held a quick meeting while his swamper turned the team around.

"There are folks that don't want us to get through with this freight," the boss said. "It will be used to cut through some rock ledge to build a road that will bypass their town."

All the wagons were covered with canvas and Kyle had no idea what they were carrying. It turned out that they had drill rods and blasting powder in the wagons. The canvas covers were waterproofed with some type of oil that had a strong odor. Any smell of the blasting powder would be masked by this. No doubt the drill rod was secured so it wouldn't move around in the wagon, possibly making a spark that could blow the whole works up.

That explained the ease with which Kyle was able to get a job on the train. There are men who do not like hauling explosives. The slim man didn't care what was being carried, though he wouldn't have minded knowing. He would have avoided some of the bigger bumps.

A couple of hours were lost getting things turned around and then the wagons headed out on the longer bypass. Kyle had a new respect for his cargo. It didn't seem to make a difference to Josh. That evening they stopped and still had a few hours on the bypass before getting back to the road. The boss had another meeting before supper.

"We may have some men waiting once we get back to the road," Campbell said. "They may have clubs, or they might have long guns. We don't want to get in a shooting fight with them, so keep your damn fingers off the trigger. I don't want no accidental shooting."

While he didn't say it, he didn't want an errant shot to set off the powder in one of the wagons. As it was, for safety the sides had been made from thick planks and would most likely prevent a ball from going through unless it was shot at point-blank range.

"Are we supposed to let one of them shoot us before we do anything?" one of the teamsters asked.

The boss clenched his teeth, and his face turned red. Finally, he replied, "There ain't going to be any shooting. They don't want to shoot and we ain't going to shoot. They could have ambushed us going over the short cut and killed some of our mules. Maybe even a driver or two, and remember, I was right in the front. Instead, they just blocked it. I do not think this problem has come to a shooting thing."

Grumbling, the men started towards their wagons. Campbell then added, "When we get close to the road, we'll tighten up between wagons."

There wasn't much talking that evening during supper. Josh seemed his normal self and dug into his plate of beans. "Are you concerned about tomorrow?" Kyle asked.

"Naw," the lad said, swallowing his mouth full of food. "I got you there and I know you don't miss when shooting. You will protect me."

I wish I was as confident in my shooting as you are, the slim man thought.

While the cook cleaned up the boss had everyone with a weapon gather behind the wagons. "When I give the command, I want everyone to fire whatever you are carrying," the boss told them.

Kyle handed the pistol to Josh. "I don't know how to shoot," the lad whispered.

"Pull it to full cock and just aim it in the air. At the command, pull the trigger," he told the lad.

There was a total of five weapons, and at the command they all fired, making a loud sound that could be heard all the way to the road. Josh had the pistol in the other hand and was shaking the one that had been holding it. "That thing kicks," he said.

Laughing at the lad, Kyle reloaded

both guns. The slim man knew that Campbell wanted to make sure that everyone had a fresh load in their long guns. If it came to shooting, he didn't want any misfires.

While laying out the whiffletrees and harnesses after the firing, the men were quiet. Their commands to the mules were the only sounds. The man driving the second wagon was in a discussion with the boss.

Josh was securing the final straps on the mules when Campbell came walking over. Taking Kyle aside, he said, "I got a proposition for you. The men on wagon two want to move back. Hank says they got no long guns and don't want to be sitting ducks toward the front. Will you take that position?"

"I understand these men are teamsters not soldiers," the slim man said. "I wouldn't want them to be in the way if it came to shooting. I'll take the position behind you. Hell, if you want, I'll even go first."

The boss didn't seem to appreciate the offer and replied, "I lead my wagons. Just pull up when you're ready."

Sitting next to Josh, Kyle flipped the reins and said, "Git up."

The team strained in their harnesses and the wagon slowly moved up, taking the second wagon spot. As they passed the other wagon both men nodded to them. Kyle and Josh nodded back. A slight tug on the reins and a "Whoa," stopped the team behind the boss' wagon.

"Will we be in more danger being second?" Josh asked.

"When I was in the Battle of Plattsburgh it didn't matter where you were," the slim man replied. "When the last cannon stopped firing and if you were still standing, you were one of the lucky ones."

"Were you still standing?" the lad asked.

"I'm here, aren't I?" Kyle replied. Then he continued, "Actually I wasn't standing. I was down and wounded."

"That doesn't make me feel any better," Josh told him.

"If the shooting starts, and I don't think it will, get off the wagon and put the mules between you and them," the slim man told him.

"They might hit the mules," the lad said.

"Better than them hitting a wagon full of blasting powder," Kyle told him.

Another motivation the slim man had for suggesting Josh shield behind the mules was he didn't want to draw fire towards his dapple-gray tied to the back of the wagon.

The wagons went ahead slowly toward the road. The breeze brought the smell of smoke from a campfire. The Kyle reached back and got the Charleville and handed it to

Josh. "What do I do with this?" the lad asked.

"Just carry it like you know what you're doing. If trouble comes keep it with you when you get behind the mules. I'll be right along to fire it," the slim man said.

The slim man looked back at his horse tied to the back of his wagon. As the wagons slowly rolled on toward the road, he toyed with the idea of letting it loose. Odds were that the horse would follow the wagons. The nagging worry that he had was if it did not follow, how could he leave Josh alone while he went after it?

Through the tree-lined bypass the intersection of the road became visible. There was no one in sight waiting for them. Kyle hoped that harassing the progress of the wagons would satisfy the disgruntled townspeople.

The boss' wagon slowed even more as it turned onto the road. It bounced over the ruts as it turned. The wagon continued ahead slowly. Then Kyle's wagon entered the road. About three hundred paces up the road was a line of men with clubs and muskets standing across the roadway.

"Don't stop, boss," the slim man whispered. "Call their bluff. They'll fall back."

"If they don't?" he heard Josh say.

"Then folks are going to get hurt and we are going to hurt them," Kyle told him.

Only four of the men were brandishing muskets. He saw a couple of pitchforks and several clubs. He handed the reins to the lad and took the Charleville. He then handed the pistol to Josh. "If it comes to shooting, put a ball into anyone that had a musket. Wait, though. I am going to kill the big bastard in the middle."

Kyles mental frame was back in the war: You don't let them get the first volley if at all possible and when you shoot, you shoot to kill. The lead wagon continued toward the line of men. The slim man had the long gun at the ready and all he had to do was raise it to his shoulder and squeeze the trigger.

He saw uncertainty in the line of men. The big man in the middle had stepped back, using another to give him some cover. The mules from the first wagon were only a step away from the line when it finally broke and the townsmen moved to each side.

They raised their clubs and shouted. Muskets where held high and pitchforks stabbed in the air, but none of the three touched the mules or wagons. "Look straight ahead, Josh," Kyle told him. "Do not make eye contact. Just keep driving."

After several tense minutes, the townsmen were left behind and the lad could not help but look back. "They are heading for the pass," he exclaimed.

"They are going to clean up the mess

they made on the short cut," the slim man said. "There are other wagons coming that they want to be able to take it."

"How did they know that we were carrying the drill rod and blasting powder?" Josh asked. "There are lots of wagons that come this way."

"Word of moving this kind of freight travels fast," Kyle said. "My guess is that there were folks from the town in Harrisburg watching and waiting for the shipment. Once they knew it was coming, they rode to let the townsmen know."

The rest of the trip to Albany was uneventful. They got two days of rain and one of the men on another wagon had an extra hat and gave it to Josh. Another had an extra ground cloth and put a slit in it so the lad could slip it over his head and keep some of the rain off him.

Albany was a bustling city. It was located at the northern navigable waters of the Hudson River. Kyle thought it was reminiscent of Boston but with fewer church steeples. It lacked the ocean on its east side, but it was the hub of distribution for the north and west of the city.

The slim man got his pay and collected his gear. He was now about a week from Boston and there was a decent road between the two cities. The dapple-gray was in fair condition after having grain twice a day and whatever it could find grazing. He did need to think about having it shoed.

It was midday and there was some kind of eating place near the north end of the freight office. Kyle found several of the drivers and swampers already having a midday meal and coffee. Josh was sitting alone to one side.

Walking over to join him, the slim man said, "You got money and now I suppose you don't know what to spend it on first."

The lad's face brightened up and he said, "I ain't ever had so much money before. I don't want to spend it and have to start all over again."

"You did a good job on the trip," he told the lad. "You know the job of a swamper, and you are a pretty good driver. I am sure you can get more work and earn regular money."

A pretty, freckle-faced girl came over. "The special is beef stew with rutabagas. I like the stew better with potatoes but the cook had to clean out the root cellar."

"I am partial to rutabaga, so I will have the stew and some coffee," Kyle told her.

She looked at Josh and his face turned bright red. "Would you like the same?" she asked him.

Stammering a little, the lad said, "Yes . . . yes, please."

"She is a pretty girl, and the cook is probably her pa and keeps a close eye on her,"

Kyle told him.

"I ain't talked to women much," Josh told him. "They just tie my tongue all up."

"That's not a bad thing," the slim man told him. "You will get in less trouble that way."

The stew came and was quite good. It had been some time since Kyle had eaten beef and the cook had been generous with it. The meal included bread to dunk into the gravy. Both looked forward to the meal, and they chewed in silence.

Wiping the last of the gravy from the bottom of the bowl with bread, the slim man stuffed it into his mouth and washed it down with the last of his coffee. "What are your plans?" he asked the lad.

"The boss asked me if I'd be making the return trip and I told him I would," Josh replied.

"I'm glad to hear it," Kyle told him. "You are good with the mules, and if the driver needs to be spelled, you can drive."

"I was thinking more of the regular meals," the lad said, pushing his bowl away.

"The weather is getting colder," the slim man said. "You will need a coat, another set of clothes, some socks, blankets and such."

"You could leave me one of your blankets," Josh kidded. Then he got serious. "I don't think my money will cover all that."

"I was about to go and get a haircut and

hot bath," Kyle said. "Why don't you join me?"

"You sure are in a hurry to spend my money," the lad complained.

Laughing at the sandy-haired young man, his older mentor replied, "Some things are important and being clean is one of them."

Kyle picked up the cost of the meals. They stopped at the mercantile for some new clothes, long johns, socks, and a coat before continuing to the barber. An hour later they left wearing their new clothing, having left the old ones to be laundered.

The street they walked down offered lots of pleasures that a man could partake of, but Kyle didn't think they would be a good influence for the young lad with money in his pockets. Instead, they went back to the mercantile.

"Are we going after more clothes?" the lad asked.

"Blankets and a ground cloth," the slim man told him.

"All I got left is $6," Josh complained.

"You will have three left after we leave the store," Kyle told him. "But you will have all you need to get by on the road."

The lad's reply was a snort as they walked in. Two blankets and a ground cloth cost another $3 and Josh glared at his mentor as he doled them out. Kyle had picked up a few things and paid for them after the lad had already gone outside.

He found him sitting on a bench in front of the store. Looking up, Josh said, "Now I got lots of stuff to carry, but most of my money is gone."

"Will you need the stuff?" the slim man asked.

"Some of it maybe, . . . well, maybe all of it, but I could have waited until I had more money," the lad muttered.

"You spent well, Josh," he told him. "You bought things you needed and will be able to use now and in the future. When winter sets in you will need some choppers to keep your hands warm and a tuque for your head."

"With what?" the lad questioned. "We spent most of my money."

"You will get paid again when you finish the next trip," Kyle pointed out. "You have $3 left now and if you spend carefully and have another $3 left from your next pay, that will be $6 in case an emergency comes up. Maybe you will be able to save even more money on some trips."

Slowly this logic sank in. The young lad had been thinking very shortsightedly and could only see what he had left now. "Well, maybe," Josh said, still in a bit of a huff.

"You helped me a lot during the trip, spelling me from driving and I have a couple things here as a thank you," the slim man told him.

Kyle placed a broad belt, a shooting bag, and a knife with sheath between the two of them. The knife was a trading knife, but it would be plenty serviceable for the young lad. Josh picked them up one at a time, his brow furled.

"You will need money to go to Boston," he said. "You shouldn't be spending money on me."

"The way I see it," Kyle replied. "You will need a place to carry all the money you will be earning, and the bag will work for that. In an emergency you might need to cut a mule out of a harness, and for that you'll need a knife. Lastly, you need a place to carry things, and the broad belt will not only keep your coat closed in the winter, but it will also be a place to carry your knife. Later on, maybe a short axe."

The generosity of his mentor left the lad speechless. Little was left to do but show Josh the proper way to roll up a bedroll so he could store extra items and keep the weather off it. The two walked to the livery leading the dapple-gray, Kyle made arrangements to have the horse shoed, and for a dollar the two of them were able to sleep in the loft.

The next morning, the clean laundry was picked up, and after a quick goodbye the lad was off to the freight office to be assigned to a wagon. They would be departing before noon. Kyle remained near the smithy and watched him make shoes and shod his horse.

"I had to do a lot of work on the hooves," the smithy said. "How'd you come to neglecting the animal?"

The comment was hurtful, but the man was right. "I ran out of money in search of a woman," he replied.

The smithy plunged the red-hot shoe into the water, creating a plume of steam. "I guess that would be a good excuse. Did you find her?" the man asked.

"I did not," Kyle told him. "I suppose it was not meant to be. I was in the war when she left."

"Which side were you fighting for?" the smithy asked.

The slim man was getting tired of being asked that question, but he did have an English accent. "I was on the *Eagle* fighting for the Americans."

The smithy stopped, his red, weathered face almost becoming pale. "The *Eagle*? Did you know John Wilber?"

Kyle nodded. "He was on the cannons . . ." The slim man's voice broke. He was on the cannons and was killed in the Battle of Plattsburgh. "Was he your brother?" he asked the man.

The smithy began to hammer the metal shoe. After a moment he looked up. "He was. John was supposed to work with me when he got back."

As the man finished fashioning the shoes, he asked Kyle about his brother's last days. The slim man wished he had known the man better, but he was able to fill in some information about the brother. "He died a hero at the cannon. He never abandoned his post," Kyle told him.

Without looking up, the smithy asked, "Did he get some good licks on the Brits before it happened?"

This Kyle could answer. "Yes, he did. His battery sent the first broadside into the British ship *Confiance* as it tried to get into position, and then several more as the battle went on."

"That would be John wanting to get the first shots in," the smithy said.

With the shoes ready, the man got to work shaping the hooves and putting them on. Kyle watched as excess hoof was cut away with a knife or removed with a coarse rasp. The smithy had stopped asking questions and the slim man was thankful. Not only was his knowledge of John Wilber limited, but the memories of the battle were not his favorite thoughts.

The smithy charged him $5 for shoeing the horse. Kyle had never paid that much for the service, but he had never neglected the animal as he had this past year, and four new shoes were needed. Feeling good about having the horse taken care of, he left the blacksmith shop. The smithy gave him a heartfelt thank you for being there with his brother and sharing what he knew about his last hours.

The slim man was anxious to get on the road, but it was late afternoon and he still had to purchase supplies for the trip. He headed for the livery. The dapple-gray could do with some more hay and grain. He would leave first thing in the morning.

CHAPTER THREE

Kyle was on the third day in route to Boston. The last night in Albany he had made the mistake of having a few drinks. One thing had led to another, and the slim man had woken up with a headache and a pretty, slightly plump lady in the morning.

His good advice to Josh about always saving some money for emergencies had been forgotten and he was down to just a couple of dollars in his shooting bag. He had supplies that would last to Boston and a few days more. His horse was in good shape and Kyle was thankful that it was properly shoed.

He left the road just short of a town called Auburn. He had no money to spend on a night in town. Kyle found a place in a stand of elm trees, some towering over 40 feet above his camp. The night threatened to be cold, due to clear skies. Collecting fallen branches, the slim man built up a larger fire than he would normally make for his meals.

He put on a pot of beans with enough to eat for breakfast also. While the weather had been cold, the rain had held off. It was too early for snow, but that too would be covering the ground soon. The horse was cropping some late fall grass near a small opening.

"Don't wander too far," Kyle called to it.

Brooding a little, the slim man watched the pot as it started to steam. A few days ago, he had arrived in Albany and was paid for driving the wagon. That pay should have gotten him to Boston with plenty to spare. Somehow, he had managed to go through all but a couple of dollars.

Why did he feel that he had to spend the money on Josh? The lad was happy with what he had and would have gotten things as he needed them. It was almost like Kyle was sending one of his own off into the world and felt he had to make sure the lad had what he needed.

He reached into his shooting bag and took out what remained of a twist of tobacco. The slim man usually took a chew after supper, but right now he had to do something to get his mind off his own troubles.

As he rolled the chaw in his cheek, Kyle wandered around the stand of elm collecting more branches. He heard a wagon come and go on the road. He didn't want to attract the attention of those going by and was having second thoughts about the large fire he'd built. Dropping the branches near the fire, the slim man dug through his saddlebag and got the brush for his horse. He hoped keeping busy would take his mind off other things.

The next morning, Kyle rode away from his makeshift camp feeling a little more optimistic about his future. Things really weren't so bad. He had food and clothing. His horse was in good shape and soon he would be riding into Boston where he had friends.

After more than a year, Kyle finally looked down on the city of Boston from near Bunker Hill. He had read stories about the early battle of the revolution and how 1,000 British soldiers had been killed or wounded on the slopes right in front of him. Now it was a pleasant view of Boston, the cries of the wounded and dying long gone.

Taking a drink from his waterbag, Kyle looked at the score of sailing ships anchored in the bay. He saw a three-mast schooner slowly moving out of the bay as they worked to set their sails. He felt a whisp of regret that his days at sea were cut short when the *Spencer* had been seized by the British. The escape from the ship before he and two others could be impressed into the Royal Navy had changed the whole course of his life.

Riding down into the city, the slim man

figured he needed to take care of his horse first. The bay doors were open on Billy's livery. The sunshine brought warmth and light to the inside of the long building. The hostler as pumping water into the trough.

Looking up, he asked, "Is that you, Kyle?"

"It is, Billy," the slim man replied. "I am glad to be back here in Boston."

Swinging down from the dapple-gray, he led it to the water. While the horse drank, Kyle gave him a quick history of the past year. "Too bad you didn't find her," the hostler replied.

"Will a couple of dollars get the horse boarding and feed for two days?" Kyle asked.

"It sure will," Billy replied, "but you're going to stick around longer than that."

Leading the horse to a stall, Kyle stripped the gear off and placed it alongside. "I'll come back in a bit and brush the animal," the slim man said.

"I can do that for you," the hostler said. "Bring back a bottle and we'll catch up on things."

Taking the last of his money out of his shooting bag, he handed it to the hostler. "If I don't get back tonight, I will do that soon."

Hurrying out of the livery, Kyle headed for the Raven, which was located in the steamier part of town along with several establishments offering gambling and ladies of the night. His lifelong friend managed the place. The two of them had never gotten rich as privateers, but things had worked out for Kit.

When the two of them worked their way to Boston on a ship named the *Spencer*, his friend had met a woman whose father had control of much of the waterfront. He'd fallen in love and married her. His name became Christopher, and he now helped his father-in-law run the business.

The street had the familiar smells of cheap perfume from the ladies hanging out in front of the taverns. They called to him as he went by, but Kyle just waved and smiled and continued towards the Raven.

Two women stood on the porch of the Raven and immediately gave all their attention to him as Kyle stepped up. "Maybe later, ladies," he said. "I got to see the boss first."

It took a moment for his eyes to adjust to the dim light of the interior. He was able to see that his friend wasn't at his usual seat at the end of the bar. Walking up to the bar, Sam the bartender noticed him and brought over an ale.

"Thank you," Kyle said. In here he was never allowed to buy his own drinks. "Will Christopher be back soon?" he asked.

"He and his missus went to New York for a couple weeks," the bartender said. "Mr.

Trent will be in soon and he may be able to help you."

"Mr. Trent?" Kyle asked.

Then there was a squeal, and he heard his name. "Kyle Oliver! You're back!"

It was Lisa, a shapely, blond woman who he had spent many enjoyable nights with. Smiling, he said, "Yes I am, Lisa."

She came up close and then said, "Ooh. Did you just get in from the road?"

Under his seven-day growth of whiskers, the slim man blushed. He had been sleeping in his clothes for a week, and until she reacted he hadn't thought about it. "I was just about to go and get a shave and bath," he lied to her.

"No, you won't," she said, pouting. "I'll have a bath drawn for you upstairs and I will shave you myself. I'm sure we have some clean clothes that will fit you. I'll have these back clean by morning."

If he'd some money in his shooting bag, Kyle would have quickly agreed and insisted on giving her some money for the services. But he had no money, and at some point she would realize that.

Forcing a smile, he said, "Normally I would not pass up an offer like that, but I am late for meeting someone and just made a quick stop to say hello to Christopher."

She wrinkled her nose and picked something off his shoulder. "Are you sure you are in that much of a hurry? I'd make you happy you stayed."

"You are making me feel awful, but I'm sorry. I have to go," he pleaded.

Getting up, he left the full ale on the bar and tried to give her another smile as he left. Just outside he walked blindly as he hurried away and bumped into a man coming to the Raven. "Careful mister," the man said.

"Hello, Mr. Trent," the girls behind him called sweetly.

Kyle took a second look at the man who was almost a head shorter than him. "Danny!"

Mr. Trent had a smirk on his face. "You look and smell like a man I came out of Canada with," Danny said. "How the hell are you, Kyle?"

"Can you walk with me, Danny?" the slim man asked.

Calling to the ladies, Mr. Trent said, "Let Sam and Lisa know I'll be back shortly."

Danny had been just a young lad when he had joined Kyle and a friend Jago during their escape from the British. With wanted posters for desertion plastered all along the St. Lawrence River in Canada, they'd kept on the run. Eventually Jago headed south to his brother's logging camp while Danny and Kyle spent the fall trapping and a pleasant winter with two Ojibwa women. Spring had come with those looking for the reward closing in on them The two trappers had narrowly escaped across the St. Lawrence River to the safety of America.

As the two of them headed up the street, Kyle asked, "Do I call you Danny, or Mr. Trent?"

"Christopher wants me to go by Daniel or Mr. Trent, but Daniel seemed too formal," his friend replied.

"And Mr. Trent is not?" the slim man questioned.

"When we're not with folks, just call me Danny," his brown-haired friend told him.

"I've got a problem, Danny. I spent the summer looking for a lady in Virginia and let myself run out of money," Kyle told him.

"I can fix that," his friend said. "How much do you need?'

Realizing that he'd done a poor job of introducing his problem, Kyle tried again. "I don't want to borrow money. What I need is work, preferably on a ship."

"I can get you a good job right here in Boston," Danny told him. "I can authorize an advance, sort of a loan on your pay and you can stay right here working with me and Christopher."

Was he being stubborn, or was it from the desire to survive on his own, Kyle did not know. But he needed to be independent and owing no man. He had done it well since he was 15 and now at 20 he had gotten himself into a bind.

"What I need is a ship to crew on," the slim man said. "If you know of one, that favor I would appreciate."

The two men stopped and Danny looked at his friend, frustration on his face. "I still owe you for our time in Canada. You spent more than I did so we could go trapping, and I never fully paid you back."

Smiling, Kyle said, "Get me a job on a ship and we will be even."

Nodding, the slim man headed up the street alone. He was getting hungry and there was food in his saddlebags at the livery. Along the way back, he saw the barracks that he'd wintered in while crewing on the *Spencer*. That was before the trouble of the ship being seized.

Billy was enjoying the warmth of the sun as he sat in front of the livery. "I got some coffee on inside. Grab yourself a cup and join me."

While walking back from the Raven, Kyle had been going over his assets. Right now, he was money poor, but he did have assets. He had all his gear and a horse. He wished he still had the leather vest. That could have been a quick sale to get him enough to get cleaned up.

Sitting on a chair near the hostler, Kyle tasted the coffee. It was strong, the way he'd learned to like it. "I might have to help you with your chores tonight."

The hostler looked over and smiled, his damaged lip making it crooked. "Other than feeding the stock, I got most of them done," Billy replied.

"If I feed them, will that get me a night in the loft?" Kyle asked.

"Hell, you don't have to do nothing to sleep in the loft," the hostler told him. "You got a horse here. You can spend both nights if you want. Of course, I do draw the line about bringing women in." Then Billy laughed so hard it bent him over.

"I got some groceries and can make us both supper," Kyle offered.

"You didn't bring back a bottle," the hostler noted.

"Well, tonight we drink coffee," the slim man told him. "We'll see what tomorrow brings."

That night Kyle lay in the loft, unable to sleep. He was pondering his situation. Somehow, he needed to earn some money so he could at least clean up. Until then he did not feel he could go back to the Raven, where friends were.

For now he could go down to the docks and make a dollar a day loading and unloading freight. Doing so would upset Danny, and if Christopher found out he too would be unhappy. Maybe it was time to get rid of some of his gear.

He had a pistol he could sell. He could let the saddlebags go and use flour sacks to carry his supplies. As he was slipping off to sleep, a thought came that he knew was his solution. It saddened him, but he had no choice.

The sound of Billy at the potbelly stove woke the slim man. Sitting up, he looked around the loft. The smell of the hay was pleasant. After shaking his blankets out and rolling them up, Kyle climbed down the ladder.

"I heard you moving around," the hostler said. "I was trying to be quiet lighting the stove. You looked like you could use some sleep last night."

"That I could," he told the hostler, "But sleep did not come easy. I've got some side meat if you want me to fry that up for our breakfast."

"I got water on heating for porridge," Billy said. "Maybe tomorrow morning."

The bay doors were mostly closed to keep out the cold wind blowing, so the two men sat in the dim light near the potbelly stove. "How are you doing?" the hostler asked.

"Just fine," Kyle told him. "I am planning on getting onto a ship soon."

"When was the last time you slept in my loft and not in that fancy room they got above the Raven?" Billy asked. "You ain't talking of it, but something is wrong."

Trying to keep things light, Kyle asked, "Could it be I like your company?"

"More than that pretty blond at the Raven? I don't think so," the hostler replied.

Blushing at the realization of how observant the old man was, Kyle thought about the solution he'd come up with last night. "I would like to sell my horse to you."

There was a long pause before the hostler replied. "If it is money you need, I can help you out. You don't have to sell your horse."

Kyle knew it was time to come clean with Billy. "I do need money. I was chasing a dream all summer and left myself in bad shape. But that is not why I want to sell the horse. I plan to go out to sea and won't be needing a horse."

"Men go to sea all the time, but they always come back, and when you do you will need the horse," Billy told him.

"I plan to be gone a long time," Kyle told him. "When and if I come back, I will come and see what you have to sell."

The porridge was done, and the two men sat in the dim light eating. Suddenly, the hostler spoke. "I shouldn't have asked about the bottle."

"You have been more than kind to me," he told Billy. "I realized while sleeping in your loft that in the future I will not need a horse. I don't expect too much for the animal. The dapple-gray has some years on it, but it is a good-tempered horse and its teeth are in good shape."

"How about the rest of your gear?" the hostler asked.

"I plan to keep it, and hopefully the ship I get on will allow me to stow it," Kyle told him.

"So, you do see a horse in your future," Billy replied. "Why don't you let me rent the horse from you so I can use it if a customer is looking to go riding for an afternoon?"

While he smiled, Kyle wished that the old hostler wouldn't try and be so helpful. The decision to sell the horse was painful enough without him making it difficult. "Just give me a price on the horse," the slim man said. "Whatever the price is, I won't be insulted and please don't offer more than it is worth."

In silence the two ate their porridge. A gust of wind rattled the bay doors. Neither man noticed. With the last spoonful swallowed, Billy cleared his throat. "Are you in debt?"

The question bothered Kyle, but he tried to shrug it off. "No, I am not. Had I spent a night at the Raven, I would have felt I was."

"The horse is worth, $50 maybe $60," Billy told him.

"That is if you sold it," the slim man

pointed out. "You have to make something on the animal."

"Like you said, it is a good-tempered horse," the hostler replied, "I would keep it and rent it out."

"The deal sounds fair to me," Kyle told him. "I will also provide you with a bottle to seal it."

The tension the two men felt during the dealing quickly ebbed and the two were soon laughing and talking of other subjects. The slim man spent the morning helping the hostler clean the stalls. It felt good to be working, loading the wooden wheelbarrow and pushing it up the planks to dump it onto the manure pile.

When the chores were finished, Billy went over to his scarred rolltop desk. There was the sound of a tin box being opened. When the man came back, he handed Kyle six $10 gold eagles for his horse. The slim man wanted to give him back one of the coins in the worst way, but he realized his need was stronger than his pride.

Billy had him sign a paper giving the hostler ownership of the horse and the deal was done. The two men sat with a cup of coffee in front of the livery. "I want to thank you for buying the horse," Kyle told him.

"If you need it before you get on a ship, it's yours to use at no charge," Billy said. "Also, if you can't take the saddle and other gear on the ship, I will store it for you or buy it."

"Thanks for the offers, but I think I will be all set," Kyle told him.

By noon, Kyle was at a bath and barber. His extra set of clothing had several small rips and was worn thin on the knees and elbows. The slim man left them at the livery and bought new clothing on the way to the barber.

With a shave, haircut, and bath, Kyle felt ready to face the world. He still had four gold coins and change left. He had prepaid to have his other clothing laundercd. Stepping out into the street, he breathed deep. It had all the smells of the city and the sun was shining.

He walked down the street toward the Raven but decided to stop and see Gus first. Gus was Christophers father-in-law's brother. He owned a quiet tavern which featured gambling but no ladies. The balding, heavyset man was behind the bar. A white-haired man with a trimmed beard was playing at the tinny piano.

"I'll have an ale, Gus," the slim man said.

The owner went to draw the beverage and didn't recognize Kyle. The slim man took a seat at the bar and anticipated the frothy brew. Placing the correct change on the bar he waited for Gus.

The heavyset man set the ale down and squinted at his customer. "Do I know you?"

"You do," the slim man said. "I'm Kyle, a friend of Christopher's."

"I thought that was you," Gus replied. "Christopher and his wife are in New York. He is helping my brother set up some kind of business deal."

"I saw Danny and Lisa yesterday," Kyle told the man.

"Mr. Trent is now in charge of the Raven," Gus replied. "And the girls work for Lisa. Christopher has been moved up and only comes to the Raven a few hours a week."

Sipping the ale, Kyle realized that things in Boston had changed. Everyone was moving up and making more money while he remained the same, just getting by. He was happy for his friends after learning that they were doing well. He wondered how he would have liked to be addressed as Mr. Oliver. Actually, he did not mind the sound of it. His father had been called Mr. Oliver.

With the ale finished, it was time to go to the Raven. He half-hoped that Danny and Lisa weren't there. Kyle looked down at his clothing. He was dressed like a dock worker, but that should be okay, he'd be dressed like many of their regular customers.

The anticipation of seeing his friend Kit was missing. It would still be nice to know a couple of people. The women in front flirted as he passed them. Kyle smiled and kidded them. Stepping into the dimly lit establishment, he saw that Danny was sitting in the seat that Christopher used to occupy. He did not see Lisa anywhere.

Sam saw him and had an ale waiting near Danny before the slim man sat. Danny looked over and smiled. "I thought you'd be in here last night."

"Bill and I were catching up on old times," he told his friend.

Smiling that familiar smile, Danny said, "Lisa is going to give you heck when she sees you."

Someone from the gambling tables called to Mr. Trent and Danny said, "I'll be right back."

Sam came over and looked concerned. "Was there something wrong with the ale the other day? You didn't touch it."

Giving the bartender a broad smile, Kyle said, "I was having some problems that day and must not have been thinking right. A man should never pass up one of your ales."

The bartender seemed relieved as he headed away to serve another customer. Danny came back and turned to the slim man. "I might have found you a ship. It is hauling cargo for St. Louis by way of New Orleans."

"I've never been to New Orleans," Kyle told him. "That sounds just fine. When does it sail?"

"In three days," Danny told him. "The captain is Grayson. He runs a clean ship. He requires references. He won't take on drunks or slackers. I told him you'd see him by tomorrow."

What Danny said made it sound like a done deal. "I appreciate you doing that. Consider us even for Canada."

Then Kyle heard a lady's voice. "Where have you been, Kyle Oliver!"

Turning, the slim man saw the beautiful, blond Lisa coming toward him. "You left here in a bad way and made me worry. I thought you'd left town."

Grinning at her, Kyle said, "I would never leave town without spending some time with you."

Danny said, "You two have fun. I have work to do."

Sitting at a table, the slim man bought her a lady's drink and had another ale. "I see you didn't take me up on the offer of a shave and bath," she said.

"It was just foolish pride," he told her. "I figured I should take the first layer off myself."

The rest of the night was a bit of a blur. Not much money was spent, but with a slight headache, Kyle woke the next morning in the room upstairs with the beautiful Lisa next to him. It was like old times. Breakfast was served and fresh clothing was laid out.

"I just wore the things one day," he told her. Lisa smiled and said, "They'll take them in some, so they fit a little better. They're made one size fits all, and you do not need a big size."

In order to get dressed, the slim man had to put on tailored slacks, a white shirt and calf-high boots. In the full-length mirror he did look good, but he wondered if the ship's captain would feel the same way. The outfit was topped off with a felt hat.

It was almost noon when he came down into the tavern. He left Lisa to let herself get a little more sleep. Two men were cleaning up from the night before in the tavern. One of them came over quickly and asked, "Can I get you something, sir?"

"I am all set," he told the man and headed for the door. The sun was bright, and Kyle squinted as he headed up the street.

He realized that Danny had not given him the name of the ship. "The captain's name should be enough," the slim man muttered.

For a moment before heading down to find the ship, Kyle debated if he should go to the livery and get his old, worn clothes that he hadn't discarded yet. Anxious to find the ship, he decided to go as is. Near the docks he saw an office with a man writing in a ledger.

Knocking on the sliding window, Kyle waited until the man finished what he was writing and then slid it open. "Can I help you, sir?" the man asked.

Sir, Kyle thought. *Why would he call me sir?*

"I am looking for Captain Grayson's ship," the slim man replied.

"It's the ketch tied up on the south wharf," the man told him.

Thanking him, Kyle headed for the south wharf. The calf-high boots were hurting his feet, the cool wind was blowing through his shirt, and the felt hat was heavy on his head. Now Kyle regretted not going and changing into the old clothes.

The slim man knew what a ketch looked like. It was a two-masted ship with a mizzen mounted on the main mast for maneuverability. Kyle knew that it needed only a half-dozen men to sail the ship. The length could vary quite a bit, and he wondered how long the ship he hoped to sail on would be.

Kyle saw what he guessed was the ketch being loaded with wooden boxes filled with cargo. The ship appeared to be around 100 feet-long and its size reminded him of the *Eagle*, he had served on in the war. Instead of square sails, it had triangular sails. He did see gun ports along the side. As he got closer, he noticed a man at the stern watching him. Walking toward the ketch, Kyle called out, "Are you Captain Grayson?"

"I am," the man said, "And who are you?"

"My name's Kyle Oliver," the slim man said. "Mr. Trent spoke to you about me."

The man gave him a cold look as Kyle got closer and replied, "Mr. Trent said he had an experienced sailor to fill my crew. I am not looking for a dandy to stand around looking good."

"I must apologize for my appearance," Kyle told him. "I spent the night at the Raven and a helpful woman named Lisa stole my regular clothes and left these to wear."

"I don't take on crew members that chase and drink when going ashore," the captain said. "Too many of them forget how to get back to the ship."

"I sailed on the *Spencer* with Captain Holmes and was on the *Eagle* during the Battle of Plattsburgh," Kyle told him. "I have never missed a ship's movement and have no intention of doing so on your ship."

The captain's facial expression changed a little but still wasn't friendly. "Wasn't Holmes' ship seized by the British?"

"It was, Captain Grayson. I escaped being impressed by the Royal Navy along with Mr. Trent, by going over the side and swimming to shore," Kyle replied.

"Be here at 8 tomorrow morning. We sail with the tide at 10. Dress appropriately, Mr. Oliver," the captain warned him.

"I have a saddle and some other gear," Kyle told him. "Can I bring them aboard?"

"Our extra space is limited," Captain Grayson said. "Keep the gear to a minimum."

As he left, the slim man glanced back. The captain had gone forward. He noticed that the name of the ship was *Fancy*.

His first stop after leaving the *Fancy* was the livery. Billy was showing the dapple-gray to a smartly dressed gentleman. "It's a well-behaved horse and your trail ride should be most enjoyable."

The man said, "I'll send someone to get it tomorrow morning."

As the man left the livery, Kyle felt a twinge on regret having sold the horse. He fully knew that he'd had no choice.

The hostler saw him and smiled. "This horse is already making me money."

Kyle pulled a pint of whiskey from his shooting bag. "I thought we'd have a drink on the sale."

With the horse in the stall, Billy hurried toward his desk. "I got a couple cups."

The two men spent the rest of the morning killing the bottle and telling stories. They were on the second drink when the hostler remarked, "Where in the hell did you get them clothes? I hope you didn't go out and spend your horse money on them."

Laughing, the slim man told him about Lisa getting him dressed this morning. He also talked of leaving on the *Fancy* and that the captain was not impressed by what he was wearing. "Did he think he was taking on a gentleman?" Billy asked, chuckling.

"No, he didn't," Kyle replied. "I believe he called me a dandy."

With the pint gone and a nice buzz on, the slim man let the hostler know he'd be coming for his gear in the morning. He had been planning on spending another enjoyable night at the Raven, but what had been three days according to Danny turned out to be tomorrow. The slim man did not want to be hungover or late his first day on the ship.

Lisa was talking with her ladies when Kyle entered the Raven. "Have Sam get you an ale and a special for me. I will be right with you," she told him.

A special was code for a drink with alcohol in it. Evidently, Lisa was having a tough day. Sam brought the drinks over to the table as Kyle sat down. "Has Danny been in?" he asked.

"Mr. Trent had a meeting and said he'd be back in a couple hours. I believe it was issues with a worker his wife hired," Sam told him.

The statement floored the slim man. Danny married? Why didn't he say anything when they met? Lisa came over and sat heavily and put both hands around the drink. "I am going to need this. Sometimes those ladies can find more ways to make my life difficult."

Then she smiled. "You looked good walking in here."

"Thank you for the compliment, but I will need my regular clothes back," he told her. "The captain of the ship I'm signing on to was not impressed with my outfit."

She took a small sip and gave him the sweetest smile. "He was probably jealous of you."

"When did, Danny . . . Mr. Trent get married?" he asked her.

"Let see," she said. "It was before he took over for Christopher. Maybe six months ago."

"Funny he didn't mention it to me," Kyle told her.

"It was a nice wedding," Lisa told him. "He married a friend of Christopher's wife. They seem really happy. Mr. Trent doesn't even look at the other ladies anymore."

"When are you going to get married?" he asked her.

Lisa motioned Sam and he brought over two more drinks. "My drinks are costing you quite a lot. You better change the subject," she told him.

The piano player started and soon men from the docks would be coming in. Danny came back and asked Kyle to give him a minute. The world around the slim man continued on while he was just standing still. Lisa took his hand and squeezed it.

Finishing her drink, Lisa had to go to work. Danny waved him over to the bar. Sam brought another ale and something for Mr. Trent. The two men toasted each other and drank. Setting the ale down, Kyle said, "I heard you were married."

"I am," his friend replied. "I was just talking to a builder that is putting a nursery in our house. Della is three months now."

The whiskey earlier and the ale probably made Kyle more emotional about the news than it probably should have, but the slim man's eyes filled with tears and he said, "I am so damn happy for you."

Danny blushed and whispered, "Now don't be doing that. It is just a baby."

"You and Kit both married," Kyle said. "Your kids will probably be calling Jago and me their old bachelor uncles."

"I got a letter from Jago," his friend said. "He plans to get married after logging's over."

Well, that didn't make the slim man feel any better about not getting on with his life. Three of his best friends would be married and he didn't even have a special gal. Danny commenced to tell Kyle about his wife and their place in Boston. He said it had plenty of room and he was welcome to stay with them when in town.

Sam brought another ale and the slim man stared at it. There was no way he was going to be on the ship at 8:00 a.m. He got to thinking, *The hell with it. I might as well stay right here in Boston and be a drunk. I'll sell my saddle and gear and have money for a little while.*

He felt someone warm next to him, "Come with me upstairs. Norma will watch over the ladies, and I will order us some supper."

Kyle said his goodbyes to Danny, Sam, and anyone else who would listen on the way to the stairs. In the apartment upstairs, she ordered their meal and scheduled him a bath. He said, "I forgot my ale. Sam will think there was something wrong with it."

"Sam will save it for you," Lisa said. "Now let's get you into something more comfortable."

She started by pulling off his boots. "Those things really hurt my feet," he said.

Soon Kyle was sitting in a robe and their meal arrived. The sliced roast beef was tender, and the carrots and new potatoes had a nice butter sauce on them. Hot tea was served with the meal.

The slim man got to talking about searching for Karen Green as they ate. After he earned some money on the ship, maybe he should look for her again next summer. Talking some with his hands, the robe fell open, exposing his scarred body, the results of the war.

With the meal finished and some hot tea down the man, Lisa led him to his hot bath. Gently, she bathed Kyle, tracing her fingers over some of the scars, while he fought the urge to doze off in the comfort of the warm water. Suddenly he asked, "Did I tell you about looking for Karen in Virginia?"

"You did at supper," she said faintly.

With the bath finished, she dried him off, and with a little difficulty got the slim man into night clothes. Pulling the covers back, the two of them lay on the bed. Kyle held her close and kissed her shoulder. She felt his whiskers and wished she had shaved him.

She heard him say, "I got to rest for just a second and then I will be ready."

Lisa sat cradling his head as Kyle softly snored. "You asked when I was going to get married?" she softly said. "It will be when you come back to Boston to stay."

* * *

Kyle woke and was not sure where he was. He heard someone moving around the room. It was still dark outside, and a candle was burning in the next room. Sitting up, he rubbed his sore head. "Lisa, what time is it?" he called out.

The man who took care of the baths and things came to the door. "I have coffee ready for you and your clothing is on the end of the bed."

"Where is Lisa?" he asked.

"Miss Lisa will be back before you leave," the man told him. "We do not have much time, so please get dressed."

"I can't wear the dandy clothes," Kyle muttered as he threw off the covers. Then he saw his new clothing neatly folded. Getting into his clean long johns, Kyle sat heavily back onto the bed. "You ain't going to make it to the ship," he scolded himself. "You haven't got the gear from Billy's or anything."

The pants and shirt fit well. The bagginess he usually lived with was gone. He found his wool coat with his tuque in the side pocket. Once he had the clothes on, he reached for his boots. The worn boots had been sealed and polished, ready for life on a ship.

Walking into the next room with the coat under his arm, Kyle saw a breakfast waiting for him. "I won't have time to eat," he told the man. "I have to get to the livery."

"Your gear has been gotten and is waiting for you downstairs," the man told him.

The lamps were turned up and Kyle could see the tall clock and its slow swinging pendulum near the door. It was only 6:30. He had plenty of time to get to the *Fancy*. He wondered what took Lisa away. He tried to remember last night, but somewhere between the bath and getting to the bed, things got fuzzy. He ate hoping she would show up.

As the clock struck seven, Kyle headed downstairs, knowing he would have to hurry. He had to carry his stuff to the ship. The slim man noticed his gear and saddle near the door. Then Lisa stepped in.

"I see you woke up," she kidded him. "I thought we'd have to carry you into the carriage."

"I am sorry about last night," he told her. "I don't think I was very good company."

She just grinned and reached into a bag she was carrying. "I got you some parting gifts," she said.

There were two twists of tobacco and a pocket watch. Kyle looked at her and said, "That is too much."

"Maybe it is," she replied, "but maybe when you get back you can make it up to me." He kept the watch while she put the tobacco back into the bag and handed it to him.

The man who had been upstairs came down, and while they were saying goodbyes, the man put the saddle and gear into the carriage. Lisa watched him and said, "I should have had your blankets laundered." The she looked at Kyle and said, "You didn't have dirty clothes in your gear."

"No," he told her. "Just a very worn set of clothing that I will probably toss off the ship once we are underway."

Then Danny came in. He also came bearing gifts. There was a fob for the watch and a new skinning knife and sheath. Handing them to Kyle, he said, "Lisa told me about the watch, and I knew you'd need a fob. If you are still using that old skinning knife, I figured you could use a new one."

Smiling, the slim man said, "I am still using the old one and the blade is getting pretty thin. I want to thank you both and I am overwhelmed. It won't be too long before I am back, and then I will make it up to you for your generous gifts."

The speech making was over, and by his new watch he had 40 minutes to get to the ship. He put Danny's gifts into the bag. Lisa gave him the warmest hug and he could see the tears in her eyes. Danny just gave him a hearty handshake and told him to be safe.

As the carriage drew him away from the Raven, Kyle had a strange feeling it might be a long time before he crossed its threshold again. He felt bad that he had missed Kit, but next time he would spend some time in Boston and catch up with everyone.

He opened the bag to take another look at the knife. He noticed something else in the bottom of the bag. Taking them out, there were two letters and a note. The note was from Lisa and just said, 'These letters came for you some months ago.'

One was from Rebecca and the other from Karen Green! Kyle asked the, driver to stop. What was in the letters could change everything. He opened Rebeccas first.

Dear Kyle,

I hope this letter finds you in good health. My family and I are all well. I could not understand when you left our village. Many people called you a thief and other terrible things. I know that you are not and finally the truth of the two men that went with you has come out.

I write to tell you that I have met someone, and he has asked me to marry him. My parents like him, and he going to be a clergy and has been working with our pastor in our church.

It might be wrong to say this considering I am getting married, but you are often in my dreams,

and I will always cherish
our walk on the upper
path just before you left.
Best Wishes, Rebecca

Kyle slowly folded the letter and put it back into the bag. Then with a shaking hand, he took Karen's letter out.

Kyle,
I received word that you came back to the cabin and left a note wanting to know where I was in Virginia. The note said you could be reached at the Raven in Boston.
What you did for me was appreciated. I was in a very bad way at the time. I have put that behind me and just wanted to thank you.
Karen

Folding the letter, the slim man looked it over for any marking that would tell him what town it might have come from. For all he knew, the letter may have arrived in Boston several months ago. He almost had the carriage turn around so he could ask Lisa.

Then realization sunk in. Both women

had gone on with their lives. There was no reason to know when the letters came. Placing them into the bag, he stared ahead, a heavy feeling in his chest. Since the war he had put his life on hold searching for something he could not have. Kyle told the driver to continue on.

CHAPTER FOUR

The slim man arrived at the ship well before 8:00 a.m. and found the captain already near the gangplank. He had a ship's log and each man coming aboard had to sign their name or make their mark in it. Glancing along the inside of the bulwark, Kyle saw that while there were gun ports, there were no cannons.

Amid the commotion on the ship, thoughts of the letters were quickly forgotten. It was time for him to get on with his life. Kyle was told to store his saddle and extra gear in a forward compartment. His saddle bags were to be hung near his hammock and the Charleville was kept on a rack fastened to the bulkhead.

The ketch was a two-masted ship, with a taller mainmast forward and a shorter mizenmast aft. Shrouds from the main deck to the top of the masts on each side held them in place, along with fore and aft lines. The aft mast was stepped forward of the rudder post. Captain Grayson's ketch had an enclosure built around the quarterdeck so the wheel was out of the weather, and necessary charts and maps could be stored. It had shuttered windows that when open gave a wide view from all sides.

Just in front of the aft enclosure was a raised compartment that was the quarters for the captain and his first mate. Amidships were cargo holes covered by tarps to keep the weather out. On top of the tarp was the ship's boat lashed down, keel up. Forward of the main sail were crew's quarters, the mess, anchor rope or chain locker, and storage compartments for line, extra sails, tools, and other items needed to maintain and repair the ketch.

Things were busy on the ship prior to getting underway. Everything that wasn't secure had to be stowed or tied down. Their cook, Barny, had brought out some cornbread and a large pot of coffee and left it near the gangplank. Other than Kyle, two other men had spent the night ashore. Both were married.

Kyle learned that *Fancy* had been a bomb ketch and was captured from the British by the American navy. After the war it had been stripped of all armament and sold. Captain Jon Grayson had purchased it and converted it to carry cargo.

Near the gangplank, an old, weathered sailor called Pop was eating a large chunk of corn bread and drinking coffee. Kyle asked him, "Where are the rest of the crew? Other than captain, first mate, and cook, I see only four of us."

"Under fair weather conditions, the *Fancy* can be sailed by two men and one of them will be on the wheel."

"Why are there four then?" Kyle asked.

Laughing, the old sailor replied, "It ain't always fair weather."

As the tide started going out, sails on both the main and mizzen masts had to be raised. The main sail was first. After removing the ties securing the sail, one of the crewmen jumped the halyard line by grabbing it as high as possible and pulling down. At the same time, a second crewman tailed it by snubbing the halyard around a belaying pin.

Again, the first crew member reached as high as he could and again pulled down the halyard as the second took up the slack. As the two men continued the sail was pulled up towards the head at the top of the mast. If necessary, the first crewman could put his foot against the mast and pull the halyard away if his weight wasn't enough to bring it all the way to the top while the second man continued to pull in the slack.

It happened fast and then the two men moved to the mizzen mast. The first two mainsails filled with the wind as the two men pulled up the headsails.

While this was happening the captain asked, "Are you familiar with the wheel, Oliver?"

"I am, captain," Kyle replied, feeling desperate to be doing something to help.

"Stand by the wheel and wait for my instructions," Grayson told him.

Standing in the enclosure, the slim man watched the crew rush around trimming the sails as the captain shouted orders. Finally, "weigh anchor" was heard and two men manned the windlass, raising the anchor off the seabed. Another man guided the heavy rope down an opening into the storage compartment.

Kyle stood by waiting for a command. He looked over the compass and noted the lubber line. To get the feel, he rotated the rudder back and forth using the 8 handles on the wheel. A look from the captain stopped him from continuing.

With the sails pulled tight and the lines secured on the fife rail, the boat slowly swung around downwind, the crew ducking as the ship jibed and the boom swung from port to starboard.

The captain shouted, "Steer three

degrees to port!"

The slim man did so as the ship cut through the waves. As it rolled some, Kyle took a wider stance to prevent himself from falling to one side or the other. It felt good to be underway. He looked forward to seeing new places.

After they were out of the bay and on the open ocean, the captain came to the quarterdeck. He stood watching the first mate calling out commands to optimize the sails. All the shutters were open and the clean ocean air blew through the quarterdeck.

The design of the ketch was made for open waters and the *Fancy* rode well through the waves. The captain had let Kyle know that there would be two-hour watches at the wheel. If the winds were steady the wheel could be lashed. He then went down to his quarters below.

Ward came to the quarter deck and watched as the land slowly shrank to a thin line on the horizon. "It's a two-week trip to New Orleans," he said. "The captain usually likes to pull into Charleston for water and fresh vegetables. Most often he is gone for one night. He has been known to spend two or three. We think he has a lady friend there."

"Does he come back with vegetables?" Kyle asked.

"It never fails," the man said, chuckling. "Before he comes back a local merchant shows up with what we need."

They had been sailing for almost three hours before a crewman named Sol came and relieved him. The man had a wiry build and had kind of a rolling step. "The first mate told me you had the wheel lashed, so I finished up what I was working on," the man said.

"I did not mind," Kyle told him.

He had actually enjoyed watching the ship cut through the water. Once down on the main deck the first mate took the slim man around and explained all the rigging and why sails were set the way they were. Kyle told him that he'd sailed on a square rigger and had spent a lot of time aloft.

The first mate, Elias, smiled and said, "The only time you go aloft on the *Fancy* is if something gets tangled or broken on the mast."

Kyle looked up at the top of the main mast and the narrow shrouds. He figured it would be quite a climb to get to the top. The slim man found some similarities between the ships he'd been on and the ketch. The biggest advantage of the *Fancy* was most everything was done from the main deck using lines run through pulleys and secured to belaying pins. There were no brace lines that required men on both the port and starboard side of the ship to trim the sails.

The slim man saw smoke coming from a pipe leading to the lower compartment. The cook was working on their next meal. Everyone seemed to have something to do, and Kyle looked around for something to keep himself busy. The first mate waved him over.

"The deck needs a wash down," Elias told him. "You'll find a bucket and some line in the forward compartment. Scoop water from over the side and give the deck a good rinsing."

Looking around, the slim man had to agree that there was debris on the main deck left from loading the cargo, but one good rainstorm would take care of that. Not wanting to question the first mate, Kyle found the bucket and line and was soon ready to give the deck a saltwater washdown.

Tossing the bucket over the side, the line quickly became tight as the ship cut through the waves and it was almost pulled out of Kyle's hands. Holding the line with a death grip, he managed to bring it up. He turned and saw that all the other crew members were watching him.

Sol was laughing. "We were sure you were going to go over the side with your bucket."

Taking the ribbing in good humor, the slim man said, "Just keep yourselves clear or I'll wash you along with the deck."

He dumped the water in a sweeping motion, flooding a wide section. The water flowed over the side through the scuppers, taking debris with it. Getting the next bucket, Kyle realized he couldn't let it go as far toward the stern and pulled it up sooner. The bucket was not as full, but at least it didn't try and take him overboard.

While he might have thought it was busy work washing down the deck, Kyle had to admit it looked a lot better after doing so. Stowing the line and bucket, a lanky man named Rene called him over to help him with mending a sail,

By the end of the day, Kyle was exhausted from fighting the continuous movement of the boat. It didn't help that he had drank too much the day before. Pop was at the wheel and Kyle had another turn after their supper.

Descending the ladder down to the forward compartment, the slim man caught the smell of the coming meal. He had expected some kind of soup, but instead there was ham, and something called a yam that he hadn't had before, a pot of boiled greens, and biscuits. His surprise was complete. He had never had that kind of chow on the *Spencer*, nor the *Eagle*.

There were two narrow tables with a bench next to the galley, one fixed against the starboard bulkhead and the other against the port bulkhead. The compartment was barely high enough to clear Kyle's head. The open hatch and an oil lamp provided light in the compartment.

Coffee was served with the meal. The slim man sipped some and it was strong just as he liked. Luca was sitting next to him and the two of them were wolfing down their meal. Kyle looked over and said, "I can't believe we get this kind of chow. It's like a holiday."

"Cookie got a deal on a big ham and had to make it today," Luca replied. "We'll see it again for the next few meals."

"That is okay with me," Kyle told him. "I do like ham."

With the meal finished, the slim man headed for his watch. He relieved Pop who asked, "How was the ham?"

"Damn good and we even left some for you," he kidded.

It was getting dark, and the *Fancy* continued to sail just within sight of land. Once in a while Kyle could see the light from a building on shore. A candle burned inside an enclosure near the compass to give light needed to read it. The shutters had been closed on the aft windows to prevent the cold wind from blowing in.

On the horizon, Kyle could see a bank of clouds and lightning flashing within them. Running lights were lit to let other ships see them in the dark. Memories of being on the *Eagle* came back to the slim man as he felt the familiar motions and sounds of the ship. Only now there was not the stress of an upcoming battle.

Ward was familiar with bomb ships and told Kyle that this ship had been one under another name in the British navy. The bow had been reinforced to support 10-inch mortars that fired explosive shells inland toward enemy defenses or cities. The ship also had had some cannons for defense against attacks. As a result, the ship was a little slower than its sleek counterparts, but it made a good cargo ship.

In anticipation of the coming storm, the crew reefed the sails, which could slow their progress slightly, but it would protect the sails, lines, and masts from potential damage. The captain had taken the ship out further from shore to prevent the blinding storm from driving them into the shallows and onto the rocks.

The wind was whipping up larger waves as Kyle was relieved. He had to support himself as he worked his way toward the sleeping compartment. While the air outside had been cool, the heat from Barny's cooking remained. The slim man climbed onto his hammock after kicking off his boots and lay there with his blankets rolled up at the foot.

The storm hit a few hours before daylight and the ship plunged through the waves, sending water running down the deck. The hammocks swung, making sleeping difficult. When the waves raised the bow and then descended, those sleeping forward almost felt weightless until the action reversed, and they were forced into their hammock. Kyle woke and grabbed onto the braided line fastening the hammock to the bulkhead to prevent being rocked out onto the deck.

There was the sound of water running and sloshing. They would be manning the pumps come daylight. Maybe even sooner. Sure enough, the command to "Man the pumps," came before it even got light. He steadied himself against the bulkhead. Near a lamp, Kyle looked at his watch. It was 5:00 a.m.

There were port and starboard pumps and two men to operate them. They were just aft of the cargo, which gave some protection against the waves and stinging rain. Kyle wished he had his foul weather gear that he had used while fishing in the channel. Now his only protection was his ground tarp with his head through the slit in the middle. His tuque prevented the rain from beating on his head.

Kyle and the cook stood on opposite sides of the pump and worked the T-handles up and down, bringing water from the bilges onto the deck and spilling out of the scuppers. For an hour, the four men pumped, barely keeping up with the water that the crashing waves caused to leak back down.

The rain stopped and now the ship only had to deal with the waves. The slim man's arms and back ached from working the pump's rocker arm. The cook hadn't said a thing and Kyle didn't dare to complain. He just kept on doing his share pushing down and lifting the handles

An hour after daylight, the command to "cease pumping" came. The first mate had been going around the deck for an hour, searching out and securing any opportunity to keep water outside. The tarps covering the cargo were one of the main culprits. Lashing them down with more ties seemed to help.

The waves continued to break over the bow and the thoroughly soaked crew went below to do their best to dry off. The cook stripped to the waist and worked at getting the fire going in the stove so he could make some breakfast. His pots and covers had to be tied down to the stove to prevent them from splashing everywhere or falling off.

Kyle sat on one end of the bench and was wringing his clothes and tuque out into a bucket. Little of the ship's work could be done with these conditions. By noon, the wind and wave action subsided enough for the crew to go on deck. The captain ordered that the sails be put back up.

Going to the main sail, the slim man began to untie the reef lines. Sol and Rene pulled the sail back to the top. The lanky Rene jumped the halyard because he was taller. In turn all the sails were brought back up. Working in the soggy clothing, Kyle could feel the wool chafing him. He was now glad he had his old, worn, and still dry clothing, because before he went on watch he was going to put them on.

The weather was sunny and calm when the ship reached the harbor near Charleston, SC. The ship's boat was put into the water. Pop and Sol rowed the captain to the wharf. About an hour later they returned with two buckets of beer, a leg of lamb and some fresh vegetables.

As it turned out, this was the only time that Captain Grayson allowed drinking on his ship. The cook prepared the lamb for roasting, and the fall vegetables would be boiled before the lamb was finished. Then, with their mugs filled with beer, the crew began to play cards. Kyle played for a while, losing nearly $2, so he decided to have a chew and watch.

Luca knew several Irish songs and had a good voice. Once he'd lost enough money, he sat next to Kyle and began to sing. Many of the song the slim man was familiar with and tried to help with the singing.

That night, with full bellies and enough beer to feel mellow, they headed for their hammocks. Those who had won money couldn't help but remind those who'd lost about it. The first mate wished them a good night and chose to sit on the quarter deck, more or less on watch, and smoking his pipe.

Only one day was lost with the captain being on shore and soon the *Fancy* was again cutting the waves and sailing south. Pop pointed out the various ports as they passed them, and when going along the Keys Kyle was impressed with the tropical islands poking out of the sea.

When passing around the end of the Keys, the *Fancy* slowed some due to an unfavorable wind. There was a shout, "Boats ahead!"

The captain was on the quarterdeck and Kyle was at the wheel. He could see muskets bristling out of the small pirogues and men were rowing hard to intercept the *Fancy*. Grayson was looking at them with his spyglass. "They intend to board us," the captain told him.

Kyle's Chesterfield was in the compartment as well as his pistol. He wished that he had the pistol in his belt. The captain shouted, "Get your long guns and man the rail, starboard side!"

Ward was going by just below the quarterdeck and the slim man called to him, "Bring me my shooting bag!"

Moments later the bag was tossed onto the deck in front of Kyle and the crew were loading their long guns. Lashing the wheel, the slim man loaded the pistol and stuck it into his belt. Again, grabbing the wheel, Kyle waited for instructions. The *Fancy* was quickly closing on the two small pirogues.

So far, the ship had been running a course that would take them just in front of the boats. The captain asked, "Do you see the third pirogue waiting for us beyond these two?"

Kyle had not, but now he did. "Yes, captain, I do."

"They plan to intercept us on both sides. They'll fire a round and then latch onto us with hooks, board us and kill everyone with cutlasses." Grayson told him with a strange calmness.

"We can turn hard to port and go wide of them," Kyle suggested.

"Doing so we will lose much of the wind we have, and that is probably their plan. I'm sure there are more boats waiting in that direction," the captain told him. "They are like a pack of wolves, intent of taking down a larger prey. I will not play their game."

"Steady at the wheel," he told Kyle. They continued to close, and the slim man could almost see their leering, angry faces.

"Steer to ram the first boat on my command," Grayson instructed. Only moments later he said, "Now!"

Kyle tuned the wheel slightly to port,

losing little of what speed they had. As he closed in on them, the men in the small pirogue abandoned their oars and took up their muskets. Two men on the second pirogue were swinging grappling hooks around, intent on latching onto the ship.

The men on the first boat fired a round just moments before the *Fancy* reached them, then men's screams filled the air. The crewmen on the *Fancy* fired at the second boat, hitting one of the men swinging a grappling hook. The second man threw his, but it deflected off the side of the ship.

There was a slight jar as the ship cut through the small vessel. The shattered craft and struggling men swept by on both side of the ship. Quickly the debris was left behind as the *Fancy* made the turn below the keys and continued into the Gulf.

The captain put away his spyglass and said to Kyle, "There is no reason to have a reinforced bow unless you are willing to use it."

The slim man gripped the handles of the wheel, in disbelief of what he had just been instructed to do. The crew below set their long guns aside and were busy trimming the sails as the ship was steered on a new course across th emerald, green Gulf waters.

CHAPTER FIVE

A day out of New Orleans the captain came to the quarter deck while Kyle was at the wheel. "I imagine you won't be making the trip back with us," Grayson said.

While Kyle hadn't spoken to anyone about whether he was sailing back or not, most of the crew assumed he would. They had talked of the *Fancy* making another round trip before winter and there was money to be made.

Unsure himself, Kyle asked, "Why do you think that?"

"A man that brings all his gear with him, is thinking one way," the captain said. "I need to know when we hit the docks so I can hire another man on."

That night the slim man was sitting on the main deck with Rene, drinking a cup of coffee and having a chew. He still wasn't sure he had an answer for the captain. He had joined the ship, figuring that he would, but now with the question posed to him, he realized he had an option of not doing so.

Waiting for a letter had always been Kyle's motivation to get back to Boston. Now the contents of the two letters made the trip less important. Of course he had friends there, but even they had moved on and the days of joining them to drink and flirt with the ladies were gone.

"The captain wants to know if I am making the trip back to Boston," he told the lanky man.

"I won't be," Rene told him. "The captain knows that. He only pays us $20 for one way. Those going round trip get $25 each way. For me, this completes a round trip."

Kyle had been told $25 when he first spoke to the captain, but at that time only a round trip was in his plans. If he didn't make the return trip, he would lose $5. That was not so much money, but mentally, the slim man already had it in his shooting bag.

The slim man spat over the rail and took a drink of coffee. He then asked, "What will you do in New Orleans?"

"I got a place on the Bienvenue Bayou," Rene replied. Then he smiled and continued. "I was born a Frenchman right here in 1797, two days before Christmas."

"Your folks were from France then,"

Kyle said.

"My father was. He came here as a soldier and stayed when he got out. My mother was born in New Orleans," the lanky man said. "This was French territory then. To my surprise, I became American in 1803 when France sold it."

The two were silent for a minute or two. Then Rene continued, "A year ago, I was a few miles from my place fighting for America against the British."

Then, smiling, he added, "Against your countrymen. We sent them running."

"That's okay," the slim man said. "I was on Lake Champlain fighting against my countrymen in a bay near Plattsburgh."

Changing the subject, Rene told him, "I figure to spend the winter trapping. Come spring I will sign on to some boats going up the Mississippi to St. Louis."

"Why St. Louis?' Kyle asked.

"Because I have never been there," his fellow crewman told him. "Men go there to hunt buffalo. Maybe I will do that."

"Trapping and hunting buffalo," the slim man said. "It sounds like a good life."

"If you decide to stay in New Orleans," Rene said, "you could spend the winter trapping with me."

"I have done trapping before," Kyle told him. The lanky man just looked at him and smiled.

It was mid-November when the *Fancy* sailed the nine miles up the Mississippi River and the crew caught sight of the wharfs in New Orleans. Kyle had told the captain that he wouldn't be making the return trip. Grayson did not seem upset and just wished him well.

With the $20 in his shooting bag, the saddle bags over his shoulder, his blanket roll slung over the other shoulder using a piece of line, and one hand holding the saddle across his back, and the Charleville in the crook of his free arm, the heavily loaded Kyle walked away from the waterfront.

He could see warehouses, a stock yard, taverns, and rows of houses along narrow alleys reaching into the town. Rene walked beside Kyle with a seabag over his shoulder and a Baker flintlock he'd picked up from a dead British soldier after the Battle of New Orleans. For the first time the slim man noticed that his lanky friend had a rolling walk like Sol. While on the *Fancy* it had not been noticeable.

There was a mixture of smells in the air ranging from food cooking, various wastes, the swamps, and a fly-covered dog carcass left along the side of the dusty street. The two men stopped in front of a tavern.

"I could go for a drink," Rene said. "Then we'll get some supplies and find a way to get your gear hauled to my shack."

Setting his gear down in front of the tavern, Kyle asked, "Is it safe to leave my stuff here?"

Speaking French, the lanky man called a young sandy-haired boy over. Giving him a coin, he asked the lad to watch their gear.

Keeping their muzzleloaders, the two men went into the dimly lit tavern and leaned them against the well-used bar. The slim man was pleased to find out that they had ale. Soon they had two foamy brews in front of them.

"I also speak French," Kyle told his friend. "You told the boy I'd give him another coin when we left."

"I should have spoken Creole," Rene told him. "That way I could have kept you guessing."

"The boy isn't very big," the slim man pointed out. "What will he be able to do is someone takes our stuff?"

"He will let us know it is gone," his friend replied.

After a couple of ales, Rene asked the bartender if he could arrange to have a cart come and carry their gear. The bartender stuck his head out of the door and said something to the boy. Coming back to the bar, he told them, "The boy will be back with Damas shortly."

"Now who is watching our gear?" Kyle asked his friend.

"We should probably go outside and wait," Rene told him.

The sun was hot in front of the tavern. It reflected off the dusty street, causing the two to squint. They could see the *Fancy* being unloaded. The captain was talking with two men who were probably joining the crew.

The young boy came back on the run. Breathing hard, with his hand out, he said in French, "Damas is coming. My other coin, please."

Kyle gave him two bits and the lad ran off, smiling.

The creaking and groaning of a two-wheel cart was heard and from one of the alleys a slightly graying, dark-complected man came walking alongside a mule, encouraging it with a small switch.

Damas was the son of a French soldier and a Creole mother. He appeared to be in his late forties and his bare arms showed scars of a rough life. Stopping the mule near the tavern, he gave the men a quick, easy smile. "The boy says somebody needed stuff hauled."

Rene tilted back his hat and said, "Hello, Damas. My friend Kyle needs his gear hauled to my place."

"Well, Mr. Rene," the man said. "It's been six months since I saw you last. You healed real good under Miss Camille's care."

This conversation went over the slim man's head, but he nodded to the man and said, "It is a pleasure to meet you, Damas."

"What have you been doing since the war?" Rene asked the man.

"I bought me a livery," Damas told him. "I come across some money after the war."

The men's gear was put into the cart, and they followed behind as the livery man drove the mule east toward the Bienvenue Bayou. "So, you fought with Damas in the war?" Kyle asked

Rene shook his head, "We were in the same battle, but I was in the army and Damas was with the pirates."

"He said you were wounded," the slim man said. "I was wounded in the Battle of Plattsburgh."

Looking serious, the lanky man was quiet for a bit, then he said, "The battle was all but over, and we killed an awful lot of British. While they were pulling back, I foolishly climbed up on the earthen rampart and was shot by a sniper or retreating soldier."

"You couldn't know that there was still danger," the slim man told him.

As though he hadn't heard the slim man, Rene replied, "I wanted to see our handiwork. You know. All the bodies."

Kyle could understand. It was war and those coming at you were intent on killing you. In the fight, you don't think of them as men. Just as danger. Not so unlike the men in the whale boats who'd come after the *Fancy.* The slim man felt nothing when running one down.

"You want me to stop at the mercantile so you can get some supplies?" Damas asked.

"Damn," Kyle said. "I hadn't thought about that. All I got in my saddlebags is some tobacco and a handful of coffee."

The mercantile building appeared to have recently gotten several repairs. It was likely that it had suffered some during the war. The owner was sitting on the porch in a rocking chair and didn't move from it until the cart stopped

"Damas. Are you bringing me customers?" the man asked.

"I am, Mr. Carl," the hostler said. "I think they need about everything. These two just come off the *Fancy.*"

"Well, I got about everything," the merchant replied. "Things have slowed down since the war."

Stepping into the low, long building, Kyle could smell the leather goods hanging on the nearby wall. The opposite wall had shelves all along it and had various spices, tins of molasses, honey, sugar, salt, tea, and small bags of coffee beans, corn meal, rice, black beans, and other staples. Further down were tin pots, cups, coffee pots, plates, bowls, and various things one would need for cooking or baking.

Kyle found some side meat in a cupboard that was well layered with salt. He learned that in the humid climate things tended to mold quickly.

He let Rene pick most of the items they'd need and then they split the cost. His friend did not chew, so the slim man paid for tobacco separately. There were three big bags of salt and that seemed like a lot, but he figured one must need it in New Orleans. Putting most of their purchases into flour sacks, they were placed into the cart along with the salt.

They continued down the dirt road towards Rene's place. They finally reached a path that went out onto a narrow peninsula. To the left it disappeared in the moss-covered live oak and cypress trees. "This is as far as I can go," Damas told them. "I can help carry things to the shack if you want."

"You have to get back to the livery," Rene replied. "Kyle will pay you."

Giving his friend a look, the slim man dug into his shooting bag and handed the man the agreed eight bits. The gear and supplies were set next to the path. "Stop by the livery," he told Kyle. "I got some stuff you can put on the saddle so the leather won't mold."

He had only been in the area for less than two hours and already he had been warned about mold twice. Kyle realized that there might be several other things he should be aware of.

The peninsula went out about an eighth of a mile and turned slightly to the south. At the end he saw the weathered shack. The clapboards were gray and slightly curled. The shingle roof was covered with a green moss. There was a shuttered window to the side of the back wall with a shooting notch in the center. A lean-to extended just over half the width of the wall. It was large enough to keep a couple of horses.

The first load of gear was placed down near the lean-to. "I will go back and get the rest of our supplies," Kyle offered. "You can go and unlock your place and start bringing things in."

As Kyle started up the trail, he heard Rene say, "It ain't locked."

It took two trips due to the bags of salt. When the slim man got back with the last two bags, he saw that everything else had been brought in. One of the double doors of the lean-to was open and inside he saw one bag of salt, so he placed the others next to it and closed the door.

Walking around the side, he saw that there was a stone chimney for a fireplace, in the front there was a covered porch that extended out over the water. He also passed a small building that appeared to be the outhouse.

Stepping onto the porch, Kyle saw the

clinker-built boat lying keel up. "Is it watertight?" he called to his friend.

"It will be once we soak it overnight," Rene called back. "Come on in and see your new home."

There was another shuttered window on the porch side and a plank door swung open into the shack. Kyle had to duck under the door header as he stepped into the single room cabin. It was eerily like the cabin in the woods.

Rather than a double bed on the left side, there were two bunks. There was a large table in the middle of the room, and on the far wall were pegs to hang clothes and a dry sink with shelves above and below it. To the right was the fireplace that he'd noticed coming in.

It was not high enough to have a loft, but in the rafters there were bamboo poles for fishing and a few other things. Two oars leaned in the corner near the fireplace. Overall, the shack was in good condition. The shack was built off the ground to prevent the bayou water from reaching it. He noticed that it needed to be swept, and some scrubbing wouldn't have hurt.

Shaking off the critical thoughts, Kyle had to admit that the place looked much homier than the stone cottage with the dirt floor where he had lived back in England. His gear was lying just inside the door and Rene was putting the supplies on the shelves.

"Which bunk is mine?" Kyle asked.

"I use the one on the left," Rene replied. "My pa used the one on the right until he died."

That was more than the slim man needed to know. He stored his saddle and other gear in the far-right corner at the end of his bunk. Rene picked up a wooden pail and blew and shook the dust from it. "I will show you where the spring is. The water out front can be a little brackish at high tide."

Just to the right of the cabin was a spring with its clear water rolling to the surface. Dipping the bucket and scooping it full, Rene set it down and tasted the contents. "Pretty good," he said.

As he walked back to the cabin carrying the bucket, the lanky man said, "I used to have a circle of slabs pounded into the bottom around the spring and the water was always perfectly clear of salt. They rotted away and I got to get some more slab wood."

Setting the bucket onto the dry sink, Rene said, "Lets rig a couple of poles and catch some supper."

It wasn't long and the two of them were sitting on the edge of the porch with two lines in the water. Small pieces of side meat were used for bait. The lines had hardly been in the water when the first fish hit. They brought up two plump catfish.

"The bayou will provide us with many

meals," Rene said as he tossed his line back into the water.

"This is one big swamp," Kyle commented. "How far back does it go?"

Laughing, his friend said, "It's a bayou, not a swamp. Around its edges you might find some swamps."

"What's the difference?" the slim man asked.

"The best way I can explain it is that the bayou is a slow-flowing river. If you dropped a block of wood in front of the shack here and watched it long enough, it would end up in the Gulf," Rene told him.

"If the water is always flowing out, how is the water brackish?" Kyle asked. "Are there deposits of salt underneath?"

"Tides," the lanky friend replied. "Look at the supports that hold up the porch. The water goes up and down, but fresh water keeps flowing in from the northwest and the springs. If you go a few miles to the other side of New Orleans the water is always fresh."

"The water has a darkish color to it," Kyle observed. "Is that from the Mississippi River?"

"My father always told me that it was tannin from the leaves of the cypress trees," his friend told him.

By this time, they had six fish on the stringer tied to the porch. "These fish will make a lot of soup," the slim man said.

"We'll fry up four of them for our supper," Rene replied. "The other two can stay on the stringer for our breakfast."

"I haven't used my new knife yet," Kyle told him. "I will clean the fish."

There was a small table at one end of the porch that overhung the edge of the porch floor. After the slim man had gutted the catfish, he used a second bucket to wash off the small table. Small fish came to the surface to gobble up the smaller bits of meat.

To the slim man's surprise, on the table in the shack were several parsnips. "I planted the parsnips last spring, and they are ready. I also have some potatoes we need to dig," Rene proudly said.

"I didn't notice a garden," Kyle told him.

"It's off the northwest corner of the lean-to," was the reply.

They found that a bird had made a nest using sticks and Spanish moss when they lit the fire. It was quickly cleaned out by poking a pole up the chimney. The fried fish and parsnips made an excellent meal.

Both men rolled their blankets out onto the floor that night. The hay in the hay ticks was musty and they would have to be refilled with fresh, dry hay. The next morning the two men had brought chairs to the porch and were sitting with coffee.

"How far are the beaver we're going to

trap?" Kyle asked.

"No beaver around here," Rene replied. "Gators would eat them. We are going after the gators."

"Do we row around with the boat and see them on the shore and shoot them?" the slim man asked.

"We could do that," the lanky man replied. "Instead, we put out baits and then the next day we haul in the ones we catch and shoot them."

"Before we do that, we have to walk into town and buy some hay," Kyle said. "I don't see any place around here that we could cut some."

After cleaning up from breakfast, the slim man swept the cabin while Rene emptied the hay from the ticks onto the garden, and then after washing them hung them to dry on the porch.

Their long guns were left on pegs in the cabin as they headed for the livery. Kyle had the pistol in his belt and his knife in its sheath. Rene had his empty army knapsack on his back to carry a few supplies they might need.

They waved to the owner of the mercantile as they passed him sitting on his porch. The slim man was thirsty. "Let's stop at the tavern for an ale."

"I got a better place we can stop," Rene told him. "It's not too far from the livery."

They walked through a narrow street of New Orleans that opened into a wider dirt boulevard. Kyle noticed the livery at the top of the boulevard. His friend pointed to another place.

"There's the La Maison saloon," the lanky man said. "They've got about anything a man might want."

A young man about 15 years-old jumped up when he saw them and called out, "Come on in, gentlemen. We have the best drinks and the prettiest women for your pleasure."

Rene dug out a coin and handed it to the young man. Kyle noticed the same young boy with wavy, sandy hair sitting on a small stool watching them. Entering the saloon, Kyle said, "They start them young here. The lad on the stool couldn't have been 10 years-old yet."

"That's the piano player's kid," his friend replied. "I imagine he hopes to take over the front porch someday. They call in customers and sweep the mud off the porch so things look nice."

"Why did you give the older one a coin?" the slim man asked.

"He's been here for a couple years and all he works for is tips," Rene told him. "He's an orphan left by one of the women that used to work here. I figure he needs the money."

Memories of Danny came to Kyle's

mind. He had been an orphan on the streets of Boston. There was no place like the La Maison to work for tips. Stepping into the saloon, the slim man saw tables for gambling, a thin, old man playing the piano, and a long, polished bar at the back.

The owner was Tully, and he was watching the bar while his bartender was stocking the backbar and mixing up the lady's drink. "What can I get you two gents?" he asked.

"Ale if you got it," Kyle said. Rene just nodded in agreement.

After leaving a coin on the bar, the two men took their drinks and moved to one of the tables. The dimly lit bar was cool, and it felt good to sit for a while.

The slim man looked around. "Where are the ladies?"

"It is not even noon yet," Rene replied. "They are still sleeping. If you are in need, I am sure Tully will wake one up for you."

Blushing slightly, the slim man said, "I was just asking. I am just fine."

A white-haired man came in and the owner asked him, "Aren't you a little early Doc?"

"I got a bit of a cough this morning and figured a little brandy would fix me right up," the man said.

Speaking low, Rene said, "That's Doc Randle. He took the ball out of my shoulder."

"I thought a woman named Camille fixed you up," Kyle replied.

Again, keeping his voice low, the lanky friend said, "Not so loud. He took it out and then it got sour. She fixed me up from that. The doc doesn't think much of Miss Camille. People say she is a voodoo queen, and she uses magic or spells to fix things. Truth is, she knew of some herbs or something that took out what I had."

After finishing the brandy, the doc left, and through the open door Kyle could see the young man holding Randles horse and buggy. *That should be good for a tip*, Kyle thought.

Just as the two men got up to leave, one of the ladies came down the stairs. She glanced at them and shook her head before heading toward a back room. As they left the young man called to them, "See you again soon."

The hostler was humming a tune and cleaning stalls when they came in. The wooden wheelbarrow was about ready to be emptied. Damas looked up and said, "Let me get rid of this and I will be right back."

There were planks at the back door that ran up to a pile of manure. Leaving the wheelbarrow on the planks, the man came back and said, "Are you after the stuff for your saddle?"

"That and some hay for our ticks," Kyle told him.

"I got a horse being shoed that I got to get to its owner first thing this afternoon," the hostler replied. "I will have the hay there by late afternoon. Hopefully, you weren't thinking of filling the ticks before that."

Smiling, Rene said, "That will be fine. My friend will settle up with you."

The slim man gave him a look, thinking, *When do you start paying?* Then he realized he was staying at Rene's shack. So far, rent-free.

Kyle left with a tin of powder with a smell he did not recognize. When he got back, he figured he'd rub some onto the leather. There next stop was at the mercantile.

The slim man needed a hat. That last night in Boston he'd lost his someplace. All he had now was his tuque. Rene had a felt hat with some wear to it, but it still served him well. The mercantile had straw, felt, and leather hats. Felt was lighter than leather and still kept the sun and rain off pretty well, and it was also cheaper than leather.

Choosing the felt hat, he headed for the counter. He also needed some gunpowder and lead. The owner got the items and Kyle dug into his shooting bag.

"That's a mighty small possible bag you got," the man observed.

"It's a shooting bag," the slim man replied.

"Around here we call them possible

bags," the owner replied. "They hold everything you might possibly need."

Smiling, Kyle told him, "I guess I don't need as much as some."

Rene came to the counter with a bag of flour. The slim man paid for everything.

The two men spent the afternoon fishing. The lanky man wanted big ones to bait the hooks for gators. Kyle had asked him what they'd do with the gators they got and was told that they would sell the skins and the meat they didn't need.

The slim man wasn't sure he'd care for gator. He'd seen large lizards in Martinique when he was a crewman. The *Spencer* had went there to load on rum. They did not look like something one would want to eat.

The boat on the porch was put into the water and slowly water seeped between the dry boards. At first, they had to bail it frequently, but by the time Damas brought the hay, the seepage had slowed significantly.

The hay was brought on the mule. The hostler had a packsaddle with a rack that held enough hay to fill the two ticks. The key advantage was that the mule could be led right to the shack.

With the hay in the ticks and put onto the bunks, the two men went back to fishing for bait and bailing the boat. Kyle made fish soup that evening for the meal. Fresh dug potatoes were part of the soup.

The next morning, Rene declared the boat seaworthy. A small box near the shack on the porch had a hinged lid and contained the hooks for catching gators. Each hook had a short chain leader that rope was tied to.

Using a file, the tips of the hooks were touched up. With four hooks, and catfish that had laid on the deck for a night to get a little ripe, the two set out in the rowboat in search of places to leave the baited hooks.

The shack had barely been out of sight, when Kyle asked, "How do we find our way back? Everything looks the same around us."

Rene kept rowing and said, "In time everything will look familiar to you. Each tree has its own look. No two small islands look the same."

About that time, they pulled up to one of the islands. Two catfish were impaled onto a hook. The lanky man stepped off the boat and the bait was hung just off the water on a small bush. He then secured a rope to a small cypress, leaving a little slack.

Kyle looked around trying to pick out landmarks or trees that were unique. They all kind of looked alike. "This island has three young cypresses," Rene said. "The gators like to warm themselves on it and I generally have good luck."

Another baited hook was left hanging at the base of a larger cypress and the rope was tied around it. As they rowed away, Kyle figured he had a pretty good idea where the shack was.

Two more baits were placed, and Rene asked his friend if he wanted to row. "I would like to, and I'll bring us right back to the shack."

By the time the two men had changed places, the slim man wasn't quite so sure. In the dense tree canopy it was difficult to use shadows for direction. When they left the shack, the breeze was coming from the north. Now it was still. There was moss on the trunks, but most had it all the way around near the base.

Meanwhile the boat was turning on its own. There was a slight current. *Was the tide coming in or going out?* He wondered.

"Okay Rene," Kyle said. "I could start rowing, but there is a chance I might be going in the wrong direction. Which way is home?"

His friend said, "The tide is coming in." Then he pointed, "That way is north."

"Is the shack north of us?" Kyle asked.

"No, it is west of us," his friend replied.

"I would be lost and starve in this damn bayou," the slim man said.

"You got the pistol," Rene said. "You could shoot something and cook it on any one of the islands."

"Sure," Kyle laughed. "Then the tide would come up and cover the island and put out my fire."

After rowing for what seemed like a long time, the island with the three young cypresses came into view. Only now most of the island was half-covered with water and the rope around the one was barely visible.

"We got to be close," he told Rene. "This was the first bait we placed."

"See, I told you," his friend replied. "There are lots of things in the bayou that will tell you where you are"

CHAPTER SIX

The next morning, Kyle woke before daylight tossing and turning restlessly, anxious to see if they'd caught any gators. Finally, he heard Rene say, "For crying out loud. How the hell is a man supposed to sleep with all the noise you're making?"

"I keep thinking about the gators," the slim man said. "What if we don't catch any?"

"What did you do when you didn't catch any beaver?" Rene asked.

"We'd check the set and maybe move the trap," Kyle replied.

"Think about moving the baits, but do it quietly," his friend said, pulling the covers over his head.

Not much later, both men were out of the bunks and Kyle was making coffee. "After I finish with the coffee, I'll make some side meat and frying pan bread," he offered.

Rene opened the door and looked out. The fog-shrouded bayou looked ghostly. "The fog should lift in an hour or so, then we can check our baits."

"What can we get for a gator skin?" Kyle asked.

"There are two ways to skin them," his friend replied. "We can skin it to leave the horns or leave the belly."

"What's the difference?" the slim man asked.

"We slit it open from the back for the belly. The belly skin is what they want," Rene said. "If they want the horns on the skin, then we slit it from the stomach."

"How do we know which one to do?" Kyle asked.

"I generally skin them all for the belly," he told his friend. "There's more demand for that."

"On the beaver we took what meat we could and ate it," the slim man said.

"A good-size gator has lots of meat. The white meat, like the jaw muscles and some of what are called loins on a deer, are very good. The darker meat is a little stronger, but it is still good eating," Rene explained.

"What do we do if we get too many gators?" Kyle asked. "Often in a pond we would catch two maybe three beavers."

"Gators are more solitary reptiles,"

Rene said. "In the spring, when they're mating, they tend to come together, but other than that in the area we put baits, we'll be lucky to get one."

While eating their breakfast, Kyle said, "We always knew where the beavers were. There was sign were they chewed on trees, and then the lodges. You could tell if it was an active lodge by canals that they came in and out of the ponds, and fresh chips near stumps." Then the slim man laughed. "Of course, the slapping of their tails would give them away."

"We look for signs with gators too," Rene told him. "When they come out of the water, we can see a trail where their tail dragged, or where the grass has been pushed down. In the evening you can hear their grunting."

"Did you see any of that yesterday?" Kyle asked.

"I did not," his friend replied. "I did hear grunting, but sound can travel a long way."

While waiting for the fog to lift, the two men sat on the porch with the last of the coffee. A blue heron glided out of the fog, landing near the edge to watch for a mcal. The songs of birds, quacking ducks and other noisy inhabitants of the bayou filled the air.

Suddenly, Rene began to talk of the war. "We fought just a few miles from here.

It was a foggy morning like this. We could hear them coming somewhere in the fog."

Kyle was reminded of how blinding the fog in the channel could be, how fast it could roll in and how lost he'd feel. Then, his lanky friend interrupted his thoughts and continued. "We were all praying that the fog would lift. In the distance we heard shots and cannon fire. Then the fog lifted as though providence had heard our prayers, and there they were. Rows and rows of men in red coats. We just started shooting and loading as fast as we could."

Then the two sat in silence as the fog around them began drifting away, like low clouds on the bayou. The two men set out to check their baits. Kyle had his Charleville, and pistol loaded and ready. The first one, at the small island with three trees, had the hook with bait pulled onto the island and one of the catfish was gone.

"Looks like the gator was full after one fish," the slim man said.

"My guess is an otter," Rene said. "I should have hung it farther over the water."

As the boat bumped up against the shore, the lanky man looked near the bait. "It's an otter," he said. "Lots of little tracks. We'll want to move this one."

The hook with the rotting fish was placed into the boat. It smelled bad, but the slim man hoped it would draw in a gator wherever they put it in next. The next one that had been put out tied to the cypress tree had not been touched. The two catfish were still on the hook with flies buzzing around them.

While heading for the third set, Rene kept an eye out for a place to put the bait that the otter had gotten into. Kyle was rowing at his direction and suddenly the lanky man said, "I see a gator trail."

Another catfish was taken from the bucket and pushed onto the hook. The slim man could see where the tall grass had been pushed down. It was a bigger island with several large cypress trees. One tree on the edge of the island had died years ago and its hollowed trunk still reach up over 30 feet. A wood duck had made a perfectly round hole about 10 feet above the water and built a nest.

They worked their way between the cypress knees to a place where they could hang the bait and secure the rope. With the bait placed, Kyle pushed the boat away from the island and cypress knees and then rowed towards their third bait.

The third place was near a tributary that flowed into the bayou. Their bait had fallen off the stub of a branch were it had been hung. Rene pulled it up with thoughts of placing it elsewhere. To their surprise, most of the meat had been eaten off the catfish, leaving only a skeleton.

The lanky man took the oar and poked at the bottom. "I'll be damned. The bottom is rocky, and we got crawdads!"

"What the hell are crawdads?" Kyle asked.

"I'm not sure what they'd be called in England, but they are a crayfish. Kinda like a shrimp," Rene told him.

"I take it they are good to eat," the slim man replied.

"They are and when we come back this way, I'll put in a trap for them," his friend said.

The empty hook was removed from near the tributary. For a half-hour Kyle rowed, looking for a place to put the bait. Suddenly there was a loud splash. "Did you see it?" Rene asked. "It was a good-size gator!"

"Should we wait for it to come back up?" Kyle asked.

"It can stay down for hours," his friend told him. "We can put the bait anywhere around here. We know there's a gator."

With that bait placed on a bush hanging over the water, they headed for the last set. Well short of it, Rene whispered. "We might have something."

Kyle quit rowing. "Why are we whispering?"

"Habit, I guess," his friend replied. "Is your pistol ready?"

"Wouldn't I use the muzzleloader?" the slim man asked.

"There is a small spot on the head you have to hit to kill a gator," Rene told him. "You could kill it with a pocket gun. Your British pistol will be plenty to kill it."

Using his knife, the lanky man scratched out the shape of a gator head. Pointing with the knife, he said, "Right here on the head. You want to hit its small brain or spine."

Kyle thought that the boat might be moving and the gator pulling to get off the hook and that small of a target might be hard to hit. "What happens if I miss?"

"We'll have a damn angry gator and a fight on our hands to get another shot," Rene replied.

The slim man pulled the pistol out of his belt. His friend used one of the oars to push the boat close to the tree and windfall where the bait had been placed. The turtles on the windfall log splashed into the water, startling Kyle, who had his eyes intently on the rope. The rope connected to the hook and chain had been pulled to the far side of the tree.

"Stcady yourself and keep any splashing water away from your pistol," Rene said as he reached for the rope.

There was slight slack in the rope and as soon as the lanky man pulled it tight all hell broke loose in the shallow bayou. Kyle saw the tail flash out of the water and the gator began to roll.

The rope had been jerked from Rene's hand. He grabbed it again and pulled for all he was worth. The rowboat bumped against the cypress tree and then swung around it as the lanky man pulled in the rope. Kyle had put the pistol back into his belt and hung on to the gunwales.

The gator lashed its tail and churned up the sediment from the bottom, turning the tannin-colored water to a muddy brown. The fight reminded Kyle of the time he had caught a large tuna in the channel back in England.

The gator finally exhausted, Rene was able to bring it next to the boat. The hook and chain were in its mouth from trying to swallow the catfish. Rene was between him and the gator and when he moved to the side of the boat to try and shoot, the rowboat leaned dangerously over.

"Just a second," the lanky man said. "Let me move in a little."

Still gripping the rope, Rene let a little slip through his hands, and he moved away from the side. This started another fight and splashing from the gator. When it stopped it was on its back.

"Don't shoot yet," his friend warned him. A couple jerks on the rope had the gator fighting again. When it stopped the gator was on its belly and the head was halfway up the side of the boat.

Gasping for air, Rene said, "Take your shot."

Kyle knew that when he shot the gator would make one more attempt to flee. He could see the spot his friend had instructed him to shoot. He adjusted his angle so if the shot went through, it wouldn't hit the boat. With the pistol cocked, the slim man took aim and pulled the trigger. Smoke of the powder masked his target and he felt the boat move under him and he grabbed the gunwale again.

Then everything was still, and as the smoke drifted away he could see the gator lying still beside the boat. He quickly began to reload the pistol. The slim man worried that he had only stunned it and wanted to be ready to take another shot.

"It's done, Kyle," Rene told him. "Good shot."

The rope from the gator was tied to the stern and the slim man rowed for the cabin. "Just tell me if I'm going the wrong way. I don't want to drag this bastard all over the bayou."

The gator was eight-feet long, maybe more, Kyle judged. The head looked damn big right behind the boat. He figured that it wouldn't be easy for one man to handle it.

"When I get a deer, I always look forward to the liver for my next meal. How does the liver taste on a beast like this?" he asked.

"The liver!" Rene scoffed. "We don't take nothing out of the innards of a gator."

I suppose I best not ask about the heart, he thought.

Kyle was beginning to get a little arm weary by the time the shack came into view. The late November nights were cool, and Rene told him that they would hang the gator overnight.

The slim man almost asked about gutting it first so it would cool faster, but then he remembered the "don't take nothing out of the innards" statement. The bow bumped against the porch and the lanky friend got out of the boat and tied it up.

The slime-covered gator was dragged and slid onto the porch. "You get a bucket of water, and I'll get the soap and the brush."

Even though the request brought up questions, Kyle figured he'd just wait and see what came next. He returned with the water about the same time as Rene came out of the cabin. "I forgot where I had put the brushes."

Placing the bucket near the gator, Kyle was still in awe when he looked at it. He had shot elk in the past which were bigger, but not as aggressive looking. The lanky man poured a white powder into the water, and using the end of the brush, he stirred it. The brushes looked like something you'd use on a horse or to scrub the floor.

"That smells like the stuff Damas gave me for the saddle," the slim man said.

"It is mostly borax and then something to help it suds up," Rene said as he began to scrub the carcass.

Taking a second brush, Kyle started on the other side. They scrubbed it from head to tail and then rolled it over to scrub the belly. Dipping buckets of water from in front of the porch, the gator was rinsed.

For the first time the slim man noticed a wooden pully lashed to one of the porch rafters. Rene tied a rope to the tail, and then ran it through the pulley and the two men pulled the gator up. The rafters were about 10 feet off the porch floor and the gators nose was just barely off the floor.

More buckets of water were gotten and tossed onto the carcass. "That should do it," Rene told him. "We'll skin it in the morning and when done, we will harvest some meat."

"Is there much meat on the gator? Its legs are kind of small," Kyle replied.

"You will be surprised how much meat we'll get. Some we can salt down and we'll make jerky out of the rest," his friend said.

The rest of the day was spent around the shack. A 10-foot plank table was gotten from the lean-to and put onto the porch. Rene worked on two wood and wire crawdad traps. Kyle did some cleaning and spent time in the garden digging potatoes.

Late afternoon, his lanky friend said, "The traps are ready. All I need is a couple of catfish and we can go out and put them near the tree."

The slim man had just finished washing the potatoes and spread them out on the long table to dry. "Will we be checking the baits?" he asked.

"We will go by them," Rene replied. "This time of day they spend time sunning themselves. But you never know."

As they rowed away, Kyle looked back at the dark green behemoth hanging on the porch. Seeing it gave him the same feeling he'd gotten when looking at the bear he'd shot in Canada.

At the first tree, there were white ibis wading in the shallow water, searching the bottom with their curved bills looking for crustaceans for their meal. Rene debated whether he should move the bait. He decided to give it another day. They reached the tributary, put a catfish into each trap and dropped them to the bottom. A line from each was tied to a cypress knee.

They went past the island where they'd heard the splash in the morning. Staying well away, the lanky man suddenly pointed. "There it is," he said.

Kyle had the Charleville. "Do you want me to take a shot?" he asked as he looked at the dark, horned form lying on the island.

"No," his friend said. "Give it time. It will find our bait."

The other two baits, which included the one that they'd had before, had not been disturbed so they continued toward the shack. "There are folks in New Orleans that will buy whole gators or their meat."

"You never said how much we can get for a gator skin," Kyle reminded him.

"It depends on the size and condition of the skin," Rene replied. "A small one will get us four bits a foot while the one we got should get us six bits a foot."

"How much will folks pay for a whole gator?" the slim man asked.

"Ones we would be willing to sell would go for $5 to $10. We wouldn't sell a bigger one. We could get money for the meat. I figured that we'd get about one to two bits per pound," his friend said.

"I imagine there wouldn't be much meat on smaller ones," Kyle replied.

"We would only take the skin off smaller ones," Rene told him. Then he thought and added, "Maybe the cheeks and loins."

Once back at the shack, the slim man tried to imagine a bigger gator hanging there. Its head would be lying on the porch floor. A cold wind began to blow, and it would be good for cooling the gator.

While they made their supper, Rene said, "If this wind cools the water too much, the crawdads will stay under their rocks, and we won't get too many."

"It's good that we got the traps in today," Kyle said.

After having a restless sleep the night before, this night the slim man slept like a log. He was still in dreamland when his friend kicked the foot of the bunk. "Time to get up. We've got a gator to skin."

Breakfast was coffee and cornmeal mush. After dishes were done Kyle got his short axe out of his gear and then the two men worked on the edges of their knives with whetstones. Both knew a sharp knife makes skinning easier, yet it does increase the chance of cutting through the skin much greater.

With beaver, elk, or deer, one tries to avoid it, but it does not decrease the value that much. With a gator skin, a hole in the belly can cut the value in half. With everything ready, they took the last of the coffee out on the porch and sat enjoying the morning. Kyle chewed and spat into the bayou water.

"I noticed that you got your axe out of your gear," the lanky man commented.

"Hell, I didn't know what all you need when skinning a gator," Kyle replied.

"It might help when taking the head

off," Rene told him.

With the last drink of coffee, they set their cups down and began. The gator was lowered and put onto the table belly-down. The carcass was firm and stiff and had begun to bloat. Looking at the bullet hole, Rene smiled. "You shot well."

One man was on each side. Slits were made along the horned back leaving one row. At this time there was not a lot of demand for the horns or scutes. Kyle was surprised how tough the skin was. Cuts were made down the legs and around the legs, just above feet.

The lanky man made the cuts around the head. Slowly the two men began pulling back the skin, making rhythmic slashes to separate the skin from the carcass. They tried to take as little meat and fat with the skin as possible. All of that would have to be scraped off.

Once the skin was peeled down both sides and down the legs, the gator was rolled onto its side and Rene finished skinning around his side. Then rolling it onto the other side, Kyle finished around his. Then the carcass was laid onto its back.

Taking his time, Rene cut around the under jaw and took the skin off to the throat. Using a rag, he then wiped off the belly and looked for any damage that might have been caused while the gator lived in the bayou. He smiled. There was very little damage.

The skin was taken from the belly area and then the entire skin was dropped to the porch floor. "We'll take the meat before we flesh the skin," Rene said.

Kyle did not see a lot of meat. Per his friend's instructions he went and got two buckets. The first meat taken was the jaw muscles, or cheeks. Those alone were almost five pounds of meat. Then Rene cut along each side of the tail just above and below the back legs. He removed the choice meat, which was like the tenderloins.

The remaining meat all along the tail was not prime but still good, and once done just the tail bone remained. The hook and chain were removed from the throat and tossed near the wall. Turning the gator over again, Rene removed the shoulder and rib meat. Stepping back, the two men looked at the two buckets of meat.

"We could get a little more off the legs and belly," the lanky man said, "but that is tougher and stronger meat. I would keep it if I was starving, but we are not."

The slim man was impressed how fast the gator was skinned and the meat taken off from it. He was also pleased with the amount of meat they'd gotten. Cloths were put over the two buckets to keep the flies off, the head was removed, and the carcass was slid into the water. He could not believe that the whole process was done without cutting into the body cavity.

The table was rinsed off with a third bucket and some more borax and the brushes were used to wash the blood and fat from it. Then the skin was spread out, the fat and meaty side up.

Knives could be used to scrape it, but the razor-sharp blades might create holes. Rene brought out two more tools. They were flat iron blades with a handle on each end. The blades were not sharp but had a square edge that worked well to remove flesh and fat.

Kyle kept the skin flat and spread out while his friend expertly scraped and removed what was left from the skinning. "We are going to need a bag of salt," he told the slim man.

When Kyle got back with the salt, he saw that the skin was draped over the rail built on the far side of the porch. "We let it dry for a little while and then we salt it down to continue the drying," Rene told him. "Meanwhile we will use a little of the salt for preserving the meat and head."

"The head?" Kyle asked. "Are we going to eat the head?"

"No," the lanky man laughed. "We take the tongue out and trim any meat left near the neck. Then we coat it with salt and leave it in the lean-to."

"What does the tongue taste like?" the slim man asked.

"I wouldn't know," Rene replied. "We use it for catfish bait or just toss it away."

The two men went to the lean-to and Rene pointed out two stoneware containers that would be needed to store the meat. Each container would hold a little more than a bucket. The two containers were brought around and put onto the table in the shack.

Kyle then went to the spring for a bucket of water. The meat had to be rinsed off before it was coated with salt. The pieces of meat were put into one of the containers with more salt added to each layer. Slices of the jaw and neck meat were kept out to be fried for their midday meal.

The first container was filled with salted meat using the best cuts. This was set near the dry sink with the wooden cover on. The darker meat from along the tail had been set aside to be made into jerky. Now using his knife, Rene removed the membrane that covered one side and then the long slabs were salted.

While his friend finished getting the rest of the meat ready to be dried in the sun, Kyle went to the fireplace and got a fire going to make their meal. After slicing a little side meat into the blackened frying pan, the slim man put the gator meat into the pan and the sounds of the sizzle and the smell of frying meat made him anticipate the coming meal. Next to the pan he had a pot of coffee brewing.

Shortly the two men sat to their meal. Kyle took his first bite of gator meat. The meat had a slight fishy taste, which the slim man did not mind. It was tender like chicken.

"How do you like it?" Rene asked.

"I like it," Kyle replied.

"Good," his friend said. "Because we will have a lot of it to eat."

After the meal, racks from the lean-to were put up near the garden and the thin strips of the salted, dark tail meat was hung from them to dry. A smoky fire was built upwind of the racks to offer some flavor and keep flies off.

The gator skin had dried some as well as the long table. The skin was laid out and a thick layer of salt was spread on it. The leg skin was folded in, and more salt was added. Then, starting from the tail, the skin was rolled up with care taken to make sure there was a good layer of salt all the way.

The slim man learned that the salt provided two benefits. It prevented bacteria from growing and it drew the moisture out of the skin. Two things that could decrease the value were spots of bacteria growth or bits of fat.

The skin was put onto a tarp in the lean-to next to the head and more salt was poured on both. Then the two men spent time with a bucket of borax water and scrubbed the long table and the porch boards. Once it was rinsed down, it was time to tend to the carcass.

Both men took their long guns as well as Kyle's pistol and got into the boat. Using the hook that had been removed from the gator, Rene sunk it into the carcass to use to tow it.

"Where do we take it?" the slim man asked.

"To the east, away from here toward the open water," his friend replied.

They took turns rowing the boat, and about a mile east of the shack the carcass was released to be eaten by the varmints of the bayou. They then headed for the gator baits to see if they'd had any luck overnight.

Rene had taken a bucket, anticipating having some crawdads in his traps. The first bait on the cypress tree remained the object of flies but no gators. "We move this one tomorrow," the lanky man said.

The dead cypress with the wood duck nest was next. Rene felt that this was a good spot and planned to leave it alone. They reached the crawdad traps and Kyle pushed the boat between the cypress knees while his friend stayed at the bow.

The first trap was pulled up and brought a broad smile to the lanky man's face. Opening the little trap door, he shook the contents out into the bucket, which had water at the bottom. The dark, clawed crustaceans splashed into the bucket.

"That one had over a hundred in it," Rene said as he placed another catfish into the trap and dropped it back into the water. The second trap had the same success. Some of the crawdads tried to climb out of the bucket, and with the flick of a finger they were sent back down the side. With both traps back in the water, the two men continued with hopes of bigger catches.

Returning to the shack with only the crawdads to show for their success, Rene climbed out of the boat and tied it up while Kyle placed the bucket onto the deck. The bucket was put onto the long table and both men looked in.

"The water is damn muddy," the slim man said.

"These little buggers live under rocks in the mud," his friend told him. "Go get a bucket of spring water."

Coming back with a nice, clean bucket of water, Rene transferred the crawdads a handful at a time into the bucket with clean water. With that done, it was time to check on their jerky project.

Frowning, Kyle saw that a few pieces of meat had been pulled off the rack. The fire was down to coals, so some kindling and green wood was added. His friend had remained on the porch admiring the crawdads and finally came to the back of the shack.

"We lost some meat," the slim man told him. "A weasel, mink, or raccoon took away a meal."

"I feel good about where we have our bait hung," Rene told him. "We'll soon have more gator to make jerky out of."

It wasn't an hour later when Kyle looked into the bucket of crawdads. Again, the water was filthy. "How the hell much mud was on them?" he asked.

"On them and in them," his friend said. "It will take several buckets of water to clean them out."

The rest of the day and into the evening, they changed the water on the crawdads. Each time the water was less dirty. After having a supper of gator meat, the water was changed one more time.

"By tomorrow morning they'll be ready to eat," Rene assured his friend.

Kyle pushed the rowboat away from the dock the next morning. It was time to check the baits. With luck they'd have another gator. His friend had been right. The water was much less dirty in the crawdad bucket. For good measure they rinsed them one more time. The plan was to boil them for their supper.

It was a misty day and water dripped from the cypress. They spooked two egrets that were fishing off the bank of a small island. With his expert knowledge of the bayou, Rene directed Kyle to the first trap. To their surprise, the fly covered bait was gone!

His lanky friend smiled. "We got something."

The slim man pushed the boat close to the tree, and the rope was jerked by their catch, confirming that something was on the other end. Rene took the rope and began to pull it in. Whatever it was, was smaller, but it still gave a good fight.

The gator's head came out of the water as it twisted, lashing its tail as it tried to free itself. Kyle had the pistol ready. A quick shot and the fight was over. His friend pulled the gator up alongside the boat. "It is six feet, maybe seven," he said.

"It is $3, maybe more," the slim man said.

Feeling good about the misty day, the two continued on to the next bait. They were approaching the one with the large gator they'd seen. The gator wasn't on the island and the bait still hung where they'd left it.

They bypassed the crawdad traps for now and checked the spot where they had already caught the 10-footer. The bait hung where they had put it, and they were off to the last bait.

The mist had gotten harder, and they came close to the area but couldn't be sure if the bait was there or not. Then Rene exclaimed, "Something got it!"

Could it be that they'd gotten two gators in one day? Kyle wondered.

Sure enough, they had another on the line. While his friend pulled the gator toward the boat, the slim man pulled the pistol from his belt. It was wet from the mist, and he worried that it would not fire.

It was another smaller one. Rene had it up alongside the boat, ready for Kyle. "In this mist, I am not sure if the pistol will fire."

"If not, you'll have to use a long gun," his friend said. "If they don't work we'll drag this damn thing all the way to the shack, fighting and splashing."

Kyle dried it off as best he could with his shirt and then cocked the pistol. Taking aim, he squeezed the trigger. There was a fraction of a second longer delay and then the pistol fired. The thrashing gator went limp.

The mist got harder as Kyle rowed toward the shack. How Rene managed to direct him in this weather he did not know. Water was dripping from the trees above them, their hats were dripping water onto their backs and shoulders, and the wet oars wanted to slip in the slim man's hands. Meanwhile, two gators were in tow behind them.

Climbing onto the porch out of the mist was a relief. They shook the water from their hats and moved things around in preparation for bringing the two gators onto the deck.

They would hang both of them on the same pulley.

Once slid onto the deck, they could see that the first one was seven feet and the second was just over six. Each man took one to scrub working on the long table. With the chore completed, they tied the tails together with a short piece of rope and then raised them with the pulley.

Kyle checked his watch, and it was midafternoon. A quick check of the bucket of crawdads confirmed that they had pretty well cleaned out. Heading into the shack, the slim man offered to make some coffee. On the way by the table, he took a piece of the jerky that had been left in a pot. A bite confirmed it wasn't half-bad.

"We can get some fast money for these," Rene said. "The owner of the mercantile told me he knew a couple of families that would buy a smaller one. We'd get $7 for each one."

"On a miserable day like this, that sounds pretty good," Kyle told him. "We could bring the first skin and head at the same time."

"We won't be bringing the head," his friend told him. "In the spring a man comes to town and pays good moncy for all the heads."

"What's good money?" the slim man asked.

"He pays three to five dollars for a

head," Rene told him. "I've seen a big one go for $10."

"So, we are going to bring the skin and try to sell the two we caught today?" Kyle asked.

"Yes, we are," Rene said. "We just have to make sure the buyers will come and pick them up."

The mist had stopped as the two men walked to the mercantile. The two men carried the salt-covered skin in a tarp between them.

The owner, Carl, was not in the chair on the front porch. The two men swung the tarp and dropped the skin on the porch. Their boots were caked with mud. After a futile attempt to scrape them, the two men went inside.

The owner looked up and smiled. "What can I do for you?"

"We have a gator skin out front and a couple of smaller gators if the folks you spoke of want them," Rene said.

"Well, I'd handle the sale of the two gators. Do you have them with you?" the man asked.

"No, we don't," Kyle told him. "We would need them picked up."

The owner frowned. "Picked up, you say."

"You've got a buckboard," Rene told him. "We can get them to the road."

"I don't know that I can leave the store," Carl said. "I could rent . . . loan it to you so you could bring them here."

"You said the price was $7 each," the slim man said.

"How big are they?" the owner asked.

"Seven foot each," Rene replied.

"That small," the man said. "I'll have to mark them up when I sell them."

"You can do that," Kyle told him. "We also have a 10-foot skin out front for you."

"Ten foot you say," the owner replied. "Let's take a look at it."

The skin was brought to the back of the store and rolled out onto a long counter. Brushing the salt away, the owner hemmed and hawed as he looked it over. "I'll have to make some brine," he mumbled.

Using a marked stick, he measured and remeasured the skin. "Yes, it is just a might over 10 feet. Right now, gator skin is down, but I believe I can give you . . ."

He hesitated for a bit and then smiled. "How does four bits a foot sound?"

"Not as good as 6 bits," Rene said. "During the war, I helped to keep the British from taking over your mercantile."

"You did do that," Carl replied. "Six of you stood guard around the building for a couple weeks as I recall, while I fed you boys."

For a couple of minutes the two stood looking at each other while Kyle wondered which way it was going to go. Then the owner smiled. "I did appreciate it. Six bits it is."

Wanting to get things settled, the two men went to Carl's barn and hitched his horse to the buckboard. Taking advantage of the transportation, they got four more bags of salt.

Just before dark they were back at the shack with $20. They spent $1.50 on the salt and a couple of things, including some seasoning for the crawdads.

Using the light of the fireplace, Rene boiled the crawdads and heated water for tea. Kyle sat at the table chewing on another piece of jerky. "We did alright," he commented. "A man works almost a month for $20 and we made that the first week."

"We got lucky with the two today," his lanky friend told him. "I would have expected one, but not two. If we get another one that size, we'll only get four bits a foot for the skin and a little meat. Winter is coming on and we need to make some wood, which will take away from hunting gators."

"I was just thinking," Kyle said. "If Carl sells the gators for $8 each, once the buyer skins it, they are going to get $3.50. They get the benefit of the meat, and come spring they sell the head for, let's say $4. The darn gator hasn't cost them anything and they didn't have to go out on the bayou and catch it."

"Isn't it a great country?" his friend said, smiling as he stirred the crawdads.

Then Rene announced that the crawdads were done. He dipped them out of the water and piled them onto a pie tin. The steaming red crawdads were seasoned with whatever his friend had gotten, and Kyle was ready to eat.

His first crawdad was not what he had expected. Once he pealed the shell off, the meat was chewy, and it tasted just a little like mud. The seasoning was a might hot but did a fair job of masking the taste.

Rene dug into them, peeling the crustaceans as fast as he could and wolfing them down. "Good, ain't they?" he asked with a mouth full.

"They are different," Kyle told him. "You did a fine job of boiling them."

By the end of the meal, the slim man found them more enjoyable. There were no more surprises at the taste. He only wished he had more of the hot seasoning.

CHAPTER SEVEN

The end of November was unseasonably cold and the gators had quit eating. Each day, bundled up in the woolen coats, the two men would row through the bayou waters checking their bait.

Their afternoons were spent making wood, fishing for catfish, or reading. As it turned out, Rene had quite the collection of books. Two shelves near his bunk held the variety. One day Kyle opened a leather-covered item that was handwritten in French.

While the slim man spoke some French, he was limited as far as reading the language and the handwriting of the author made the reading even more arduous. "Have you ever looked at this?" Kyle asked his friend.

"I have," Rene told him. "I got through

a couple pages and gave up. The first entry was made in 1804. The man who wrote it was going somewhere."

"Where did you get it?" the slim man asked.

"After my mother died, my father hired a man to help on our farm. He used to tell wild stories about traveling west all the way to a large ocean," Rene replied. "He tended to drink, and we figured they were tall tales. After he died, we found it in his belonging. Now I just keep it with my books, figuring someday I would try and read more."

Kyle placed it back onto the shelf. "I wish you luck with that. The handwriting is awful."

After a miserable end of November, the first two weeks of December were warm, almost hot in fact. After a few days of the warmth, Rene announced, "This weather might make the gators active again. We got to catch more catfish and get the hooks back out."

Without any activity in the bayou due to cold weather, the two men had taken all the hooks in except the one near the known large gator. Even that one they figured wouldn't be eating until spring.

It had shortened the distance they had to row to check the baits, but now it might be worth having them all out there. "There is no sense in putting the crawdad traps back out,"

Kyle figured.

"It will take a few more days for the water to warm up for the crawdad, but hell yes we will get them out," Rene replied.

The slim man left the shack, muttering, "More damn crawdads."

It felt good to be in shirt sleeves rowing the boat while setting out the bait. They caught sight of one gator swimming across their path. The head and snout slowly disappeared under the water.

"We will put one trap near here," Rene said, his voice filled with excitement.

At the island where they'd sighted the big gator, they moved and refreshed the bait. His friend figured that there must be something beneath the water that kept the gator from going by the current spot. It could be cypress knees under the water, maybe a submerged log, or some rocks.

There was a large cypress just off the island on the other side. The two men chose that to place the bait. When they went by the tributary, his lanky friend dropped the crawdad trap into the water.

"Just a few more meals, and I think you will begin to like them," Rene told him.

"That will be just about when I start making coffee with mud," Kyle replied, laughing.

The slim man no longer needed directions to row back to the shack. He had learned that every turn had a different look, and he was always aware of the winds and tides. Everything had become second nature.

That night, after a meal of salted gator meat, the two men enjoyed the evening breezes on the porch while the sun set. Some mergansers swam by, diving to chase unsuspecting fish. Rene had made some tea, and Kyle rolled his chew between sips of the hot brew.

His lanky friend was telling him about trapping in the spring, when gators were active and hungry. He also told Kyle about the wild hogs. Rene told him next fall the two of them could hunt them. He knew a man that would smoke the side meat and hams.

It sounded like a good plan to Kyle. It was hard to imagine hogs running wild for the taking. He had never heard of that, growing up in England.

The next two days garnered one gator. Rene figured it was the one they'd seen swimming. It was over seven feet, and while his friend cleaned the crawdads, Kyle skinned the gator. With the skin in a pile on the floor, the slim man took care cutting the cheeks and tenderloins from the carcass.

Then, while Rene took the rest of the meat off the gator, Kyle got the chain and hook out. He used the short axe to break the spine from the skull while taking off the head. Laughing, the lanky friend said, "I am glad you found a use for that thing."

Together they scraped the skin and soon had it hanging over the rail to start drying. Rene washed and salted the meat while Kyle cleaned up their mess. The lanky man had put the carcass near the edge of the porch and had impaled the hook into it.

"I'll take the gator and get rid of it," Kyle called to his friend.

"You do that," Rene replied. "I will have gator and potatoes waiting when you get back."

Taking his long gun, pistol, and short axe, the slim man got into the boat and secured the carcass to the stern. Pulling on the oars, the boat glided away from the porch. This was the first time he'd taken the boat out on his own. It felt good being free to go wherever he wanted.

Close to the last place where they'd gotten rid of the 10-foot carcass, he released this one. It floated next to a raft of floating sea grass. As he rowed away, a turkey buzzard swooped in and landed on the grass, hoping for a meal. Before the raft of grass was out of sight, there were three more on it.

He started to row toward their first bait. It wouldn't hurt to check them. Then he saw it. Sunning on an island was a gator. He estimated that it was seven to eight feet-long. Curious about how close he could get to it without scaring it, he let the boat drift.

Out of habit he had put the Charleville across his lap. He might have to defend himself. As the boat slowly got closer the gator opened its jaws, revealing is bright pink mouth.

Then Kyle had a foolish thought. It was so close he could not miss the spine behind the head. Slowly he raised the long gun. Sighting right behind the head, he cocked the weapon and pulled the trigger.

Fire and smoke belched out and the recoil rocked the boat. As the smoke blew away he saw the writhing reptile as it disappeared off the far side of the island, the water churning. His first feeling was shame. This would have been a perfect place to set a bait and there would have been little doubt that they could have caught this gator. Now wounded, it had gone off into the water, possibly to die and the skin would be wasted.

Putting the long gun down, Kyle took the oars and started around the grassy island. Then he stopped. *What the hell are you doing? You have a wounded gator and an empty long gun!*

While the boat floated along, the slim man loaded the Charleville. He then checked his pistol and put the short axe on the seat next to him. Rene had talked of the danger of a wounded gator and Kyle had no idea what to expect.

Slowly, he rowed around the island,

trying to look behind him to see if there was any sign of the wounded reptile. His back crawled, expecting it to rise from the water with its pink mouth wide open, coming at him with revenge in its bloody eyes.

Then he saw it. It was on its back, just floating a short distance from the island. Was it playing dead waiting for him? Was it badly wounded but not dead and once closer it would react?

Letting the boat drift toward it, he held an oar out to prod the gator. It just bobbed in the water and did not move. Relief spread through Kyle. It was dead. Using the oar, he rolled it over and watched for movement. None came.

The wound behind the head was easy to see and the slim man reached over with a hook and sunk it into the gator. Then, tying the rope to the stern, he sat back down and took the oars. His hands were shaking. Was it excitement or remaining fear of the monster he was towing?

The sun was getting lower and he was still a mile or more from the shack. Kyle put his back into his rowing as the stress left his body. It was slowly replaced by excitement of the kill. Maybe he shouldn't have shot, but it had worked out. He had a nice gator.

After what seemed to take forever, the boat bumped up against the porch. He heard Rene inside call out, "I didn't wait for you and already ate. Yours is keeping warm in the fireplace."

"I need help out here," the slim man called back.

Coming out of the shack, his friend asked, "Did you hurt yourself?"

Then Rene saw the gator. "Was it hooked on one of the baits?" he asked. "You should have come back and got me."

"It was sunning on an island, and I shot it," Kyle replied. "I probably shouldn't have, but it let me get too close."

"You did great!" Rene exclaimed. "That's got to be all of nine feet."

With the boat tied, the two men pulled the gator onto the porch. "I didn't check the other baits," Kyle told him. "I ran across this gator first."

"Come morning will be soon enough to check them," his lanky friend said. "Go eat your supper while I scrub this bugger."

The potatoes and meat had been next to the fire for far too long and were somewhat dried out. Eating from the pan, the slim man scraped the food loose and stuck it into his mouth. It took a lot of chewing, but he finally finished his meal.

Rene was tossing water over the gator to rinse off the borax solution. Soon the two men had it hanging from the pulley. "This one should add enough meat to take us most of the way through the winter."

"If it stays warm, chances are good that we'll get one or two more," Kyle told him.

Both men were too wound up to sleep, so they made another pot of coffee and went out to the porch. The slim man retold the story of getting the gator. As he described his concerns, his lanky friend found humor in them.

"You were wise to be cautious," Rene told him. "Most often a gator will swim away from you, but a wounded one may go after what hurt it."

That night, Kyle slept restlessly. He kept seeing the wide-open pink mouth in his dreams.

The next morning, their first task was to process the gator. The two men lifted it onto the long table, and after a final touch up with the whetstones they began with their knives on the thick-skinned reptile.

"I told you about the man that could smoke any hogs we got," Rene reminded him. "I think we could get him to smoke gator meat. The sun's getting too low to try and make jerky, so why not have it smoked, like pork?"

"He might charge too much," Kyle said. "I believe it takes several days to make hams."

"We can give him some of the meat," his lanky friend replied. "We can keep the best parts and salt them, but the tail and such might be good that way."

As they dropped the skin to the porch floor, the slim man said, "I wonder if he smokes crawdads?"

Once the meat had been taken off the carcass, it was time to tow it away. Reaching the spot, Kyle removed the hook and pushed it away. Then Rene pulled on the oars at they went to check their baits.

They found the baits untouched, that is, except the crawdad traps. Both were full of the dark gray crustaceans. Rene talked of it being a bonus catching them this late in the season. The slim man couldn't match his excitement but was getting used to the taste of crawdads. It was a change from catfish and gator meat.

Once back at the shack, the two men headed to town carrying the gator meat. Carl at the mercantile could sell it if the man with the smoke house wouldn't do it. They found the man tending to his smoke house. He had a stove door on the outside of the log building so he could add wood without going inside.

The man was willing to smoke the meat, and after soaking it in brine could add it to what he had going from the fall butchering. For a small amount of meat and a couple of dollars the deal was made.

Their next stop was at the La Maison. It was late afternoon, and the ladies were working the customers. A sweet-smelling woman sat next to Kyle and placed her soft hand onto his.

"I'm Mary," she said. "I don't believe I've seen you here before."

"I've only been in New Orleans about a month," Kyle replied. "Most of the time I am out on the bayou hunting gators."

"Did you get enough of them to buy me a drink?" she asked as she leaned a bit closer.

Kyle was set pretty well from selling his horse, getting paid for the trip on the *Fancy*, and what they'd made catching gators. He had no intention of spending any amount on the sweet woman.

The bartender came over to the table with ales for both men and lady's drinks for the two who had sat with them. "I guess I will be buying you a drink," the slim man said. "I can't stay long so after you finish you might want to find another customer."

Honesty is a good thing. Maybe she appreciated it as she snuggled closer to him and sipped her drink.

Three ales later and several lady's drinks, Rene was still at the table and seemed to be enjoying the female company sitting with him. Kyle was trying his best to think of a way to tell sweet Mary that he wasn't interested and had to be leaving soon.

Even as she led him to a room upstairs, he was still formulating a plan to escape. But the flesh is weak, and he had no will to leave.

As he held her in the bed, she was warm and soft. He was no longer trying to think of a way to say no.

It was very late when the two men staggered into the shack, laughing and reminiscing about their evening. Kyle's shooting bag was several dollars lighter and it would not be until the next morning before that fact would hit him.

The two woke to a cold wind and headache the next day. A chill had seized the shack, Rene got up and, shivering, went over to light the fire. Once the flames were licking around the kindling, he hurried back to his bunk and pulled on the covers.

His teeth chattering, he said, "I sure could have used a warm woman this morning."

Kyle just groaned and muttered, "Sure. You would have made her get up and start the fire."

By the time they tossed off their blankets, the fire needed more wood and hadn't done much to warm the place up, but the sight and glow almost made them feel warmer.

As the two men sat in front of the fireplace waiting for the coffee to be ready, Rene complained, "This will stop any chances of getting another gator."

"I can assure you we were not thinking of that when we decided to stop at the La

Maison last night," the slim man grumbled.

"You might be right," his lanky friend replied. "But I don't think I can complain about last night."

The coffee was done, and the two men were finally starting to warm up. The first cups were drunk right next to the fire.

"We got a skin to bring into town and we should probably bring in the baits," Kyle suggested.

"I'm sure old Carl saw us bringing the meat to Rudy," Rene said. "He may not be in a very good dickering mood. He likes to have things go through him."

"I have noticed that," the slim man replied. "You might have to remind him that you and the others protected his place again."

"You make side meat and frying pan bread for our breakfast, and I will make the crawdads for our supper," his friend suggested.

After breakfast, the two men sat on the porch in their wool coats, drinking the last of the coffee. "How much do you think we could get for an otter skin?" Kyle asked suddenly.

"I don't know," Rene replied. "Not as much as we could get for a mink or fisher."

"Hell," the slim man said, "I bet you have muskrat, and in some of the swamps we might even find beaver."

"We have no traps," the lanky man reminded him. Then he asked, "Other than beaver, have you ever trapped anything else?"

"No, I haven't," Kyle admitted. "It can't be too hard. Is there someone you know that could tell us how to do it?"

"Maybe Carl can tell us of someone when we bring him the skin," Rene replied. "If we buy the traps from him, he might give us more for the gator skin."

Plans were now made, but they still had baited hooks to bring in. Kyle fired and reloaded his long gun and pistol. His friend got out some leather gloves to keep his hands warm. Soon they were ready to go. This time they would be looking for more than just gators. They would look for homes or habitat of some fur-bearing critters.

Generally, they moved quietly through the bayou, but today they had lots to talk about. There was last night and also the prospect of trapping. Their voices echoed off the trees and traveled deep into the bayou, alerting everything that lived there that they were coming.

Kyle pointed out an otter swimming. Near the crawdad traps, Rene noticed that something had been eating the crustaceans on the bank. Hardly looking around, they reached the cypress were the large gator had been seen.

Their boat bumped against the tree and suddenly Rene exclaimed, "The bait is gone! We might have something."

Then there was dead silence in the bayou as the lanky man took the rope and gave it a tug. It was jerked out of his hand and snapped tight against the tree where it was tied! "We got something big," he whispered.

The slim man saw a swirl in the water about 20 feet away. "It's over there," he said.

"If it is as big as I think, we are going to get wet," Rene warned him.

Reaching into his shot bag, Kyle took out a small feather and put it into the nipple of the pistol to protect the load. He thought of doing so with the Charleville but could not find another feather.

He had always done this when traveling on rainy days to make sure water didn't get into the load. One could always dry the pan and put more powder in that, but it gets more difficult if the load gets wet.

His friend had leather gloves on, so that would help protect his hands. Kyle took the short axe out of his belt just in case he needed it quickly. The pistol remained in his belt. "Push the boat closer to where you saw the swirl," Rene told him.

Using an oar, Kyle pushed the boat. Whatever they had caught had allowed a little slack in the rope and the lanky man let it slip through his hand as they moved closer. Then he gripped it with both hands and pulled.

The water next to the boat exploded as

the gator lashed with its tail and began to roll. The fear now was that the rope would break, and the gator would be gone, certainly to die from the hook in its throat.

His friend hung on to the rope with a death grip, fighting the gator. Then the behemoth went under the boat, lifting it and dumping the two men into the water! Kyle, came up spitting and gasping. He heard his friend shouting, "Get back into the boat. The bastard will clamp onto your leg and take you down!"

The water was just below their hips and Kyle felt the gator scrape his leg as it went by. Scrambling, his leg burning, the slim man rolled into the boat, landing on their long guns lying in the bottom of the boat.

The rope snapped tight again and the gator came to the end, its head coming out of the water, the chain cutting into the corner of its mouth. Kyle looked down and saw that the long guns were covered with water that had splashed into the boat.

Rene said, "We might have to cut the damn thing loose."

"The long guns are of no use," the slim man told him. "I might be able to shoot the pistol."

"Wasn't that in the water?" the lanky man asked.

"The load should be dry," he answered. "All I have to do is reprime the pan."

As they sat still on the water, Kyle opened the frizzen of the flintlock pistol. To his surprise very little water had gotten into it. He blew the prime powder out, and using the top of his long johns, he wiped it.

Raising the flap of his shooting bag, he felt inside. Some water had gotten in. Taking out his powder flask, he dried it on the long johns. He put some powder into the pan, closed the frizzen and cocked the pistol.

"Are you ready?" Rene asked.

"I am," the slim man said. "I don't know if it will fire, but odds are it will if water didn't get down the barrel and past the wad."

"This gator brings its head up when it pulls the rope tight," the lanky man told him. "We'll move the boat close to the head and then I'll pull the rope. When the head comes up, shoot it."

"And if it doesn't fire?" Kyle asked.

Giving his friend a weak smile, Rene replied, "Then we'll come up with another plan."

Wiping off any additional water from the pistol, the slim man held it at the ready as Rene pushed the boat closer to the head of the gator. The rope started to move in the water. The gator was moving to the left.

Reaching into the water, his friend gripped the rope. "Get ready," he said.

Kyle was kneeling in the boat with the pistol leveled. The feather had been taken out of the nipple. He saw the rope tighten and up came the head, swinging a splashing water. The pistol fired!

Rene pushed the boat away from the thrashing gator as they watched what they hoped were its death throes. Then it went quiet. Kyle quickly began to reload the pistol. Once finished, he asked, "Are we going to try it again?"

"The rope broke from the tree," his friend said. "Do you think you hit the gator?"

"I am confident that I hit it somewhere between the snout and the back of its head," the slim man replied.

"If I can get the rope, we will get one more shot," Rene told him. "Then it will realize it is free and will swim away."

As the lanky man reached for the rope, in slow motion the gator floated to the surface, its white belly up. "I think it is dead," Rene whispered. "I am going to poke it with the oar. Get ready in case."

The shot had been true and the gator was dead. The lanky man exclaimed, "Great shot!"

"Awe, it was nothing," Kyle replied. "The gator was close."

Then he heaved a sigh of relief and said, "Thank God."

The two men began to laugh, releasing the tension that had built up. There were shouts of, "We did it!"

"Do you want to row back with our trophy kill?" Rene asked.

"You best do it," Kyle replied. "I am shaking too much, and my leg is killing me."

Looking over, Rene asked, "Are you hurt? The water near you is all bloody."

"Get me back to the shack and I'll take care of it," the slim man replied.

With the gator tied to the stern, the lanky man pulled hard on the oars and the boat cut through the bayou water. Once back at the shack, he jumped out and tied the boat. He reached out to Kyle and helped him to the porch. Their wool coats and long guns remained in the boat.

Kyle pulled up the pantleg and Rene gasped. "It got you with its claws."

"I'll put something on it and then help you with the gator," the slim man told him.

"We'll get something on the leg and then we will go and see Camille. The gator claws are filthy, and you'll be in trouble if we don't get that attended to," Rene said sternly.

The lanky man ran into the shack, came out with a clean cloth and tied it around the leg. Kyle could feel something squishing in his boot and didn't know if it was bayou water or blood.

The two men headed up the path towards town. Luck was with them, a buckboard was coming up the road, heading into town. Flagging it down, the two men climbed into the back and the driver headed for town with the horse at a trot.

Camille had a nice house with a courtyard and some buildings in the back. Rene pounded on the door and a moment later a slim, olive skinned woman with black hair tied in a bun opened the door.

"What is the all the noise, Rene?" she asked.

"My friend here had his leg scratched by a gator," the lanky man said, gasping for breath.

"Bring him in and have him take off his pants," she instructed.

Kyle was in a neat looking parlor. "I should take my pants off outside," he said. "I will make a mess in here. Maybe I could just pull up my pantleg."

Camille came back with a pan of hot water and some cloths. "What is this?" she asked, her dark eyes flashing. "Get those boots, socks, and pants off right now."

"Yes, ma'am," the slim man said as he untied the boots and place them nearby on the varnished wooden floor. Blood and bayou water ran onto the floor from his socks. He then stepped out of his pants, feeling uncomfortable in his long johns.

She instructed him to sit on a nearby wooden chair. With scissors, she cut the long john leg at the knee and exposed the injury. Kyle looked down and almost felt faint. His bloody leg had deep blue claw marks in it.

Noticing his reaction Camille said, "Look away while I take care of the leg."

The hot cloth made the cuts sting as she cleaned them. He sat looking at the ceiling, forcing himself to think about the gator left floating behind the boat. He wished that they had pulled it onto the porch before leaving.

The woman got up, took Rene aside and spoke quietly with him. His friend went out the door without saying a word. "You will have some scars to remember this day," she told him. "We need to get the filthy water off you. I will have a bath made."

Leaving him sitting in the chair, she went out of the room. A man dressed in dark pants and a white shirt came into the room and picked up the boots, socks, pants, and long john leg and took them away. Kyle bent forward to look at the bandage. The leg was throbbing, and he reached down to feel it.

"Do not touch your leg with those filthy hands," Camille warned him. "Your bath will be ready shortly. Would you like some tea while you wait?"

The slim man was thirsty. "Yes, I would."

A young girl, about 16 years-old, came back with the tea. "My aunt had me put honey in it."

Thanking her, he looked away as he

held the tea. The young girl was stunning and had a dress that clung to her figure. He was sure that Camille could read his thoughts. After all, she was a voodoo queen.

He had just finished the tea when the man came back. He took the cup and saucer and asked Kyle to follow him. In the next room was a bronze bathtub. It reminded him of the one upstairs of the Raven.

The water was quite hot and had a smell to it. The man left the room with the dishes and Kyle removed the rest of his clothing. He slowly got into the water. As hot as it was, it took time, but he was finally sitting back in the odorous water. The wound on his leg began to sting. It had to be whatever was in the water.

He had been given a bar of soap and a cloth. The man came back with scissors and a razor. "Miss Camille has asked me to trim your hair and give you a shave. She believes men heal better when properly groomed."

Soon Kyle's blond hair was cut to the middle of his ears and the man stropped the razor in preparation for the shave. "Would you like me to leave the moustache?"

Kyle had tried a moustache once before, but with his blond hair it was hardly visible. He wondered if his hair had gotten darker. "Yes," he said. Please leave it."

He did not see a single hair fall into the water. The hot water now felt very good and the slim man scrubbed himself from head to toe, avoiding the bandaged area.

The man came back with a towel for Kyle to dry himself. He was given some kind of white pants and a white shirt to put on, along with fleece lined slippers. The slim man was feeling pretty good, except for the throbbing leg.

The man came back and asked Kyle to follow him. They went back into the parlor, which now showed no evidence of the muddy, bloody water. Camille asked him to sit back on the wooden chair.

She brough a cushioned stool and put his foot up on it. "This might hurt some," she told him.

The original bandage was removed, and the leg was patted dry. "The wound isn't as deep as I originally feared," Camille told him. "I am going to wrap the leg with a poultice. It will give you some pain while it is working. If you want, I can give you something to help you sleep."

As she began to apply the poultice, Kyle winced and asked her, "Where are my boots? I will need them to walk back to the shack."

"Your shack, where unwashed men sleep?" she asked. "I do not think so. You will be staying here for a few days."

The slim man would have liked to argue but, dressed in the thin white clothes, no long johns, and no boots, he was in a weak position. "Is Rene coming back?"

"Of course not," she said. "He has an alligator to take care of."

Learning that gave him some relief. Still concerned, he told her, "Rene will need help with the gator. It is over 10 feet-long."

She smiled and replied, "He said all of 12 feet. Your friend will be back in three days. In the meantime, you will be a guest in my cabin."

Feeling desperate at having his every move controlled, Kyle asked, "When do I get my clothes and boots back?"

"You'll have no need for them while you are here, but I am having them laundered and repaired," she told him. "You should have them by late tomorrow."

"Then I will be gone," the slim man muttered to himself.

"No, you will not," she told him. "Not if you want to keep that leg."

He blushed at the reprimand. Somehow, she had heard him. Kyle had to remember that her hearing was very good. "You are right," he told her. "I will leave when you tell me to."

"Now, would you like to eat in the cabin, or with us in the house?" Camille asked.

He had not seen the cabin and did not know how far away it was. Not wanting to cause her any more trouble, he said, "In the house, thank you."

She looked at him and cocked her head. "You have good manners. Your parents must have taught you well before they passed."

A shock went through his body. How would she know that his parents had died. Was that something she pulled out of his mind with those dark eyes? Feeling he should say something he replied, "Yes. Yes, they were good, God-fearing people."

With a hint of a smile, she told him, "Horst will show you to the cabin. He will light the stove so you can make more tea or coffee."

That was when he realized that he didn't know where his shooting bag was. It had his flint, steel, and his money! Kyle decided that he wouldn't ask about it unless it wasn't returned when he got his clothes.

The man came and led the slim man to the cabin. It was next to the house, with just the drive separating them. It had two rooms separated by a curtained doorway. The front room had a small table with three chairs and a six-plate stove. He saw what would have been the dry sink, but it had a pump mounted on it to draw water. The was a single window in the room with stiffly starched curtains.

Horst went through the curtained doorway and Kyle followed. The back room had a cot on each side, a side table with a pitcher and bowl. There was a stand near one of the cots with an oil lamp for light. He also saw a shelf with several books. There was another door, which he'd learn led to the outhouse.

There were also some pegs for hanging clothes alongside the curtained doorway. He thought, *I won't need those. She hasn't given me any clothes.*

While the man lit the stove, Kyle had to admit that this cabin was probably the nicest place he'd stayed in. Even his folk's home hadn't been as nice, and no place had a pump in the kitchen.

Then as Horst clanked metal on metal at the stove, the slim man remembered the place above the Raven. *No,* he thought. *That was just a place to sleep and do . . . whatever.*

Before he left, the man showed Kyle where the coffee pot was and where the needed supplies were to make coffee or tea. Then he left. They day was cool and the heat felt good from the six-plate stove. He noted the box with additional wood in it.

He walked around the room, looking at pictures on the wall. They were all paintings of the bayou. He then went to the back room and looked in the mirror. He twitched his moustache. The blond hair still didn't stand out on his face. *Maybe if I let it grow longer,* Kyle thought.

He sat on a cot and looked around. Suddenly memories of Karen Green came to mind. This place would be perfect if she was here. Only they would have a double bed. He lay back onto the cot, thinking of her.

"You're sleeping," a sweet voice said, startling Kyle. "I knocked but you didn't answer."

Swinging his legs to the floor, he sat up. The leg throbbed. "I guess I was, and no, I didn't hear the knock," the slim man said.

It was the stunning girl. "Aunt Camille sent me to tell you that the meal will be ready in 15 minutes.

He reached for his watch and remembered that he did not have his clothes. "I will be right along," he told her.

She smiled and left the room.

Kyle went to the kitchen and tried the pump. Clean, cool water spurted out into the sink and went away down the drain. There was a dish pan next to the sink and he placed it inside to fill it. After washing the sleep from his face, he dried with a towel hanging nearby.

Damn convenient, he thought as he headed out of the cabin. He had no idea how long he'd slept, but the sun was low in the western sky. He walked across the dirt driveway. Reaching the door, Kyle wondered if he should knock. Suddenly it opened and there was Horst.

"Everyone is in the dining room," he told the slim man.

As he walked through the parlor, Kyle looked down at the white pants and shirt he was wearing. These were not the proper clothing to wear for supper. They were more suited for sleeping.

He stepped into the dining room and saw Camille sitting with her niece and another young child around eight years-old.

"Kyle, we were just talking, and I don't believe I ever introduced you to my niece, Desiree, and the younger one is Gabrielle, my daughter," she told him.

With a slight bow before sitting down, the slim man said, "It is a pleasure meeting you both. And Desiree I enjoyed the tea."

"It was chamomile," Camille told him. "It might have made you sleepy."

Smiling, Kyle replied, "It did. I believe I slept the afternoon away."

A woman dressed on a long, dark, flaring skirt and a white blouse came into the room with a tureen filled with a clear bouillon soup. Taking a bowl from each, she filled and returned it. Kyle figured he'd be pretty hungry after a meal of soup.

"Thank you, Anna," Camille said, and the woman took the tureen away.

The soup was very good. There was bread in the middle of the table and Kyle would have liked to have dunked some in the soup, but nobody else took some and he wasn't sure he should.

Anna appeared again and took the bowls away. She then came back with a tray carrying small plates with three crawdads on each. There was a red sauce beside them. She put one in front of everyone but Gabrielle.

Camille smiled and explained, "She doesn't like the crawfish." Then turning to her daughter, she said, "Just have some bread."

Clear soup and crawdads, Kyle thought. *I am going to starve.* Then to Camille he said, "I believe I'll have some bread also." He tried to take one of the bigger pieces. He noticed the young girl placed it on a small plate near her. He did the same.

The crawdads, or crawfish as she had called them, were not a favorite of the slim man. He found that they had been cut, which made it very easy to remove the shell. He noticed that they used a small fork to do so and spear the meat to eat it. They also dunked it into the red sauce. He did the same. The red sauce had a little bite to it and the crawdads tasted quite good.

As he ate the three crawdads, he wondered what they did differently than Rene? There was butter and an odd-shaped knife near it. After Gabrielle used and returned it, Kyle did the same, putting butter on his bread.

Between the soup, crawdads, and bread, the slim man knew that he would not starve. He just hoped breakfast was bigger. Then Anna took the small plates and used silverware away. Moments later she was back with a tray with a sliced ham, surrounded by peeled potatoes. Horst came out with a smaller dish filled with boiled greens and plates.

Soon, Kyle had a plate filled with a generous portion of ham, a couple of potatoes with a sauce poured over them, and some greens. Camille said, "Please take some more bread." Not wanting to disappoint her, he did so.

After buttering it, he took a bite before starting the meal. The creamy butter was something he seldom had. This had a sweet taste and was just lightly salted. After surveying what silverware each used and how they used it, Kyle dug in.

He found that they talked a lot while eating, but never with their mouths full. It made the meal last longer but was quite nice. He was asked several questions about where he was from. He talked about growing up in England and fishing in the channel. There was no talk of the war that had just ended.

Then everyone went to the parlor and tea was served with cookies that Kyle did not recognize, but they were very good. Then Desiree took the young girl and left the room.

Camille looked at Kyle and said, "I got the feeling that you were uncomfortable at the meal."

"It was something I'm not used to," he admitted. "Once I attended such a meal while in Boston and the man next to me suggested that I watch what others do before making a move."

"Well, it worked," she said. "I didn't see one mistake on the silverware. If you would like, I can have your meals brought to the cabin."

"Maybe that would be best," he told her. "I won't need all the things before the main stuff."

"You seemed to like the crawfish," Camille said. "Not everybody does."

"They were the best I have eaten," he told her. "Rene does something that makes them taste a little . . . different." He figured it wouldn't be right to say like mud.

"There is quite a process to get the bayou mud out of them," she replied, smiling.

The two continued to make small talk and Kyle was looking for the opportunity to excuse himself and go back to the cabin. Then Camille got up. "We will look at the leg again. I have another poultice I want to put on it."

There in the parlor, she lifted the white pants leg and removed the bandage. Slowly, she peeled the poultice off. He saw that the leg was bruised, and the inside of the poultice was stained with blood and something yellow.

Horst showed up with a basin of hot

water and some cloths. Putting the leg onto the cushioned stool, Camille bathed it. Kyle had to grit his teeth a few times. Then the new poultice was put one. He flinched at the sting.

"I should have warned you," she told him. "This will prevent infection."

With the bandage back onto the leg, it was time to go back to the cabin. "I will have some tea sent out that will help you sleep."

CHAPTER EIGHT

The tea along with a full belly from supper, did its job. Shortly after lying down, Kyle was asleep. The discomfort of the leg would wake him when he moved but did not keep him up.

He woke early, having to use the outhouse. Returning to the cabin, he found a flint and steel on a small shelf behind the stove and got the fire going. Then using the pump to get water, he put on a pot of water for coffee. Impressed with the ease with which everything could be done, he went to the back room to make his bed and noticed the books.

Kyle found a book on the shelf that was about the Lewis and Clark expedition. He could only imagine what it must have been like exploring uncharted lands. Kyle sat at the table with his coffee and the book.

There was a soft knock on the door. Getting up quickly, he opened it. It was Anna with his breakfast. He stepped back and she put the tray onto the table. "I just made some coffee," Kyle told her. "Would you join me in a cup?"

Before responding, she smiled at him, her hazel eyes looking into his. "Thank you, but I cannot. I must bring breakfast to Miss Camille."

Then, quickly, she turned and was gone. He liked the way she turned. The breakfast was eggs folded over ham and cheese. She had also brought toasted bread with a small dish of jam.

It was very satisfying. He washed the dishes and tray and left them near the sink. Kyle paced around the front room, wondering if he should go to the house and ask about his shooting bag and clothes.

Deciding against it, he sat back at the table and picked up the book. It wasn't as much of a story as a documentation of the trip. It was still interesting, and he envisioned paddling up the Missouri River, heading towards the unknown.

Just before noon there was another knock on the door. Again, it was Anna. She was carrying his folded clothing with the boots on top and the shooting bag.

Seeing her loaded down, Kyle quickly

took the clothing and boots. She set the shot bag onto the table. Anna turned and said, "Miss Camille would like you to join her for a midday meal. It will be in a half-hour. Your watch is in the bag."

"Did she want me to change into my clothes?" Kyle asked.

"You may want to," she told him. "Then we will wash what you've got on."

She looked him up and down when she said that, and Kyle realized what he was wearing was almost nothing. She turned and left, her skirt flaring some.

"Thank you, Anna," he called as the door closed.

Kyle thought she was a curious woman. With her beauty and gentle manners, she shouldn't be working for Camille. She should be someone's wife. Shaking it off, he turned to his stuff.

The first thing he checked was the shooting bag. It felt softer when he picked it up. Dumping it out onto the cot, he found everything was there and had been cleaned and dried. His money was all there in a small leather sack. The letters were water-stained but in readable condition. He was sure that Camille knew more about him from reading them.

He put everything back into the bag. Then he picked up his boots off his clothing. They looked almost new and were also soft.

The leather laces had been replaced. Kyle also found that his holey socks had been replaced with new wool socks. The pant leg had been neatly sewn up and one could hardly tell where the tears had been.

He had left his broad belt, knife, and the pistol at the cabin. He should find out what they used to soften the leather and use some on his belt. Suddenly, he remembered being asked to join Camille. He did not want to wear the white things.

Quickly, he put on the long johns. The one leg left the bandage exposed. He then put on his pants, shirt, new socks, and boots. He felt almost normal again. The watch was back in his pocket, and he headed for the house.

He knocked and Horst answered the door. "Miss Camille is in the dining room."

Kyle hurried there and found her alone. She had been drinking tea. "Will your niece and daughter be joining us?" he asked.

Smiling, Camille said, "It will just be us. Desiree and Gabrielle are visiting friends."

The meal was much lighter that the evening meal had been. Kyle often had only a piece of jerky for his midday meal, so this was fine. Anna brought out bowls of thick soup and fresh-baked biscuits with honey on the side.

"If you would like more, I can have something made for you," she said, noticing him looking at what was served.

"This will be fine," Kyle assured her.

"I see you have your clothing back on," Camille told him. "Now that they are not soaked with bayou water, they look good on you."

"I left my broad belt back at the shack and am having a little trouble keeping my pants up," told her.

"I believe I have some belts around here that you could use," she told him.

The thick soup was good. It had potatoes and ham in it, probably from the prior meal. Anna came back out with tea for him and some more for Camille. When she stood near him, he noticed she smelled very nice.

"Thank you," he told her.

She smiled and returned to the kitchen.

"She is a very nice girl," Camille told him. "Anna has been with me for four years now."

"You are fortunate," Kyle replied. "You having her and Horst seems very good."

A thoughtful look came to her face. "He is now," she said. "Six years ago, when he first came, he had problems, but we worked them out."

Doing the math as he ate his soup, the slim man realized that both must have been rather young when they came. Somewhat younger than her niece, Desiree.

The meal was finished, and Anna came and collected the bowls. "Would either of you like more tea?" she asked.

"None for me," Camille replied.

"I wouldn't mind another cup," Kyle said, knowing that it was only so he'd be able to see her one more time.

He had taken an extra biscuit and would eat it with the tea. When she brought the tea, Anna was going to take the honey away. The slim man reached out and touched her hand. "I would like that for my tea and biscuit."

She withdrew her hand quickly and said, "As you wish." He saw that she was smiling as she entered the kitchen.

"Horst said you had scars on your back," Camille said. "Did you get them in the war?"

"I did," Kyle replied, busying himself stirring honey into his tea.

"You sound British," Camille told him. "Was it American firing that wounded you?"

He smiled. It was a normal thing to think with his accent. "I was on the *Eagle*, an American ship in the Battle of Plattsburgh."

"And where is Plattsburgh?" she asked.

Kyle told her more about the battle and that it was fought on Lake Champlain just below Montreal. "It was then that I realized I felt more acceptance from Americans than my birthplace, in England," he concluded.

"My father was Acadiana and he, along with others, were forced out of Canada around 1765," Camille told him. "He married a woman that was Creole and French. My mother had the gift, and she passed it on to me."

She did not explain "the gift" and Kyle did not ask her what it was. This gift probably had something to do with voodoo.

With the meal finished, the slim man got up to leave. "I need to look at your leg," Camille told him. "Have a seat in the parlor."

She disappeared for just a moment and then came into the room. Camille had him put his leg onto the cushioned stool. The pant leg was folded up to the knee. She had just started removing the bandage and poultice when Horst came in with a bowl of hot water, cloths and a belt hanging over his arm.

The claw marks stung much less as she washed them. "There is no fever in the leg and that is a good sign," she told him.

Rather than a poultice, Camille swabbed the wounded area with something that made the sting return, but not as much as the poultice. Making a pad out of a small piece of cloth, she placed it on the claw marks and then wrapped the leg, securing the bandage by ripping the end and tying it around the leg.

"If the pad doesn't show any sign of weeping by tomorrow, you can go back to your

. . . shack," she told him. "I will send Horst to let Rene know how you are doing, and he will bring your blankets back to be properly cleaned."

She sure did like washing, he thought. Then Kyle replied, "I appreciate you letting Rene know. Have Horst ask him how long the gator ended up measuring."

In response to his request, she gave him a quick smile and a nod. "Now you need to keep off the leg and should go back to the cabin."

Kyle had hoped to see Anna again before he left, but she did not appear. When he got to the cabin, the slim man hesitated as he stepped in. Someone had been there since he'd left. The place had been neatened up and everything was in its place. He also found that the sheets on his cot had been changed. One other thing was that the white pants and shirt were gone.

The slim man looked at the belt. I was hand crafted with designs pressed into the leather. He put it around his waist and it fit perfectly. "Damn, she must have measured me," he muttered.

Kyle sat at the table and picked up the book. His leg throbbed a little, so he put it up onto one of the other chairs. He continued to read about Lewis and Clark. There were some sketches showing maps of the route. He was awed by how long they had spent on the

Missouri River. The slim man knew little about the Louisiana Purchase in 1803, but it must have been a lot of land.

That evening, the slim man was dozing on the cot after reading for a couple of hours. A knock on the door woke him. Before he could get up and answer it, Anna came in with his supper.

He noticed that the tray included a pot of tea and two cups. She smiled and said, "I thought I would have some tea while you ate."

For a moment he was speechless, and she got a concerned look as though she thought he didn't want her to. Finding his voice, Kyle said, "I would like that very much."

Smiling, she placed the supper onto the table and poured two cups of tea. She put a little honey into each. He looked at his meal, and it was fish, boiled potatoes, and some greens. The fish was not catfish, but when he tasted it, it was very good.

"Miss Camille says that you will be leaving tomorrow," Anna said, her face showing some disappointment.

"She thinks it has healed enough," Kyle told her. "You have made my stay here most enjoyable."

"You were the perfect guest," Anna said, smiling broadly. "You were no trouble at all."

After some small talk, the meal was

finished, and Anna poured the last of the tea into their cups. Having never been too adept at making conversation with a lady, the slim man racked his brain for something to say to keep her longer.

He had already talked about growing up in England, then he remembered what was mentioned at the midday meal. "Miss Camille said that you came to her four years ago."

A cloud went over her face, and she stared at her empty cup. Suddenly, he feared that she was about to leave. "We don't have to talk about that." Struggling to say anything that might detain her, he blurted out, "Rene and I are going to trap otter and muskrat this winter."

Giving him a half-smile because of his attempt to change the subject, she asked. "Why won't you be catching more alligators?"

"They quit eating in the cold weather," he told her. "I think they might even sleep a lot."

Unable to think of something else to say, he just kept smiling at her, desperation on his face. Then she said, "I don't mind your asking about me."

"Oh. I don't want to pry," Kyle told her, wishing he could take her hand. He remembered that when he'd tried it before, Anna had withdrawn her hand.

Looking past her at the window, he saw that it was getting dark. He didn't dare get up and light a lamp. That would be a signal for her to leave.

"I was in a bad way when I met Miss Camille. I had been beaten and someone I did not know brought me to her," Anna told him.

"The person that beat you must have been a coward," Kyle told her, keeping his voice low.

Then she took his hand. "It was over money. I told him he had cheated me, and he did not agree, making a point by beating me."

"You could have had him arrested," the slim man told her.

"A girl like me couldn't go to the sheriff," Anna replied. "He would have said I deserved the beating."

In the dim room, Kyle could see the tears running down her cheeks. He was glad that he hadn't lit a lamp.

"So that is how you ended up with Miss Camille," he said. "You found someone very good to work for."

"No, I do not work for her," Anna said. "She lets me stay here and I try and help out. If I need money for something, she gives it to me."

Curious about the man, Kyle asked, "Does Horst have the same deal?"

"He does," she replied. "Miss Camille taught both of us to read and write. We learned working with numbers."

Now it was dark in the room. "Will she

let you leave?" he asked.

"Yes, she will," Anna said, her voice seeming to lift. "If we have family to go to, she will pay for our trip and give us some money to live on until we can find work."

While Kyle didn't say so, it sounded like Miss Camille treated them almost like family, except they were expected to do some work while staying with her.

Then in a low voice, Anna said, "I can't stay with you tonight. It would worry Miss Camille."

"I understand," Kyle told her, even though he wished she would.

Slowly, she pulled her hand back and stood up in the dark. Then he heard her footsteps as she went to the door. "Thank you," she said. "I enjoyed our visit."

Then the door opened and closed. Anna was gone. His thoughts of the two of them on the cot holding each other would not happen. That's okay, he told himself. It would have been wrong to ask her to stay.

Kyle did not see Anna again before he left the next day. Miss Camille declared that the wound was healing nicely, and the pad showed no seepage. His clean blankets had been brought to the cabin

With the blankets rolled and tied with line allowing them to be slung over one shoulder and his shooting bag over the other, he left. When he was leaving the house, Kyle had asked Camille what he owed. She had smiled and said, 'I have already made a deal with Rene to cover your expenses."

Walking back to the shack, Kyle felt some distress. It wasn't Rene's fault that he'd been injured. His friend should not be paying for her healing him. Arriving at the shack, he found the boat gone and there was no evidence of the big gator.

Inside the shack everything was about like he'd left it except his bunk was stripped of covers. He tossed the blankets onto it. There was a partial pot of coffee near the fireplace and the coals were cold. Putting some tinder and kindling into the fireplace, he got a fire going and put the pot near it.

He went to check his gear and saw the Charleville leaning in the corner, cleaned and ready to load. There was also the pistol, short axe, hat, and broad belt. Something was bothering Kyle but he couldn't figure out what it was.

The coffee was hot and he poured some into a tin cup. Then he stood and looked at the room. What was wrong came to him. The place was dirty. There was dust, cobwebs, the dry sink had dried food on it, and the windows were so dirty that one could hardly tell the shutters were open.

Had it been like this when he left? he wondered. The slim man knew it had been. Gulping the coffee down, he put the cup onto the dry sink and got the broom. For the next two hours Kyle swept, dusted, washed windows, and in general did his damnedest to clean the shack.

Once finished, it wasn't the cabin, but it was much cleaner. Even the coffee pot was washed and sitting in the fireplace with water for tonight's meal.

Kyle was sitting on the porch with the pole, trying to catch their supper when he heard the oars in the locks as Rene rowed back. He got up and caught the line as his friend tossed it to him. Quickly, the boat was tied up and Rene climbed out.

"Welcome back," he said. "It looks like Camille did a good job of getting you back on your feet."

"She has a way about healing folks," Kyle agreed.

"What did you think of that Anna?" Rene asked.

Not really liking the way he asked the question, the slim man replied. "I found her a very nice lady."

"Better than what we had at the La Maison," his friend said laughing.

Desperately wanting to change the subject, Kyle asked, "Did you pay for me staying there?"

"We paid for it," the lanky man replied. "Camille did it for the head of the big gator. I guess she can make some kind of voodoo with it."

Hoping to see it, Kyle asked, "Did you already bring it to her?"

"Horst took it," Rene replied. "Now there's a man that Camille turned around. He'd have been hung by now without her help."

The slim man smiled like he understood what his friend was talking about. He was still stuck on the way he talked about Anna. Attempting to change the subject, Kyle asked, "What were you doing on the bayou?"

"Looking for muskrat huts," he friend replied. West about a mile there's a small canal that goes into a swamp. It has several huts. I figure we can put otter traps anywhere by just leaving a trap with fish hanging over it."

"Did you get the traps?" Kyle asked.

"I figured we'd get them with some of the money we get for the 12-foot gator skin. It's lying in the lean-to," his friend replied.

"Who helped you skin it?" the slim man asked.

"Damas came over after I told him of your injury," Rene told him. "I think he really came over to see the big bastard. All he wanted for doing it was some of the meat."

"I would have liked to have seen the head on that gator," Kyle said, showing his disappointment. "That okay, though. I appreciate you taking care of everything."

"That's what partners do," Rene replied.

* * *

The mercantile owner, Carl, gave them $10 for the big gator skin. Kyle was sure he did it because he knew he was getting some of the money back when they bought traps. After an hour of dickering, they ended up with six traps and a promise that they'd sell the furs through him.

He'd give them two bits for a muskrat skin and $1.50 for an otter. They had to make boards to stretch them. Carl had a couple of old ones and tossed them in with the deal.

For the rest of the week, the two men made boards. After they had two dozen, they were ready to start trapping. They decided to put out two traps for otter and four for muskrat. The first otter trap was set where they'd lost the catfish on the gator set.

The slim man had never trapped otter, and he had no idea of how one would do it. When Rene made some stakes for the trap, Kyle didn't question it. When they rowed back and forth where the otter had gotten the catfish, he wondered what his friend was looking for.

"There it is," his lanky friend said.

What he was pointing at was a place where the otter came out of the water on a regular basis. Kyle soon realized that the one that had stolen the catfish hadn't come out of the water near there, but rather right here, and then went across the grassy island to the gator set.

Pulling the boat up onto the shore a short distance away from the exit spot, Rene walked into the water over to it and set the trap in the water next to the otter exit. He then brought the chain out into the water and slid the stake through the ring and pounded it into the bottom. Now just like a beaver if caught in the trap, the otter would go to the safety of the water and the weight of the trap would drown it.

"That's just like a beaver set," Kyle said.

"It is," Rene replied. "Only we don't have castor to draw it in. We'll put some fish just above the trap on a short stick. If you find an active cross over where the otter go from one place to another, you don't need any bait at all."

Kyle rowed around while Rene looked for another place where the otter came in and out to put the second trap. The slim man realized he was lucky his friend knew about setting the otter traps. The slim man would have set them on the grassy island, and if he was lucky enough to catch one, it would be alive and very angry.

Once the second trap was set, they

rowed back to the shack. "It's my birthday tomorrow," Rene told him.

"That must mean Christmas is two days way," Kyle replied.

"When I was growing up, that had always been a problem. My folks didn't have a lot of money and gifts weren't easy to get. I always got one to cover both days," his lanky friend said. "They did let me choose which day I got it. It was always on my birthday. It came sooner."

"I would like to go to church on Christmas Eve," Kyle told him. "I always did that in England. Mostly because Rebecca would be there, but I'd like to think I'd have gone anyway."

"I won't be doing anything that night," Rene replied. "I'll go with you."

They decided to wait until after Christmas to set the muskrat traps. According to what Carl had told them, the little rodents were easy to catch. The slim man didn't have anything to give his friend on his birthday, so the two of them went to the tavern on the docks and Kyle bought the drinks.

They watched the men playing faro and the winners always cheered. Most of the players were not cheering. The bartender was Walt, and he kept the two men's glasses full. Late that evening the two were staggering back to the shack, singing Christmas carols.

They rowed out to check the otter traps late in the morning. Both were still feeling the effects of the night before. The traps were empty, and Kyle was glad. He did not feel like skinning anything today.

Once back at the shack, both men took a nap after some jerky for their midday meal. Kyle did his best to clean up before heading for the church. The bartender had told them that the service started at eight.

There was music as they approached the church. "I hope the sermon isn't too long," Rene said. "I might snore when I fall asleep."

"Don't worry," Kyle told him. "I'll give you an elbow if you do."

The two men weren't in a hurry to go in. Kyle had a chew in his cheek and stood in the shadows as he spat. Suddenly, he spit out the chew. His heart began to pound. Coming toward the church was Anna.

He saw that she was alone, and Kyle whispered to his friend. "It's Anna and I am going to ask her if I could sit with her."

"What if she is joining someone?" Rene asked.

"Then she will probably say no," the slim man told him. "Let's hope she isn't."

Kyle stepped out of the shadows and startled her. "I didn't mean to scare you," the slim man apologized. "I was wondering if I could sit with you?"

"You and your friend?" she asked.

"If you don't want him to sit with us, he is history," Kyle promised.

He saw her smile in the light of the lamps in front of the church. "Okay," she replied.

"That he's history?" the slim man asked, trying to clarify the okay.

"You can both sit with me, but you beside me," Anna told him.

As they followed her in, Kyle whispered to his friend. "You can't sit next to her. Stay on the other side of me."

It felt good sitting in the church and listening to the music. Kyle hadn't been to church in a long time. It was especially nice having Anna at his side. His thoughts drifted to Rebecca. This would have been the two of them one day.

The sermon was long, and Rene began to fidget. The slim man wished it could have lasted all night. Finally, the last song was sung, the benediction was said, and the people began to leave.

Anna was sitting near the aisle and waited until near the end to leave. The two men followed her, his friend whispering, "It's about time."

After shaking hands with the pastor, the three stepped out into the street. Kyle was about to ask Anna if he could walk her home when there was a tap on his shoulder. It was an old man with shaggy white hair and a beard to match.

"The man from the mercantile told me you might be looking for traps," the man said. "I quit trapping and got a bunch I'd sell cheap."

Before Kyle could reply, he heard some sharp words behind him. It sounded like Anna. Turning, he saw a rough-looking man talking to her. He heard him say, "Just one drink for old times, Anna. We always had fun."

She tried to walk away from him, and he grabbed her and spun her back around. "Are you too good . . ." The man never finished the sentence. The angry slim man was on him.

Kyle led with a right to jaw and followed with one to the stomach as he and the man went down into the dirt of the road. The rough bastard didn't seem to be fazed by the slim man's attack. The two rolled in the dust, punching, and the man tried to bite Kyle's ear but came away with a mouth full of blond hair that he ripped from his head.

Then the two men were back on their feet. A group of men who had just attended church cheered the two on. Kyle saw stars when the man hit him alongside the eye, and then with a poke of his right fist he felt the rough man's nose crunch and blood was sprayed on the two of them.

Strong hands grabbed him from behind

and the slim man fought to get free. The words, "Stop this right now!" got through to his fevered mind and he looked. It was the pastor. Others had grabbed his bloodied opponent.

The pastor was livid. "Fighting on Christmas eve at the steps of this holy place! You have the whole town to create trouble like this and you choose to do it here!"

Kyle had no idea if the man he fought was affected by the words, but the slim man was cut to the quick. The pastor was right. He should have just stepped between the man and Anna and helped her walk away.

"I'm sorry," Kyle told the pastor. "I did not think."

"You certainly did not," the man said. "When you come to church again, I expect you to conduct yourself properly."

Then the pastor walked away. The slim man could hear him talking to others and apologizing for the antics of the ruffians.

Rene was there, smiling. "I was going to jump in and help you, but you were doing alright."

"I was wrong to fight in front of Anna," he said. "She will never talk to me again."

"I believe she is waiting for you to walk her home," his friend said. "As far as I am concerned, that is the wrong way from our shack, so I leave it to you to do it."

Kyle turned and looked at Anna. He

shrugged his shoulders and walked over to her. "You can't trust me, even at church."

"It scared me when you went after that man," she said. "I was afraid his friends would jump in. Some of them carry knives."

"Maybe the lord was watching over me and kept them away," Kyle said, trying to lighten the mood.

"I think the lord was looking down and frowning," she told him, "but I want to thank you for what you did. The man was someone I knew long ago."

The two of them left the church and she accepted his arm. The slim man watched for trouble as they walked. He would be carrying the pistol from now on when he came to town.

All too soon, they reached Camille's house. "I like your perfume," he told her. "I noticed it when I was staying here."

"I can't say the same for you," Anna replied. "I think you rolled in some horse dropping while you were fighting." The way she said it made them both laugh.

Then she got serious. "There are many men that think of me the way the one did tonight. I can't have you fighting every one of them for my honor. I am not someone you should want."

Then she kissed his cheek quickly and went into the house. For the second time he saw tears. He wanted to shout after her that it did not matter, but that would only confirm to her that he knew what she had once been.

With an ache inside, he walked through the streets toward the shack. He didn't keep an eye out for trouble, Kyle half-hoped it would come.

The slim man woke on Christmas morning with one eye swollen shut. His body hurt all over from the punches he'd received. Rene was already up and lighting the fire for coffee.

Swinging his legs onto the floor, Kyle sat with his head in his hands. He had fought at the church, Anna was done with him, and his clothes were filthy and lying in a heap near his bunk. This was the worst Christmas he could remember.

His friend came over. "Merry Christmas. I got coffee going and we can fry up some of the smoked gator for breakfast. If you are up to it, you can make frying pan bread."

Kyle's reply was a groan.

Looking at his disheveled friend, the lanky man said, "Damn, those clothes stink. I hope you do something with them today. At least put them on the porch." His hope was to get some kind of response from his friend other than a groan.

"I ruined my chances with Anna," the slim man said. "She as good as told me to stay away."

"I don't think she would do that," Rene

told him. "You came to her aid. You defended her. She has got to have seen that."

"She saw a man that couldn't control himself even in front of the church," Kyle replied.

"Maybe she saw a hero and doesn't want you to get hurt fighting for her," Rene told him.

With one eye swollen shut, Kyle picked up his clothes and put them onto the porch. He then went to his pack and dug out the worn ones that he had intended to toss out. "Good thing I didn't do that," he muttered.

Dressed in the clean clothes, the slim man went to the dry sink to mix up some bread dough. The water bucket was empty. "Did you use the last of the water?" he asked his friend.

"I used it for coffee," Rene told him.

Snorting, Kyle put on his boots and headed for the spring. "Damn fine Christmas," he grumbled as the dipped the bucket and filled it.

The two men ate their Christmas breakfast with one cheerful and the other not so much. Other than the fight, something else was nagging Kyle. It was something someone had said, but he could not remember what it was.

"Your frying pan bread is getting better and better," Rene told him.

"That's because I save some for a

starter and that gets better with time," the slim man explained.

"We have to check the otter traps today," the lanky man said, around a mouthful of bread.

"Traps!" Kyle shouted. "I met a man who had traps. I never asked him his name."

"Yes," Rene said. "You were too busy defending her honor."

Then his friend got serious. "You got to know. Anna wasn't always what you see today. She lived on the street and made money anyway she could."

Kyle felt anger surge through him. He did not want to hear that about her! The look on his friend's face was not a mean one, but rather a concerned look. Rene had lived in New Orleans all his life and would know things that Kyle could not, but the slim man did not want to know anything about Anna's past.

The two ate in silence for a few minutes. Then Rene said, "The smoked gator tastes just like ham. I should have done that before."

Unsure he wanted to forgive his friend yet, Kyle just nodded.

"I saw the old man you were talking to," the lanky man told him. "His place is not far from the battlefield."

Try as he might, the slim man couldn't stay mad any longer. The old man had what they needed, and his friend knew where he lived. "He told me that he had traps and would sell them to us cheap," Kyle told him.

"That's great," Rene said. "There are lots of muskrat huts around the swamp and we could set a dozen or more."

With their breakfast finished, the two men rowed away in the cool morning air to check on the otter traps. The first one was near the island where the otter had stolen a catfish.

"We got something," Rene said.

Reaching into the water, his lanky friend pulled in the chain on the trap. It revealed the dark brown otter. The trap was opened, and the otter fell to the bottom of the boat.

While Rene admired the catch, Kyle reset the trap. When they got to the second trap, it hadn't been sprung. The two men continued back to the shack with their catch.

"We don't have a board long enough to stretch the otter," Rene pointed out.

Kyle thought for a moment. "Maybe we can skin it like a beaver and stretch it on a hoop."

"I've seen them at Carl's and they are always stretched on a board," his friend replied.

By the time the boat bumped against the porch, both men had come up with a couple more suggestions, but none were a real solution. While tying the boat, Kyle asked. "Why don't we walk to the old man's with the otter and see if he has a longer board?"

"That might be a good idea," Rene replied. "Maybe he'd like to skin it for us for a share of the fur."

"Did you forget it is Christmas?" the slim man asked.

"I know he ain't got no family," the lanky friend said. "Just maybe he would like some company."

With the otter in a bag, his new belt holding up his pants and his knife, Kyle suddenly remembered and got the pistol. The slim man felt ready for anything he might encounter in town and followed his friend to the old man's place. It was a three-mile walk to the old man's. Two miles into it, Rene said, "I hope he ain't got friends that invited him to a Christmas meal." Kyle had no reply for him, just a glare.

The old man's place was just off the road and was a small shack made of overlapping slab wood, and had a tin smoke pipe sticking out of the slanted rood. It had a small porch at the front, and from what Kyle could see, no windows. In the back there was a building almost three times the shack's size. The slim man guessed that it was used for horses and hay.

The door was halfway open, which gave the two men hope that he might be home. The old man's name was Benny. As they walked up to the building, the man came out. "I thought I heard someone coming," he said.

"You mentioned having some traps when we were at the church," Kyle told him.

The man rubbed his beard. "I did at that, but you didn't seem to be interested. When you went after the fella bothering the woman, I came home."

"I apologize for leaving you like that," the slim man said. "I kinda know her and didn't like what the man was saying."

"Most men kinda know her," the bearded man replied. "I ain't ever seen two men fight over her."

Choosing to ignore the comment, Kyle said, "We have an otter here and we realized we didn't have any boards long enough to stretch it. We figured you might."

"When you said you had an otter, I thought you might be bringing me a Christmas present," the man said, laughing.

"We are interested in muskrat traps," Rene said. "That and a board to stretch the otter."

"Come around back," the old man said.

He pulled open one of the doors on the back building and Kyle's jaw dropped. It was filled with traps, boards, and tools for skinning and fleshing. Then the old man looked at them and asked, "How you been skinning them up to now?"

Sounding almost proud, Rene replied, "This is our first one."

That got a snort out of the old man. "Damn green hands." Then he said, "Let me see what you got in the bag."

Kyle dumped the otter onto the plank floor. The man scooped it up and lay it onto a wooden table. "Nice male you got here. If you don't make a mess of skinning it, you could get $1.50 from Carl. A man comes here twice a year, and he'd give you $2."

"Is he the same one that buys gator heads?" the slim man asked.

"He does," Benny replied. "I will show you how to skin this otter for four bits."

"What are you asking for some traps and boards?" Kyle asked.

Still looking over the otter, he asked, "How many do you want?"

"That depends on what you want for each trap," Rene told him

"Two bits a trap, and I will throw the boards in," the man said.

The two were floored with the price. They had just paid a lot more for the traps from Carl. Kyle couldn't help but ask, "Is that what they usually go for?"

"No, a new one would go for $2, but I got no use for the ones I've got and could use the money," he told them.

That made the two men feel a little better. Then the old man began to sharpen his skinning knife. "I will show you how this is done."

With his skinning knife ready, he picked up something that looked like a curry comb for a horse, only a little smaller. Benny brushed the otter from stem to stern.

The two men stood watching in surprise as the old man hung the otter's back feet onto hooks and then removed the front feet. He then cut from the pad of one back foot down the leg, stopping near the butt hole. Then he did the same down the other leg. Each was then cut around and skinned down to the body.

Benny wiped the skinning blade and touched it up on his whetstone. Next, he slit up the underside of the tail nearly to the tip. Working quickly, the fur was skinned from the tail. He then started to work removing the pelt. By pulling the pelt down and quick cuts with the knife as needed, he had the pelt skinned to the front legs. Working with his fingers, he pulled the legs out of the pelt and then continued skinning towards the head.

Time was taken going past the ears and eyes, and soon, with a swipe of the knife, he cut the pelt loose from the body. Holding it up, he said, "It is that easy. Now we got to do the fleshing."

The old man had a fleshing board secured to the table and it came up at an angle to about his waist. The pelt was inside out with the fur to the inside. He held up a tool that reminded Kyle of the fleshing tool used on the gators. The working blade was dull, and gripping it on both sides, he began scraping the fat and meat off the pelt.

Working from the bottom to the nose, he removed the unwanted flesh. When necessary, he used a large skinning knife to carefully cut difficult pieces off. Once finished, Benny held it up proudly. "We got a fine-looking pelt here."

The old man then slid it over a stretching board, pulling and smoothing it. At the bottom he took some tacks that would be used to make a carriage seat, and pulled the pelt and tacked it to the board. Finally, he tacked the tail skin flat on the board.

Then stepping back with pride showing on his face, Benny said, "That's how it is done.

It had taken the old man less than 15 minutes to do it. Kyle figured that he could have done it faster, except while doing it he was explaining everything to them.

Leaving the pelt, the old man said, "Let me show you where the traps are."

On the back wall hanging from spikes were dozens of traps. They ranged from large that could be used for bear to small that would be used for a weasel. The two men were interested in the ones for muskrat. "This size will be best," the man said, pulling several off the wall and tossing them into a pile.

Then he asked, "Have you ever eaten muskrat?"

Both men shook their heads no. The old man laughed. "I survived many months on muskrat meat. It is sweet and tender."

"When trapping beaver," Kyle told him, "I ate a lot of that."

"If you liked the beaver, you will love muskrat," Benny said.

Then it was time to settle up. There was quite a stack of traps and the two assumed that the old man had kept count. Unsure what they would cost, Kyle told him, "We'll need boards also."

Benny waved his comment away. "Like I said, you can have all the boards you can carry. I spent off season making boards and ended up with more than I could ever use."

Kyle and Rene looked at each other, unsure what this was going to cost. Then the old man said, "I was about to make coffee when you two came. I will make that now and then we can talk money."

As soon as the old man was out of hearing range, the two started to count the traps. "Fifty-seven," Rene said. Doing the math in his head he said, "We'll owe him near $15."

"And we haven't talked of otter traps," the slim man said. "We would still need a couple more of those."

"We got the money, but we also have all

winter coming," the lanky friend said.

They then heard the old man calling them to come and have coffee. "We will have to give him some of the traps back and try and stay a $10 at the most," Kyle replied. "We'll have to catch 40 muskrats just to break even."

The old man had dragged three stools onto the porch. "The days nice, and I thought we might sit outside."

Kyle had noticed the tobacco stains on the man's beard. "Would you join me in a chew?" he asked.

Taking the twist from his shooting bag, the slim man handed it to Benny. Taking a big chew off it, the old man stuffed it into his mouth and rolled it into his cheek, causing it to bulge out.

Kyle then took a chew and put the twist back into his bag. Then Rene spoke up. "We can't afford all the traps that you pulled off the wall and we still need a couple more otter traps."

The old man spat off the side of the porch and took a drink of his coffee. "I figure to make money on muskrat you'll need 60 traps and 200 boards. I don't figure you'll have time to go after otter and muskrat. They are two different things. Skinning is much the same, but that's where it ends. Otter, you spend lots of time finding where they go in and out of the water. In the bayou that is a lot of rowing. With muskrats you can see their huts and they usually climb onto them and eat. You have a lot of trap setting, skinning, and stretching to do. I was never able to do both."

The three men drank their coffee in silence with only the sound of spitting heard. Then the old man spoke up, "I'll sell you 60 traps and boards for $10 and the otter. I will even throw in a couple bags to carry them in."

Rene looked at his friend and saw him nod. "We will give you $10 and the otter for 60 traps and the boards," the lanky man said.

When they went back to the building, the old man said, "You best count the traps. I might be a bit shy."

Kyle wanted to tell him they would need three more but decided to do another count. With the deal set and the traps and boards counted, they were put into two large canvas bags. The two men headed down the road towards the shack.

The bag of traps weighed over 60 pounds and Kyle had to stop a few times to rest. The boards were bulkier and weighed almost the same. While on one of the rest stops, the slim man said, "We should have had Damas come with the cart."

When passing the dock tavern, a shapely woman standing outside called to them, "If you two are Santa's helpers, come in here and we can exchange presents."

Christmas day was pretty much gone

when they reached the shack. In the dusk they dropped their burdens onto the porch and went into the shack. Exhausted, the two men sat at the table. "Whose turn is it to cook?" Rene asked.

Kyle wanted something fast like side meat, but it was Christmas. "I will boil some rice with honey. It will make a fine meal."

With the fire going, the slim man put on a pot of water for the rice. He also heated water for tea. Shadows from the fire danced around the shack. The two men went outside and sat on the porch.

The evening was quiet, with just a light breeze. There was only the occasional bump of the boat against the porch. Rene looked at his friend. "Aren't you going to have a chew?"

"I gave the twist to the old man," Kyle said. "He sold the traps so damn cheap."

"Wasn't that your last one?" his friend asked.

"Yep," the slim man replied.

Banking that muskrats would make them money; the two men pulled the otter traps the day after Christmas. When doing so, they found them empty, and it helped to confirm their decision.

* * *

It took a half-hour to row to the large swamp. After going through the canal that cut through the bridge of land that separated the two bodies of water, Kyle couldn't tell much difference from the bayou, except less trees. The banks were thick with muskrat huts and on a couple of islands they could also see huts.

The swamp was a mile wide. As they rowed around the edge of the swamp, Rene spotted several places where they had burrowed into the banks along the shore. "Where do we start?" Kyle asked, speaking rhetorically.

In the boat they had 40 single-spring traps and as many stakes to secure them. There was no lack of huts or muskrats that they startled as they rowed around the edges. Their first attempts to set the traps from the boat were in vain. Remembering the days of trapping beaver, Kyle shed his boots and pants and walked along with the traps. At any runs or slides made by the rodents he would set a trap. First, he would make an indention where it entered the water. Then just under the water he'd place the trap and stake it.

The water was knee-deep to waist-deep. The bottom was squishy mud. An advantage over beaver trapping up north was the water was not as cold. Kyle had pushed the boat and set traps two-thirds of the way around the pond when he ran out. He had even skipped some of the burrows and runs.

Climbing back into the boat, the slim man sat with the water dripping from his long johns. Rene began to row toward the canal. "How many do you think we'll catch?" the slim man asked. "We may have set too many traps."

"Do you think we will catch too many, or do you think we wasted time putting so many traps in?" the lanky friend asked.

"Yes," Kyle said. "Either one."

When they got back to the shack it was only a little after midday. Setting the traps had not taken as long as they had anticipated. Some salted gator meat and potatoes were put into a pot to boil. It was New Year's Eve and Kyle had picked up a bottle so they could have a drink with their supper.

Throughout the rest of the day, they brought the long table from the lean-to. As usual, the slim man noticed the salted gator heads sitting on stakes and they gave him a chill. It was like they were down there watching him.

They sorted the boards by size in case they got a small one. They had rigged lines across the porch to string the planks on while the pelts dried. That night, over bowls of soup and mugs of whiskey, they guessed how many they would have caught by tomorrow.

"Tomorrow it will be a new year, 1816," Rene said. "I will be glad to see 1815 gone. It has some bad memories."

"I will drink to that," Kyle said. "We are entering the year of muskrats!"

"You missed church today," his lanky friend said.

"I don't think the pastor missed me," the slim man replied.

After a pause and another drink, Rene said, "I bet Anna was there."

That kind of took Kyle's mood down. It was time to get some sleep.

The morning had a cool haziness to it. They put the rest of the traps into the boat with a pile of stakes. Kyle had a short club in case he had to use it on any of the catch. If he used the pistol, there wouldn't be enough left to skin. They did have it along in case they caught anything bigger that they had to shoot.

The slim man huddled trying to keep warm, while his friend did so by rowing. Suddenly, out of the haze the canal appeared. "I am always impressed how you find your way around in the bayou," Kyle told his friend.

As they entered the swamp the slim man began to remove his boots and pants. "You should wait to see if we caught anything before you do that," Rene suggested.

The sun was just starting to cut through the haze when they got to the first trap. It remained unsprung. "I was right," his lanky friend told him. "Aren't you glad you're not wet?"

Only a few feet further, they had a muskrat. It lay still under water. Kyle climbed over the side and slid slowly into the cool water. Squeezing the springs of the trap, he dropped the rodent into the boat. He then reset it and placed the trap back on the run.

The next two traps were empty and Kyle began to feel disappointed. Muskrat trapping wasn't as good as he had hoped. Then he found one that was still alive. Taking the small club, he quickly killed it. Dropping it into the boat, he looked at his friend. "That's two."

Then their luck changed. The slim man was kept busy emptying traps and clubbing an occasional live one. By the time they got to the end of the traps they had just under 30 rats. Kyle climbed back into the boat and looked at the pile of muskrats.

"Not bad for one night," Rene said. "We got our work cut out for this afternoon."

The slim man had to agree as he sat there dripping while his friend rowed the boat, dodging the trees and islands. They saw several muskrats swimming away to avoid them. *We'll be back tomorrow*, Kyle thought.

Best-made plans don't always work out. The two thought they were all set up to skin the muskrats. First, they had to get as much water out of the fur as possible and brush them. It took three hours before they felt dry enough. Then it took far too long to get their first ones skinned and fleshed. After they were done with the first 10, they had ruined two pelts.

It seemed like Kyle was faster at skinning, and when they would switch from one activity to the other time was lost. It was decided that the slim man would do the skinning and Rene would flesh them and put them onto a board. Both would then pin and hang them.

After a few rats, the two men got into a rhythm and the remaining muskrats were finished much faster. On the long table they pinned the skins to the boards and then strung them onto the lines to hang.

The old man had suggested letting them dry for four days. The two men figured they wouldn't keep them for any amount of time after that. They'd take them to Carl and turn them into money.

The next day when they went out, they took the rack for making jerky to keep the muskrats out of the water on the bottom of the boat. It would start the fur drying. They also brought the rest of the traps.

Kyle pushed the boat from trap to trap. Again, the had more traps with muskrat than they found empty. The ones that were empty for the second time were moved. Rene would take the muskrats, strip as much water as he could with his hands and then lay it onto the rack.

By the time they reached the last trap, they had to double stack some. Once they finished checking all the traps already in the swamp, the additional traps were set. The two men weren't sure how long the swamp would produce catches, but when it slowed down there were other swamps nearby.

They found that the checking of traps and processing the muskrats could be done by midafternoon. With so much daylight left, Kyle had finished reading the Lewis and Clark book. Then he thought of the leather-covered diary handwritten in French.

"Why don't we try and go through the book your father got from the man he hired? I'd like to see what it was about," Kyle suggested.

The two began to go through it and together they slowly translated it to English. Some of the stained or torn pages would leave some holes in the diary. The two men found it enjoyable and soon realized it was about a man on the Lewis and Clark expedition.

Six days after the first catch, they took the skins to Carl. They had 63 muskrat pelts of various sizes. The mercantile owner did a lot of hemming and hawing. "I wish they were paying more for muskrat right now. Sometimes I almost have to give them away to get rid of them."

Eight miles upriver, Rene knew of a

trading post that bought any type of fur or skin. The lanky man wondered if it would be worth renting a mule from Damas and hauling them up there once a week.

"I suppose that Scottie's trading post is having the same trouble," the lanky man said, looking the man in the eye.

"I saw him just after Christmas," the owner said. "He was also complaining about prices."

Then Carl moved a few things around on the counter before looking up. "You know, we talked about two bits a pelt and by God, I will honor that."

"That is good of you," Rene replied. "When we bring in more, will you stick to that?"

"You are a good customer, Mr. Curie," Carl said, smiling. "I will hold the price for you this season."

The two left the mercantile with $15. Kyle had spent six bits on tobacco. They were on their way to the tavern on the docks. "He must really respect you," the slim man said. "He called you Mr. Curie."

Laughing, Rene said, "He had me worried for a minute there. I heard that Scottie was paying one bit for muskrat."

As winter coolness moved in, their catch continued to get smaller. They trapped, skinned, fleshed, and stretched muskrat every day and ate the meat at night. Sunday mornings were taken off so Kyle could go to church and sit with Anna. Most of the time Rene joined him.

At the end of February, he was walking her home. She seemed excited about something. Kyle was making small talk about muskrat trapping. Camille met them at the door.

"Would you like to join us for the evening meal today?" she asked him.

He had not been in the house since his injury. "I would be pleased," he said.

"We will expect you at six," she said.

Anna gave him a quick kiss on the cheek and went inside. Kyle walked back to the shack, quite excited. He would see Anna again, even if she was only serving the meal. Then he started to hurry. They had to go check the traps.

Kyle had run behind on his laundry, and walking in the swamps each day didn't help. The ones he'd wear to church were barely acceptable. He was sure Camille would serve a fine meal. What he had on would have to do.

Rene was left finishing up when the slim man left. There was a lot of kidding about the voodoo queen putting a spell on him, and about him and Anna as he was changing back into his church clothes.

The slim man was looking down at his boots as he walked toward town. They were stained from the muskrat fat and blood. He had wiped them off as best he could, but it just made sure that there weren't chunks on them.

He felt nervous as he approached the door. He wished that he'd made some excuse not to come. Kyle knocked lightly and the door opened. It was Horst. "Miss Camille is expecting you," he said. He took his hat and coat.

The slim man was escorted to the dining room. To his surprise, Anna was seated at the table as well as Desiree and Gabrielle. Camille smiled and said, "We have been having a pleasant conversation while looking forward to your arrival."

Kyle sat and replied, "I hope I didn't keep you waiting."

"Not at all," Camille replied. "I was able to get a turkey for our meal. I hope you like it."

After over a month of muskrat and gator meat, the change sounded good. "I has been some time since I had turkey. I do like it," he told her. He also lied. He had never had turkey.

A thicker soup was served as a first course. It was brought in by a woman Kyle hadn't seen before. As the bowls were being filled Anna kept looking at him and smiling. The slim man tried not to grin too widely. Several times he felt like he was blushing at all the attention they were all giving him.

The turkey and potatoes were good, as well as the vegetables. Now Kyle could honestly say he liked turkey. A drink he did not recognize was served. He had never had citrus before. All too soon, the table was cleared and tea was served.

Then Camille said, "Anna has some good news for you."

Kyle looked at her and she was blushing. He noticed she was blinking back tears. Then Camille said, "She is having trouble telling you. Our Anna is going to school in the east."

The slim man's heart fell. Fighting showing any emotion he replied, "That is wonderful." Looking at her, he added, "You must be excited. I am very happy for you."

Her voice was a bit weak as she said, "I am looking forward to going. I will be there for nursing."

The end of the meal was tasteless as the cake was served and his tea was refilled. He just kept thinking, *She is going. She is going.*

With the meal finished, it was time to leave. Anna said, "I will walk you to the door."

When they got there, Horst was waiting with his hat and coat. "Isn't that wonderful news?" the man said. "It was Miss Camille's present to her."

"It is wonderful," Kyle said. "Miss Camille is very generous."

Anna stepped outside with the slim man. "It's cold out here. Would you like my coat?"

She shook her head no. "I will be leaving in two days," Anna told him. "A friend of Miss Camille is giving me a berth on his ship."

"Where is the school?" he asked.

"It is in Virginia," she told him. "It is supposed to be one of the best."

Virginia, Kyle thought. *Why do they always go to Virginia?* Then the slim man said, "I will miss you very much."

"I want to thank you," she said.

Confused, he asked, "For what?"

"You treated me like a lady and never asked for more than friendship," Anna told him.

"Had you only known my thoughts, you might not think of me so kindly," Kyle told her.

"If I had known your thoughts, I fear I may not have been such a lady," she said. Then she laughed. "I am talking silly now. You will always be someone special to me."

He took her hand and kissed it. Then again with the tears, she turned. Stopping with her back to him, she said, "Don't come again before I leave. It would hurt too much." Then she was gone.

The walk home was long. Kyle almost stopped at the dock tavern but forced himself to keep going. With a few drinks in him, the slim man didn't trust himself not to return to the house and beg her to stay.

Then he laughed. It was not a happy laugh as the thought, *Camille would probably turn me into a toad.*

Kyle found that working on the French diary helped him to keep his mind off Anna. Sometimes he thought he should leave on a long trip like that to help get his mind off things like the women who had been in his life.

CHAPTER NINE

The two muskrat trappers had good success until mid-February, when a cold spell hit, forcing the rodents to stay in their burrows and huts and live off stashed food. The two men pulled their traps to avoid having to check them every day for a few catches.

Kyle had saved most of his money and now had almost $200, counting the money he'd come to New Orleans with. The disappointment of Anna leaving was tempered by hard work and an occasional visit to La Maison. The sweet-smelling girl he had first met never allowed him but a few minutes alone when he got there.

At some point the slim man put the French diary together with the Lewis and Clark expedition. The long trip up the

Missouri River. The winter camps. The portage around the Great Falls. These were mentioned in the diary, but from a much more personal view. There was a good deal of complaining.

One morning, over bowls of porridge, Rene asked, "How old are you?"

"I'm not sure," Kyle admitted. I was born toward the end of August in 1793. It's not something I think about."

"Well, you're something over 20," his friend said. Then he furled his brow as he worked the numbers in his head. "On your next birthday you'll be 23, so that makes you 22 now."

Hearing his friend put a slight shock through the slim man. "How the hell did that happen?" he said in disbelief. "I was 17 when I left England. Men I knew in their twenties were married with children."

"Maybe that shaggy moustache that you're eating with our porridge makes you look older," Rene kidded him.

Wiping the moustache with his hand, Kyle realized that it had gotten more pronounced.

After the meal, the two went outside to warm in the morning sun. "If it warms up some, we'll have to put the traps out again," the slim man said.

"Last time I was in town, I saw cargo being moved up the river," Rene told him. "I plan to join them to St. Louis."

Staring thoughtfully at the bayou water, the slim man replied, "I hadn't thought so much about going to St. Louis. I've been thinking about getting on a ship back to Boston."

"Don't feel you have to leave just because I am," Rene told him. "You can stay in the shack as long as you want. Hell, when I come back the place will be clean and warm."

"We still have the gator head to sell," Kyle reminded him.

"He should be in town now," his lanky friend said. "I am glad you mentioned it. We can take them to him today. I need to go and talk to the cargo folks anyway."

They hung the salty heads onto a pole, and with one on each end the two headed for town. The man gave them $5 for each head. Walking away, Kyle said, "They pay almost as much for the head as we got for the skins."

On the way back Rene led the way along the cargo docks. An older bald, man with a neatly trimmed moustache and beard watched them. As they passed him the man asked, "Are the two of you looking for work?"

To the lanky man's surprise, Kyle replied, "We are."

"I lost some men coming down from St. Louis and need strong lads like you two to get back there. My name's Jacob and the trip upriver will be three to four months, depending on the wind and current. I got a good cook, and the crew is better than some. I don't allow hard drinking except during a layover."

Kyle thought about the three months or more, then asked, "What do you pay for one way?"

"Why would you want to go one way?" the man asked. "Going up is the hard part. Coming back is only four to six weeks. That's where you make your money."

The slim man figured a laborer made near $30 a month. He had understood that going up would take four months. He was sure that Captain Jacob wouldn't pay $120.

"What do you pay for the trip up?" Kyle repeated.

"Same pay up and down," the man said. "It's top wages at $75."

The lanky man was looking doubtful. The slim man continued asking, "That includes two meals a day?

"It does," Jacob replied.

"I've got a saddle and some other gear," Kyle told him. "Is that a problem?"

"I ain't responsible if some bastard steals them to buy whiskey," the captain warned him.

"When do we leave?" the slim man asked.

"Daylight tomorrow," the man told him.

"I'll be here," Kyle said. He then looked at his shocked friend. "Are you in, Rene?"

"I guess I am," the lanky man replied.

As the two of them walked toward the shack, Rene said, "I didn't think we would be leaving so fast. I was just going to make some inquiries. That's a lot of months for $75."

"We wanted to go to St. Louis," Kyle told him. "Now we know we'll be well fed for three or four months. In the end we will be there."

The keelboat was something over 60 feet long and 15 feet wide. There was a small shelter forward with a mast secured to it. The boat had locks for three sweeps on each side to row when the sail couldn't be used. There were set poles that were used to push the boat off snags or sandbars. There were coils of rope to string out ahead of the boat and be tied to a tree to manually pull it along.

The cargo was covered with canvas secured to the sides with openings where necessary for rowing. There was room for the 12-man crew to take shelter under the canvas and to sleep.

The cook and captain stayed in the cabin toward the stern and lived there year-round. Owning a keelboat was a significant investment; therefore, many of the captains were the owners and the boat became their homes. The cook, Claude, got the benefit because the captain's quarters had the only stove.

One of the crew was the bosun named Wade, and he knew the river as well as the captain. The bosun would assign the men their stations throughout the day. He also took his turn at the sweeps and set poles. The six sweeps propelled the keelboat and the seventh one was used at the stern as a rudder.

The bosun slept in the forward rope locker, which held the crew's personal gear. On cold, wet nights, several of the crew would pack into the cramped space to get out of the weather. The less senior crewmen had only a dry spot under the cargo canvas.

Aft there was a whale boat for hauling the hawsers ahead to tie them to trees. The deck was kept clear to prevent tripping when rushing to one method of propelling the keelboat to another.

Kyle was assigned to the aft set pole when pushing off from the wharf. The bosun watched the flatboats floating down the river as they were guided into dock. When he saw an opening, he called out, "Push away." Gripping the long pole, the slim man pushed away, making sure that the bow moved out farther.

Then, still using the poles, with three men on each side, they pushed the keelboat upriver by walking down the sides with the poles planted in the river bottom. Once they reached the stern, the pole was pulled up and carried forward to be used for the next push.

Once they were midriver, the poles were put up and the men went to the sweeps, which were long oars. With four men on each side, they pulled on the oars to propel the keelboat out from the congestion of the port. This morning the boat was blessed with a wind from the south. The single sail was raised and the men stowed the sweeps. One man at the stern continued to steer the keelboat with a sweep used as a rudder.

Kyle had been moved to the sail and assigned on the halyard to raise the yardarm. With the help of Alwyn, one of the crew, they pulled it up. Other men were on the brace lines and sheets. The captain oversaw the operation of the keelboat, and once satisfied he went to his cabin for his breakfast.

With the keelboat on course up the Mississippi River, the crew broke for breakfast. The meal was porridge with milk in it. It turned out that the cook, Claude had been able to barter for some fresh milk this morning.

Alwyn gulped his down and then went to relieve the man on the stern sweep. The captain had two fixed chairs on the roof of the forward rope locker and watched the keelboats progress.

With the boat underway and the wind pushing it, there was little to do for the crew. The set poles and sweeps had been stowed.

One of the crew went to the forward rope locker and started to move items around to make more room or, maybe to look through others gear.

Introductions were made to the Kyle and Rene during breakfast, and the slim man recognized most of them as English or Scottish. He let them know that he was from England while Rene just kept quiet, being the only one of French origin.

The winding Mississippi River soon put the wind in the wrong direction and the command was given to put out the sweeps. As Kyle put his sweep into the water, he noticed that the keelboat was hardly moving and at best only keeping up with the current.

The men at the front of each side set the pace as the boat was rowed. One man started singing a sea shanty that had the right rhythm to pull on the sweeps. Soon all were singing it. Once again, Kyle could see the boat was making way upriver. With his eyes half-closed the slim man thought about being back in England rowing his yoal.

Every half-hour, two men would relieve men on the sweeps and that would give them a half-hour break every hour and a half. Kyle and Rene, being the new crew, were put in the middle, and after an hour they took their break together.

"I thought my arms would fall off by the time we got relieved," his lanky friend said.

"When we go back it will be for an hour and a half," Kyle reminded him. "Maybe you're dipping your sweep too deep. Dip it a little less but don't make it look like you're just skimming the water."

"I think the crew knows I'm French," Rene said. "I don't think they like me."

"Tell them you're American," his friend replied. "If trouble comes, I got your back."

Midday the keelboat tied up to a tree leaning over the river. The wind had all but died, so the sail was taken down, flaked over the boom and tied. The men sprawled all over the boat, resting. The cook walked ashore along a sandbar and soon came back with two buckets of spring water. The men lifted them to the deck and with dippers drank thirstily.

Near the aft cabin there was a barrel of water, but it had taken on a taste of the wood. A light, but tasty meal was served. Kyle was beginning to understand the captain's comment of having a good cook. After an hour's break, set poles pushed the keelboat away from the tree and sandbar and the men were back to singing and rowing.

It was near sunset when the keelboat bumped up against the shore and the men climbed off, quickly building a fire. Baited handlines were tossed into the river and the men began to pull in bass and catfish. While the catfish were more like dead weight being pulled in, the bass put up quite a display, breaking the surface and diving to run.

Rene and Kyle didn't have anything to fish with and watched, cheering those with success. After a decent mess of fish were caught, the cook brought out an iron rack with legs and put it over the fire. As the men cleaned and rinsed the fish, he broiled them over the fire.

The two friends stood to the side while the crew got their plates and got broiled fish. Kyle and Rene weren't sure they were invited to eat. They hadn't caught any of the fish. Wade came by and said, "Ain't you hungry? You best get some before they're all gone."

The two men sat near the bosun and picked the sweet meat off the fish. "Are there any extra handlines?" Kyle asked.

"Most men got their own," Wade replied. "We stop near a trading post tomorrow night and they sell them there."

Once the meal was finished, the crew sat around the fire and passed a bottle. Kyle remembered the captain saying he only allowed drunkenness when the boat was on a layover. He wondered if this was considered a layover.

The two men sat a little way away from the fire and the bottle was not offered to them. That was okay, though. Some of the crew had awful, nasty-looking teeth. The slim man sat with a chew and some coffee the cook had made. He was sitting by the river and the air was comfortable. It was a good evening.

That night, Rene and Kyle found a place under the cargo tarp and rolled out their blankets. Six of the crew were able to get into the rope locker, and after a few hits on the bottle were snoring loudly.

It was raining when the two friends woke. It was sort of a steady drizzle. The sky was filled with heavy clouds, which threatened something more. The six men came out of the rope locker with rain gear on.

Kyle had had a sou'wester hat with a brim on the back, along with an oil cloth coat and pants for fishing on the channel. He could see the advantage of having them here, but they were long gone in his past.

Wade came by and said, "Get your chow from Claude and then come back here to eat it."

"Does the captain give us rain gear?" Kyle asked.

"No, he doesn't," the bosun replied. "You can get some at the trading post and the captain will give you some of your pay if you need it." Then he was gone on the run to get his breakfast.

When Kyle went to put his blankets away and get his ground tarp, the slim man had noticed that his gear had been moved to make room. It also appeared that his saddle bags had been gone through.

Kyle always carried the pistol in his

waist band and could see his long gun where he'd left it in the rope locker. The slim man kept his money in a flat leather pouch under his shirt. He had his shooting bag slung over his shoulder, so other than extra tobacco there was nothing of great value in the bags.

Both Rene and the slim man got their ground tarps with a slit in it to put over their heads to keep the rain off. That and their felt hats did a fair job. The rain was what Kyle had always called a wet rain. It wasn't hard, but it soaked everything. After breakfast, the two friends pushed the keelboat away from the sandbar and six crewmen with the oars started rowing. Slowly the heavily ladened boat moved upriver.

As the miserable day went on, Kyle found it hard to grip the sweeps. He noticed that some of the crew had gloves that helped. *Another thing I have to buy*, he thought. By midafternoon, the rain stopped, and the ground tarps came off. Shaking the water off it, the slim man put it into the rope locker. He wanted to look in the saddle bags, but time did not permit. He had to get back to the sweeps.

That evening they reached a landing with the trading post. There was a 100 foot-long wooden dock that the keelboat could tie up to. There was a flatboat tied ahead of them filled with barrels of grain and salted meat going south. It caused the keelboat to stick out about 30 feet beyond the dock.

Once everything was secured on the boat, Kyle went to the rope locker and opened his saddle bags. Everything had been dug into and the tobacco was gone. Other than that, it looked like nothing else had been taken.

The captain was standing near the gang plank and talking to the bosun. The slim man watched the men file off ahead of him. Most stopped and got money from Jacobs. He then jotted the amount in a logbook.

Kyle and Rene headed for the trading post. For being in an area that appeared to be in the middle of nowhere, the trading post was well-stocked. A sign said, "Everything For Sale Or Trade."

"Someone stole my tobacco," the slim man told his friend.

"It's a damn good thing you didn't leave your pistol or money in the bags," Rene said. "You can be sure the thief would have traded the pistol for whiskey and other things he didn't need."

"Did you see the men getting money from the captain?" Kyle asked his friend.

"I did," the lanky man said. "They might be a little short."

"I am willing to bet they spend this trip's money before they get to St. Louis and have nothing left," the slim man said. "That way they have no choice but to take the return trip. By the time they get to New Orleans they have spent the return trip money. They never catch up."

"I knew some dock workers that hung around at the tavern," Rene told him. "They gambled and drank, and every week they'd bring their pay to the bartender. Like you said, most never caught up."

Memories of being out of money after his search in Virginia went through Kyle's mind. He never wanted to be in that situation again. He went to the fishing items. The slim man took a hand line rig. It was no more than a flat piece of plank with an oval hole for the fingers and it extended out to wrap the line around. It was compact and would fit into his saddle bags.

His friend came over and picked one up. "We can use this when we get back to the shack."

Kyle got some more tobacco and some hooks for fishing. He spent some time trying on the leather gloves before choosing a pair. Each man got a pint of whiskey and then went to the counter. The slim man saw pipes on the back wall. "I'll take one of those also," he said.

Prior to coming to the trading post, Kyle had taken some coins out of the flat leather pouch. In case someone from the boat was in the trading post, he didn't want them to see where he got his money from.

They headed for the boat and saw some of the crew sitting on a log near the dock. One of them, named Leith, looked up and asked, "Will you two be going to see the women tonight?"

Looking around the area, Kyle asked, "What women?"

"About a quarter-mile behind the trading post they got a place," Leith replied. "There's a man playing piano if you want to dance with them."

The other men with him laughed and one said, "That ain't what I go there for."

There was a fire going on the shore and some of the crew were sitting around it and drinking. The two friends sat with the group and Kyle dug his bottle out of the sack their supplies were in.

As he passed it around, the slim man said, "I haven't been in a place as well stocked as this trading post."

A crewman named Eyre replied, "This stop has about everything a man could want. You should go and see the ladies."

"I'll pass and save them for the return trip," Kyle told him. Pulling the pipe from the bag, the slim man cut a piece of tobacco from the twist and filled it. Using a burning stick from the fire, he held it to the tobacco, drawing on the pipe.

The acrid smoke burned his mouth. Coughing, he stared at the pipe, questioning his purchase. His actions got a great deal of kidding from the other crewmen.

Alwyn was one of the men laughing. He then said, "I once worked for a man that wouldn't hire someone that smoked a pipe and wore a belt. When he wasn't lighting the pipe, he was pulling up his pants."

The pint got back to Kyle, and he took a drink and passed it on to Rene. With his mouth cleansed by the whiskey, the slim man took another draw on the pipe. It had gone out.

Picking up the stick again, he touched it to the pipe and drew a mouthful of smoke. Not being surprised by the experience, he did not cough. "You might be right, Alwyn. They don't stay lit. I best not let the captain see me. I wear a belt and now have a pipe."

The keelboat didn't have any rules about when the crew had to be back on board, but knowing what it feels like to pull on the sweeps with a hangover, the crew quit drinking early. Even the men who had gone to see the ladies were back. One was sporting a black eye due to a confrontation over a lady with another customer.

Kyle spent some time in the rope locker before coming back with his blankets. Rolling them out under the cargo canvas, he was chuckling. "What's so funny?" Rene asked.

"I was thinking about catching gators with hooks," the slim man said.

It made no sense to the lanky man. He just shook his head and pulled up his blanket against the cold wind.

An hour later there was cussing and shouting in the rope locker. Kyle looked over. In the moonlight he saw one of the crew, named Clyde, swearing and shaking his hands.

The commotion continued for a half-hour before things settled down. The slim man turned his back to the disturbance and dozed off with a smile on his face. The next morning, the crew had an early breakfast and a half-hour after sunup, the keelboat was pushed away from the dock.

While on his break, the bosun came over to Kyle. "What do you know about the problem last night?"

"It was the damnedest thing," the slim man replied. "What was going on?"

"Somehow Clyde got some fishhooks in his hand," Wade told him. "When I was cutting the last one out this morning, he seemed to be blaming you."

"The only hooks I have are in my saddlebags," Kyle said. "I can't see him getting them there, unless he had his hands in the bags looking for another twist of tobacco."

"You saying he stole from you?" the bosun asked.

"All I am saying is I put the hooks I bought for my handline in my saddlebags," the slim man said.

"You best be careful," Wade warned him. "Clyde's the type to hold a grudge. He's quick to pull his knife."

"I've got a knife and a pistol," Kyle told him. "I won't use either unless I have no choice."

"You should know the captain frowns on fighting between crewmen even more than heavy drinking," the bosun replied. "The last two men he let go cut each other up over something stupid."

For the next two days they were rowing against a north wind. Then they got to a section with a more severe current. Try as they might, the crew could not make any headway upriver. That was when the two friends learned what the coils of rope were for.

Kyle and Clyde were assigned to the whaleboat, hauling the rope upriver and securing it to anything solid on the shore, usually a tree. Then the crew onboard would haul the rope in, pulling the keelboat through the current.

As the two men worked in the whaleboat, Clyde glared at the slim man. The prominent pistol in the Kyle's waistband wasn't beyond his notice. The angry crewman handled the rope, and the slim man rowed. This allowed Kyle to keep an eye on Clyde.

For two days the keelboat was pulled upriver with the ropes before the current slowed and to the men's relief, they got a south wind, and the sail was put up. The aching and exhausted crew lay around the deck soaking up the spring sunshine. Kyle brought out his saddle bags and sat to one side, shielded from Clyde.

Slowly and carefully, he picked the fishhooks that he had sprinkled around in the bags and put them back into the containers he'd purchased them in. Rene sat back against the tarp, covered cargo and said, "That was an awful trick you played on Clyde."

"Damn," Kyle said as one of the hooks jabbed him. "I wasn't particularly after Clyde. I was after the man that was going through my bags. It just happened to be him."

"If looks could kill, you would be really dead by now," his lanky friend said, chuckling.

To make sure the pistol was ready to fire, Kyle had taken to shooting it each morning before breakfast and then cleaning and reloading it. He would choose an object to shoot at, and as the crew would make bets on whether he'd hit or miss, the slim man would line up on the target and squeeze the trigger.

In the past several days, he'd only missed once. Kyle would always look at Clyde after shooting, hoping to send a message that he was nobody to mess with. Even the captain would come out of his cabin to watch. One day he told the slim man, "Your shooting is better than a bosun whistle getting the men up."

With all the hooks taken care of, Kyle closed the saddle bags and set them aside. Sucking on his injured fingers, he looked at the riverbank going by. "We should come this way sometime and follow some of the smaller streams spilling into the river. I bet we would find some beaver ponds to trap."

"You don't like what we're catching now around the shack?" Rene asked.

"Beaver won't try and eat you like a gator while you're catching them," the slim man said, "and a couple of their pelts are worth eight to ten muskrat furs. In a few good ponds a man can make some money."

"I like sitting on the porch with a hot cup of coffee after a day of trapping," his friend replied. "And after the sun goes down, we have a comfortable and warm place to sleep."

Kyle lay back against the cargo and closed his eyes. He thought about the winter of trapping in Canada. He and Danny had been wanted by the Royal Navy for desertion after avoiding being impressed, and with the help of some Metis they had trapped until the ponds froze over.

The slim man wasn't sure if it was living in the wilds trapping beaver that made the nostalgic memories so satisfying or if it was the winter months spent with a beautiful

Ojibwa woman. Either way, the memories were good, and it was when he had been trapping beavers.

"Make ready to tie up!" came the command, bringing Kyle out of his thoughts. Jumping up, the slim man tossed his saddle bags into the rope locker.

The captain was pointing at the low dark clouds in western sky. "We have a hell of a storm coming!"

The slim man began helping with striking the sail as the thunder was heard and the winds began to tear at the keelboat. Other men had manned the sweeps as the bosun looked for a place to tie up on the east shore. Rushing from side to side while flaking and tying the sail to the boom as the wind tried to grab it, Kyle was suddenly tripped and went sprawling onto the deck.

"On your feet, Oliver," the bosun shouted. "This ain't no time to be lying around."

Scrambling to get up, Kyle saw the sneer on Clyde's face. No doubt he had caused him to trip. "That's one for you," the slim man muttered as he continued to tie the sail.

The boat scraped up against the brush leaning over the water. Lines were tossed out to tie the keelboat to anything solid. With the sail secured, Kyle grabbed one of the lines used to dock the boat, and leaping to shore, he scrambled up the bank and quickly tied it to the trunk of a tree using a timber hitch he'd learned while logging in Vermont.

Before the slim man could climb back onto the boat, the storm hit, viciously lashing and tearing at his clothes and the brush around him, pelleting everything with a mixture of rain and hail. His hat went flying as Kyle clung to the tree trunk to prevent being blown away.

Then as quickly as it had come, the storm passed, leaving the slim man wet and bruised from the hail and flying debris. Others who had leaped from the boat with lines started to get up. All hadn't been successful tying the keelboat, but it made little difference. The winds had been pushing the boat against the shore.

Kyle saw that the tarp covering the cargo had been ripped loose and hung over the side of the keelboat, torn and covered with dirt and branches. The captain was shouting, "Is everyone okay? Answer up!"

They had all survived and called back to Jacob. Several had cuts that would need attention, but there were no broken bones. Now the job of putting things back together began. The keelboat remained tied to the shore as the men worked at getting the cargo protected. Kyle had an awl in his bags and got that to help repair the tarps.

The rest of the day was spent undoing what a few minutes of wind had created.

Nobody cared what kind of storm it was. All they knew was that it was a big one and they had survived. With the tarp fixed as best they could, it was stretched back over the cargo. The cook had repaired the stove pipe coming from the cabin and had started making the crew's supper. It was a soup with salted pork he'd gotten from the flatboat they'd tied up next to.

With the keelboat ready to go the crew rested. Kyle sat with a chew in his cheek and exclaimed, "What the hell! Look at that!"

Rene asked, "Look at what?"

"The tree I hung on to," he said pointing. "The top was clean tore off."

* * *

Memories of the storm were soon forgotten as the monotonous days of rowing and pulling the keelboat north dulled the men's senses. It had been over a month and there were at least two more to go. Only the captain and possibly the bosun knew how far they'd traveled.

The nights were spent drinking when the crew had whiskey, or gambling on a blanket spread on the deck or shore. Kyle and Rene chose to watch the men playing cards or rolling dice. The slim man had broken in his pipe and now enjoyed a smoke in the evening. Rene continued to translate the leather diary and explain each page to his friend.

In the small tally book Kyle had gotten in New Orleans, he jotted items that Rene had translated using a stub of a pencil. "Let's figure how far our man has gotten," the slim man said.

"The big falls was mentioned," his lanky friend replied. "That would be a way up the Missouri River."

"They used boats kind of like we're on," Kyle said. "Only they were smaller."

"It seems like they drag the boats around things more than row it," his friend said, laughing.

A week later they reached a long stretch of faster water. They had noticed it coming a couple of days earlier when rowing had slowed their progress upriver. The captain talked of it being several miles. The crew didn't seem too concerned about it, but Kyle was dreading hauling out the lines and pulling the keelboat. A lot of work was done, and little progress was made each day.

Then as they pulled in for the night, the slim man learned why the crew wasn't concerned. On the bank were men with mules who for a price, would tow the boats above the fast water. A crude road had been cleared to lead the team tied to the boat. All that was required of the crew was to use set poles to prevent the keelboat from swinging out into the current or running into the bank or a sandbar.

Kyle had only seen something like this when moving ships in port, even though the method of pulling barges or boats using mules along the shore had been used in different parts of the world for years.

CHAPTER TEN

It was late March and the keel boat was sailing on a breeze from the southeast when they reached the confluence of the Mississippi and Ohio Rivers. Care had to be taken to avoid the shifting sandbars caused by the ever-changing currents.

There were cheers of excitement from the crew, knowing that they had less than 200 miles left to go. There was a small settlement that struggled to survive the spring floods each year. As the keelboat arrived, there were the sounds of hammers fixing buildings that had been damaged.

They would have a two-day layover to give the cook time to restock his larder and give the men some time to unwind. Unwinding meant having a night of heavy drinking. As the men left, several of them got some money from the captain. It was obvious that some had reached the end of this trip's money as they looked with surprise at what little the captain gave them.

As the two friends left the captain told them, "This might look like a quiet town right now, but come night there are areas that have men who prey on the boatsmen. Keep your eyes open."

The two men thanked the captain and headed for town. "The captain must think this is the first river town we've been in," Rene said. "He forgets we hired on in New Orleans."

"In New Orleans they'll hit you over the head and take your money," Kyle replied. "Maybe here they cut your throat and take your money."

"He forgets, we got each other's back," his friend told him.

The first stop was at the mercantile. Kyle hadn't been able to buy a new hat and had been wearing his tuque. While he looked at the hats, Rene was looking at the boots. The sole on one of his boots had ripped open on one side, and he had wound packaging cord that the cook had around the boot.

The slim man took a fancy to a flat-brimmed leather hat. Being a little heavier, it would be less likely to be blown off like the felt. He brought the hat to the counter and asked the owner for two twists of tobacco.

Reaching into his shirt, Kyle took out the coins to pay for his purchase. Then he noticed the jerky behind the counter. Feeling kind of hungry, he got some of that. Rene came up behind him and asked, "What do you think of these boots?"

Taking one, he looked it over. "Looks like a well-made boot."

He stepped back while the lanky man settled up. On the front porch, Rene sat with a stick of hard candy in his mouth, lacing up his new boots. Standing up, he flexed them some and smiled. "They might make a few sore spots, but they feel okay."

Leaving his old boots by the porch, Rene said, "I could use a drink."

Wearing his new hat and chewing a piece of jerky, Kyle led his friend toward the sound of a piano. The tavern had a rough look to it from too much flooding. The owner did only what he had to in order to re-open.

Standing at the warped plank bar, the two ordered whiskey. "Shot or the bottle?" the man asked.

"Leave the bottle," Kyle replied. Digging out a coin for the whiskey, he told his friend, "This one is on me."

"I'll get the next one," Rene said.

"Who the hell is going to carry us back to the boat?" the slim man asked, laughing.

The whiskey was watered down and had the sting of pepper in it. Leith and

Claude were at a table and waved them over. The two of them were already halfway through a bottle.

"The bartender said a couple of ladies come in later," Leith said.

Looking around the tavern, Kyle replied, "Well, there are the four of us and three men in the corner playing cards. They will be done with work in a damn hurry."

"I stay away from them women," the cook said. "I got a regular girl in St. Louis."

"What does she do during the months you are gone?" Leith asked him.

Claude puffed up his chest and said, "She waits for me."

The other three laughed and he didn't care for that. To sooth his feelings, Kyle told him, "I am sure she is a good, church-going woman."

"She is," the cook replied. "I don't know about church-going, but she is a good woman."

The slim man had had peppered-down whiskey before and when he drank too much he suffered for the next two days when it went through him. He laughed and joked with the others while nursing his drinks.

The bosun and Alwyn came in and joined them. "There's a place up aways that had girls dancing on a stage. They show most of their legs and everything," Alwyn told them.

"We got two coming in here later,"

Leith said. "Maybe they're some of the dancing girls who come here after they're done."

There were loud words between the three playing cards in the corner. Apparently one of them was losing. The six friends at the table ignored them. They had three empty bottles in front of them and were about to order another.

Suddenly, all hell broke loose with the card players. Two stood up, knocking their chairs over and one yelled, "You are a damn cheater!"

The bartender came around the bar with a short club and quickly had the two men on the floor with hits to their heads. The men watched as the remaining player helped the bartender drag the two men to the door and dump them into the street. Kyle noticed the bartender quickly went through the men's pockets, taking any money they had left.

The man who was blamed for cheating just nodded to the bartender and headed up the street. Claude slurred, "I saw you go through their pockets."

The bartender was an intimidating man. Glaring at his accuser, he said, "You didn't see nothing."

Wade suggested, "I think we should go and see if the ladies have finished their dance."

As they got up, the bartender hit the

top of the bar with the club and shouted, "Get the hell out of here you damn river rats!"

As they passed the two men lying in the dirt, Leith asked, "Should we help them?"

"When they wake up," Wade said, "they'll have a headache, but I doubt they'll be any smarter. You never play cards with a man that has his back to a wall."

Kyle didn't know what that meant, but as for the two men lying in the street, that was true. Then he thought, *Watch your back for the bartender.*

The slim man kept looking back, feeling it wasn't right to leave the two men, then he saw one of them trying to get up. He justified in his mind that they were probably alright.

The place with the girls dancing was in better condition. There was a waterline around the building showing how deep the spring flood had been, but inside work had been done to clean the place up.

To the left side there was a long bar. Beneath the shine there was evidence of scarring over the years. To the back there was a raised platform where two ladies in plunging dresses and flaring petticoats were dancing to the piano player.

There were several tables for customers. Half of them had customers enjoying the show and their drinks. Two other ladies moved around the room soliciting drinks and other things.

The tables were set up for four, so they grabbed two extra chairs so the group could sit together. "I'll buy the first one," Kyle offered, and he went to the bar. The heavy-set bartender had his hair greased back and sported a small goatee.

"We'll have a bottle," the slim man said.

The man's goiter bobbed when he said, "Two dollars. I'll bring it to the table."

Giving the man the money which Kyle had taken from the flat pouch before coming in, the slim man headed back to the table. A full-bosomed woman was in his chair. Leith was making conversation with her. He looked up and asked, "Could you have the man bring this lady a drink?"

Going back to the bar, he saw that the bartender was carrying six glasses and the bottle. "We'll need a drink for the lady at the table." Kyle told him.

Snorting, the bartender turned and poured a lady's drink. "That will be a dollar."

Damn expensive, he thought as he gave the man the money.

The circle around the table expanded and a chair was added for Kyle. The slim man tasted the whiskey. It was better than the last place. A little less water and no pepper. The lady was busy flirting with the entire table as she gulped down her drink. Claude bought her the next one.

Then her attention was focused on Leith. The touching, the leaning close, the breathy whisper into his ear, was witnessed by Kyle. The slim man knew Leith was short on money and was somewhat safe.

The dancing girls came off the stage and started circulating with customers. They avoided their table. They chose ones that gave them room to maneuver. Realizing that this whiskey was more potent than the peppered stuff, Kyle sipped the brew slowly. Another bottle was ordered, and it came with a lady's drink. She had turned away from Leith and was now giving all her attention to the drunk cook.

It won't do you any good, lady, he thought. *Claude has a woman in St. Louis.*

Suddenly, to his surprise, he got up with the lady and headed for a room in the back. "I thought Claude had a woman in St. Louis," Kyle told the table.

"I guess enough whisky can make a man forget almost anything," Wade replied, laughing.

When the lady came out without the cook, the slim man became worried. "Did you see that?" he asked.

The others looked at him. "See what?" Leith asked.

"She came out without Claude," the slim man said. "I am going to see what happened to him."

"He probably passed out right after he paid the lady," Alwyn told him.

"Maybe so," Kyle replied as he got up.

"Where are you going?" Rene asked.

"I'm going to go get Claude," the slim man said. "It ain't right her coming out without him."

Adjusting the pistol in his waist band, Kyle headed for the door. The bartender came around the end and said, "You can't go in there without taking a lady."

"We got a man back there and I am going in to take him out," the slim man snapped at the man. "You are welcome to go in with me, but you walk in front of me."

The bartender swore and went back behind the bar. Kyle knew he probably had a club behind it and maybe even a scatter gun. The slim man ducked through the door quickly and looked down the dim hall of curtained rooms. There was whispering behind the first curtain.

In his head he counted the ladies. He was sure they were all at the tables. Pulling back the curtain, Kyle startled two men who were going through the unconscious man's clothing, looking for money.

One of the men, with a mean ugliness to him, looked up first. He raised a club and threatened, "You best get the hell out of here or I will bust your head."

Kyle pulled the pistol and cocked it.

"Then you're the one I am going to kill," he snarled.

Both men leaped back with nowhere to go. Their eyes were big. "Toss whatever you've got in your hands on the bed."

The two men did so, and then Kyle told them, "Take your clothes off. You can keep you filthy long johns on."

"You can't make us do that," the mean ugly man said.

"You don't have to," the slim man told him. "I'm going to kill you anyway."

Quickly the two men shed their clothing. When they reached to put their boots back on, Kyle waved them away with the pistol. "Now you two leave the way you come in."

"We come in the way you did," the other man said.

Glancing to the back, Kyle saw a window. "Climb out the window and if I see you two again tonight, one of you will die and I will cut the throat of the other."

Giving them plenty of room, the slim man let the two long john-cladded men by him. The window was opened and the two of them went out, sprawling on the ground below. As they ran away, the two became brave again and shouted all kind of threats at Kyle.

Quickly, the slim man collected the coins off the bed and then he picked up the two men's clothes and kicked their boots under the bed. Pulling the door going into the tavern open, he called to the men at his table. "I need help with Claude."

Other than Wade the others were slow to respond. As the bosun went by Kyle the slim man said, "I hope he's passed out and they didn't hit him."

The bosun got Claudes arm around his neck and held him around the waist with the other arm. The drunk cook was muttering something as Wade helped him back into the tavern. Alwyn came over to help.

Kyle saw the big-bosomed lady staring at him wide-eyed. Walking up to her, he tossed the dirty clothing into her lap. "You can give these back to your friends when you see them."

After another bottle was bought, the group left, half carrying their drunk cook. The bartender glared at the slim man and was blustering about something or other, while a couple of ladies were screaming at him. Kyle ignored them.

He stopped just before leaving and turned to the other customers in the room. "She had two confederates in the back waiting to rob her customers. There ain't no other door, so they must have come in from the front and the bartender and ladies knew they were back there." He noticed the piano player laughing as he left.

Rene walked next to Kyle as they headed back to the keelboat. "These damn boots hurt my feet. I hope my old ones are still in front of the mercantile."

The next morning, the slim man woke with a slight headache and an upset stomach. Rene was still snoring as Kyle went to the water barrel and took a long drink of the stale water. The cook stuck his head out of the cabin door and looked surprisingly good after being so drunk. Claude said, "Coffee will be ready in a few minutes."

The slim man went over to the side of the boat and saw a piece of log floating by. He pulled and cocked the pistol. Took aim and pulled the trigger. Nothing happened. He looked at the weapon and muttered, "Good thing the bastards didn't challenge me last night."

Another day was spent tied up next to the river town. The crew was kept busy taking care of things that needed to be done before continuing upriver. That night a fire was built on the shore and the men sat around it, telling stories of their adventures the night before.

Clyde was quiet and sipped on a pint while he glared at Kyle. The slim man had gotten used to the behavior and figured the man would have tried something by now if he was going to.

They had about two more weeks before

reaching St. Louis. The nights this far north were cool, but the days for most part were sunny and warm. Kyle was on the sweeps and Clyde was sitting right behind him.

"Your time is coming," the slim man heard.

A couple of minutes later, Kyle was on his half-hour break and he stood back, watching the men rowing. He had hoped that the angry crewman had gotten over being stuck by the hooks, but it did not sound like it. Maybe he was going to wait until they got to St. Louis and attack him then. That way he wouldn't lose his job on the keelboat. Kyle smiled. He could quickly get lost in the crowd once on shore and never have to see Clyde again.

Less than a week out of St. Louis, moods were high on the keelboat. The men would get whatever pay they had left coming to them and have a few days off. There was a south wind and the sail was up.

Rene and Kyle were at the bow cleaning their muzzleloaders and watching the shoreline slowly go by. At one point there were two hogs with young ones playing at the edge of the water. "When we get back," his lanky friend said, "We'll hunt some in New Orleans."

"I'd like that," Kyle replied. "We could have Rudy smoke hams and side meat for us."

While the Mississippi River was wide,

one still had to keep an eye on other snags, new sandbars, and other boats. The captain or Wade most often kept watch from the chairs on top of the cabin. In times of fog, a bell that hung at the bow was rung and the bosun manned it.

Today was a beautiful day and a lazy one for the crew. Suddenly, Rene pointed. "Look at that damn flatboat. It is drifting round and round. It must have come in contact with a snag or the shore."

Seconds later the captain shouted, "Man the sweeps!"

Scrambling to their feet, the two friends tossed the cleaning stuff and their long guns into the rope compartment and took their places at one of the oars.

The first attempt was to pick up some speed and maneuver around the flatboat. As they got closer, attempting to pass it on the west side, it again began to turn. Someone on the flatboat had an oar in the water and was pulling on it for all he had and over-corrected.

"Reverse!" the captain shouted. The men spun around on the benches and pulled for all they were worth to stop and back the keelboat up. It was a glancing blow when they hit the flatboat, jarring the men and throwing them from their stations.

Clyde was propelled toward the bulwark striking his head as he went over the side. Without thinking, Kyle kicked off his boots, and dove over the bulwark and into the river. Coming up he shook the water out of his eyes and saw the men on the keelboat pointing and shouting, "He's over there!"

Kyle saw the man floating face down. The keelboat was slowly being pushed towards him by the flatboat. Swimming through the muddy water, the slim man reached Clyde, rolled him over and then, with one arm around his body, he kicked and swam with the one free arm, pulling the two of them away from the boats.

As though in slow motion, the keelboat swung around and the two men were upstream. A rope was tossed to them and landed about 10 feet away. Coughing and spitting water, Kyle pulled the seemingly lifeless body of Clyde toward it. Grabbing the rope, he treaded water and got it tied around the man's chest.

The keelboat, still against the flatboat, continued to turn slowly as they floated downstream. The men pulled on the rope, hauling Clyde onto the boat. Kyle remained in the water, having the feeling that he was being drawn under the keelboat. Desperately, he tried to swim away, but his soggy clothing hampered his progress. Then a rope splashed into the water beside him.

Grabbing it, he felt the men strain on it, pulling him up out of the river. Rough hands grabbed him, pulling the slim man over the bulwark and onto the deck. Kyle laid on the deck, coughing up the river water he'd breathed in. One of the men with a gaff hook called out, "I got his hat!"

The river water was surprisingly cold. The slim man began to shiver as the adrenalin left his body and the effects of the water were felt. Someone helped him sit up and put a whiskey bottle to his lips. The burning liquid felt good on his throat and warmed his insides.

Kyle became aware and asked, "How is Clyde?"

"You saved him," Wade replied. "He has one hell of a bump on his head, but he's awake and cussing."

Rene came with dry clothes for the slim man. After a couple of more pulls in the whiskey bottle, Kyle stripped the wet clothing off and put on the dry. Meanwhile the captain was having words with the farmer on the flatboat. The man had a load of root vegetables, salt pork, and some grain.

Prior to disengaging from the keelboat, the farmer passed over a bushel of vegetables with his apology. The sail was brought back into the wind and the keelboat again progressed upriver. Captain Jacobs and the bosun were looking over the side for any damage. Kelvin checked the cargo hold for any leakage.

All was well. It was to be expected.

The keelboat was designed for work on the river and its keel was reinforced to handle impacts against snags, rocks, sandbars, and the occasional flatboat.

That night the keelboat tied up in a small cove. The men had their handlines out and fish was caught for their supper. The cook had boiled rutabagas to go with the fish. The men sat around the fire eating. Clyde's skin had split on his forehead and had a bandage wrapped around his head.

He kept looking at Kyle, and due to the bandage and some swelling, the slim man couldn't tell if he was glaring or not. The slim man didn't care. The fish tasted great, he liked rutabagas, and he was dressed in dry, warm clothing. On the downside, it would take a day or so for his hat to dry. He couldn't believe that he hadn't tossed it off before going into the water.

The crew scattered around to relieve themselves or get something from the boat. Soon he found himself alone with Clyde. In a rough voice, the man said, "You saved me. You risked your own life to save me."

Well, Kyle didn't consider it risking his own life. He knew that he was a good swimmer and would never have gone over if he wasn't. He did not say this to Clyde. Instead, he said, "It wasn't any more than you would have done if I went over."

The man's head lowered. The slim man

knew he must be thinking if the roles were reversed, Clyde would have just waved farewell to Kyle. The slim man sat quietly. Then Clyde said, "I was mad at you for a long time. That's all in the past now."

"I appreciate that," the slim man said. Then he asked, "How is your head feeling?"

Things were settled with the man. The simple act of saving his life ended the grudge. Kyle thought of offering him a chew but chose to leave well enough alone.

* * *

The levees were crowded around St. Louis when the men rowed the boat looking for some open space. Several heavily loaded flatboats and large keelboats were heading downriver.

Above the levees was the town of St. Louis, founded by Pierre Laclede and Auguste Chouteau. It was established to collect furs purchased by trading posts placed near various tribes. Settled by the French, older buildings were built with vertical logs and then plastered, giving them a white look. A few newer buildings had started to use brick.

There were few warehouses, so cargos such as blankets, knives, long guns, various tools, cornmeal, flour, sugar, leather goods, whiskey, and other items were protected by tarps and stacked beyond the levee after being offloaded.

There were various hides and furs left uncovered a short distance away to be loaded onto waiting keelboats or flatboats. Cargo that was brought to St. Louis to be shipped further south made up the rest of what was staged beyond the levee. Kyle saw grayish stacks of what appeared to be hides. "Those are buffalo," Wade told him.

After a bit of swearing, the keelboat was able to find space on its second attempt. Kyle jumped onto the levee and handled the stern line, tying the boat up to posts driven into the dirt.

An offer was made to the crew to help offload the keelboat. Two men who had spent all their money on the way up signed on. They would make enough money for a good drunk before starting south.

Kyle was putting his $75 into his flat pouch as he walked away from the levee. "Where do you want to go first?" he asked his friend.

Rene was looking around, wide-eyed. "I don't know. It looks a lot like New Orleans."

St. Louis had been built on a rise, keeping it out of reach of the Mississippi during spring floods. Eventually the levees were built along the river to make the lower land usable for building.

"I got to find a place to put the saddle and stuff," Kyle said.

Loaded down with the saddle, long gun, and other gear, the slim man walked up the slope towards the town. They passed a man laying bricks on a new building and Kyle asked him, "Where would you recommend we find a place for the night?"

"There's a tavern with some rooms," the man said, speaking French. "If you want to sleep for little money, take the next street to the left and watch for the sign."

Rene looked at his friend. "I like the idea of the place for little money."

They took the narrow dirt street to the left. They passed an open building that might have been the tavern and they continued on. Then they saw a sign that read: "Augie's Two Bits a Night"

"That's cheap enough," Kyle said, tired of carrying his burden.

The building was narrow and long, with plank walls sealed with narrow strips of wood. Each side had three fly-specked windows. They found that the front section was split into two rooms.

To the right was what appeared to be a kitchen. Through its doorway they saw a heavy-set woman with a stained dress peeling potatoes. The room they stepped into was starkly furnished with a couple of tables, some stools, and a low counter. It was occupied by an equally heavy man in a stained shirt sitting behind the counter, reading the paper.

Hefting himself up, the man smiled, exposing several missing or rotting teeth. "They call me Augie," he said. Then asked, "You men looking for a place to stay?"

"We are," Rene said. "We'd like to see the room."

For two bits one could not be too careful and could end up with a sagging bed in a room so small one could hardly turn around in it. Smiling, the heavyset man opened the door near his counter.

Kyle's jaw dropped. The back section was an old military barracks. Two high, wooden bunks lined both walls. Each bunk was designed to sleep two soldiers. By the looks of the place, it was probably used before the War of 1812.

Rene saw the place quite differently. Walking in, he looked around the dusty, cobweb-filled room. Then he turned. "Does the two bits include a meal?"

Puffing out his chest above his big belly, the man proudly said, "It does. Ma makes breakfast every morning."

"Each of us gets the whole bunk?" the lanky man asked.

The man hesitated and then smiled. "We only got four others staying here right now. That should not be a problem. Just choose two empty ones that you want."

Nothing was clean about the place,

including the bunks that had dust and remnants of hay from past ticks. They chose two bottom bunks about halfway down the room. The other occupants had stuff on bunks further down the other side.

Sitting on his bunk with the sideboard cutting into the back of his legs, Kyle asked, "Now that we have a place to sleep, where do you want to go?"

"We will look over the sights of St. Louis," his friend said.

Placing his saddle, blankets, long gun, and saddlebags onto the bunk, the slim man was happy to be unburdened. Now he had to worry about things being stolen.

On the way out to the street, Kyle asked, "Is our gear safe in there?"

"Safe as can be," the man said. "Me and Ma keep a good eye on them that come in and out."

That assurance didn't make the slim man feel any better, but he did smile and say, "Thanks."

As they stepped out, Kyle asked his friend, "Where do you want to go first?"

"I say we walk from one end to the other and see what this town is about," the lanky man said.

An hour later the two of them were back at the cargo area. The slim man asked, "What did you think?"

"Kind of like New Orleans without the

businesses," Rene replied. "I saw a livery, some kind of a small mercantile, a place that baked bread, the church, a couple small taverns and the places that stored grain. They must have come from a different part of France. There is not much to do after you finish work."

"You go home and take care of chores there," Kyle kidded him. "I like the town. We missed some of the streets. Maybe that is where the night life is."

"It won't be too long, and I'll be ready to catch a boat back south," his lanky friend told him.

"I need some tobacco," the slim man said. "Let's go to the place that looked like a mercantile."

The log building was not plastered, but rather the seams were filled with some kind of mixture that sealed them. Stepping into the building, Kyle stopped as the smells of leather, spices, and other good things hit him, reminding him of places he'd been to in the past.

A man with thinning hair and a thick beard was putting things onto a shelf. Without looking up, he said, "I will be right with you." He spoke French.

Kyle figured he'd leave St. Louis with his French much refreshed. The slim man said in English, "I just need some tobacco. No hurry."

Rene noticed the peppermint stick on the counter. The lanky man also spent time looking at the long guns behind the counter. When Kyle came by, he said, "I should get me one of these. They look nicer than the Baker, and are also rifled."

The slim man had heard of rifled barrels and that they shot straighter. He had never had a need for that. On a rolling deck of a ship, it would have done little good. And he went by the creed that if you couldn't get close enough to game, you didn't deserve to eat it.

The man came over and introduced himself in English. "My name's Andre LaRue. Are you interested in a new long gun?"

Rene asked, "Where are they made?"

"In Lancaster, Pennsylvania," the man said. "Buffalo hunters like them. It's important to have kill shots on the buffalo so you don't end up with a wounded one stampeding the herd."

I'm using a British Baker right now," the lanky man replied.

Andre looked at Kyle. "What are you using?"

The slim man replied, "A Charleville, .69 caliber long gun."

The man looked at Rene's long gun. "The Baker is rifled and accurate to 200 yards. The Charleville is a smoothbore and accurate at 50 yards. In a battle the Baker is slower to load and will foul faster than the Charleville. You must weigh accuracy over ability to shoot faster."

Kyle didn't care for what Andre was saying and stood in silence.

Remembering the weapon he'd lost on the battlefield in New Orleans, the lanky man said, "I didn't think too much of the Springfield I was issued when I joined the army."

"Well, you made a decent trade when you got the Baker," Andre told him.

The whole conversation left Kyle less than happy. Growing up in England, only the upper class had firearms unless you were in the army. He had been so proud in Canada to be able to purchase and own the Charleville.

The two men left Andre's and continued along the dusty street. They stopped in a tavern. The owner spoke French and had stew made with lamb. The friends ordered bowls of the stew and ale. As Kyle ate, he felt that the stew lacked taste, but he did not complain. The ale made the meal.

The tavern owner's wife came from the back and asked, "How was everything?"

Both said very good despite what they might have thought. "That was a favorite when Commander Lewis and his friend Clark came in for a meal," she proudly said. "I never changed a thing."

At that point, both men's opinion of the

stew changed. If Lewis and Clark liked it, it must be good. "Did they eat here often?" Rene asked.

"No, just the once," the owner's wife replied. "They were at the fort they build about 30 mile upriver."

Smiling at the memory, she headed back into the kitchen. In a low voice, Kyle told his friend, "I understand why they didn't come back."

Over several more ales the two men talked about St. Louis and Lewis and Clark. The slim man's notebook that he'd kept while they translated the diary was in his saddle bags, and he wished he had it to add places and points to the conversation.

With too much ale under their belts, the two friends staggered along the street toward their lodging. Laughing, Rene asked, "I wonder if Lewis and Clark ever stayed at the fine two bits place?"

"Back 12 years ago it was probably the one bit place," Kyle replied. Those that lived along the street probably wondered what was so funny as the two friends proceeded to Augie's Two Bits a Night.

Morning brought the familiar headache and upset stomach as the slim man rolled out of the hard, wooden bunk. Next to him on the bunk was his saddle and other gear.

He saw the other boarders moving

around. One old man with spectacles and a beard said, "You buggers must have been having a high old time last night. You woke everyone up with your chortling."

In a hoarse voice, Kyle said, "I do apologize for waking you. We were just unwinding from a long trip up the river."

"Damn river trash," the man muttered as he headed for the front room.

Another man came from the back. "Don't mind him. He is always grouchy in the morning."

The two friends headed for the front room to have some breakfast. The owner's wife was pouring coffee and came right over when they sat at a table. "I'll be right along with your breakfast."

The meal was a thin porridge and the coffee was weak. Rene swallowed a spoonful and said, "It is more like gruel than porridge."

"Is gruel good?" Kyle asked.

"You just ate some," his friend replied. "What do you think?"

"I don't think I will look forward to gruel every morning," the slim man told him.

Finding nothing to do in St. Louis, the two men walked back to the cargo area. They were surprised at how much cargo had been moved around since they'd got in yesterday. Jacob's keelboat was being loaded with buffalo hides.

The captain saw the two men and

called to them. "If you changed your mind about the return trip, I already hired a couple of men for $40 each."

Rene called back, "I am glad you found some men. We are going buffalo hunting and wouldn't have been able to join you."

The two men walked back toward town and Kyle looked at his friend. "Buffalo hunting? When did this happen?"

"I just decided," his lanky friend replied. "I think we should go buffalo hunting."

"Do you figure that we should just walk out on the plain, shoot and skin some buffalo, and then drag the hides back here?" Kyle challenged him.

"Not exactly," Rene replied. "Maybe we could find some hunters that would let us join them."

They reached the street with the place they were staying and stopped, debating on where they should go. "Maybe Andre could help us," the slim man said.

He also wanted to go back and talk to the man about guns. Since their last visit, the Charleville had begun to be less and less the weapon he wanted. They reached the mercantile and saw the owner arranging some shelves.

Andre looked up and said, "I see you have come back."

Not wanting to waste anytime

concerning the weapon, Kyle asked, "How much is the rifle?"

"Do I have to take the Charleville in trade?" the man asked.

The slim man hadn't thought about that. Then he replied, "It is a fine long gun, but I guess I would want to trade."

"That's exactly what it will be good for," Andre told him. "Men pick them up cheap to trade for beaver pelts or maybe a bride with the tribes."

Kyle had no idea if that meant it had value or not. He followed the owner to the wall with the rifles. Taking one down that had a few scars on the stock but otherwise looked good, Andre handed it to the slim man.

"I can make you a fair deal on this one," Andre told him. "Your Charleville flintlock, and the ball mold would be worth $2. This .48 caliber, Kentucky long rifle would easily sell for $15. Because they are readily available after the war, I will take another dollar off and sell the rifle and a mold for $12."

Kyle remembered the deal he had made in Canada and realized that it wasn't as good as he had once thought.

While he held the Kentucky long rifle he was looking at another still on the wall. "How does this compare to the one on the wall?" he asked.

"Basically, the same," Andre replied. He took it down for the slim man to look at.

"It is a .54 caliber M1803 rifle made by Harper's Ferry."

Hefting the M1803 Kyle asked, "Which one would be better for hunting buffalo?"

"Buffalo hunters tend to lean toward the Harper's Ferry rifle," the owner replied. "I believe Lewis and Clark carried a similar rifle on their trip."

That clinched it. Kyle wanted the M1803. Trying to remain casual, he asked, "How does the price of the M1803 compare to the Kentucky long rifle?"

"They are less available," Andre replied. "I got this one from a man that was wounded in the war and needed money. I gave him too much for the rifle, but he was in a bad way."

This did not sound promising to the slim man. He had leaned the long rifle against the wall and was till holding the M1803. Searching his mind for something that would make it less valuable, Kyle asked, "Is this the latest version?"

The owner's face broke into a half-smile. "They made some revisions on the M1805." Then he asked, "Are you interested in trading the pistol in your waistband along with the Charleville?"

"No!" the slim man exclaimed. Catching himself, he repeated, "No. I have found it to be useful more than once."

The owner figured it was time to close

the deal. "What if I give you $3 for the Charleville, sight unseen and price the M1803 at $17."

Realizing that the deal had gone up $2, Kyle wanted the M1803. "That would include a mold?"

"It would and I will even throw in some patches," Andre replied.

Looking at Rene, the slim man said, "I best go and get the Charleville."

Off he went on a trot to get the smoothbore muzzle-loader. Reaching Augie's, he hurried in. "What's the hurry. Someone chasing you?" the heavyset owner asked.

"No," Kyle said and hurried into the back. Picking up the Charleville, he turned to go and then remembered the mold. He wondered if he should also give Andre his .69 caliber balls. Shaking his head, he realized he could melt them back down and make .54 caliber balls.

With the deal done, the slim man walked down the street carrying his new rifle. Rene asked, "Did you really want to go buffalo hunting?"

Smiling at the thought, Kyle replied, "Yes, I would, but we would need more that this rifle to do that. We wouldn't know where to go and we have nothing to carry the hides back with."

"I was talking with Andre while you went and got the Charleville," his lanky friend said. "He knows some hunters that we could join up with. They will be going out in three days."

"Did he say they needed someone to shoot the buffalo?" Kyle asked.

Laughing at his excited friend, Rene replied, "No. They need someone to skin and flesh the hides. We'd make six bits a hide."

Disappointed that he wouldn't be shooting, he thought, *I should have bought a knife.* Then he told his friend, "Let's go talk to Andre tomorrow."

The next morning Andre was eating some soup that was keeping warm on his potbelly stove. The owner looked up as they came in and said, "You two are becoming my best customers. Help yourselves to some soup."

Soon the three of them were sitting around a small table at the back of the mercantile. Between mouthfuls, Rene told him, "We have been thinking about going buffalo hunting."

Before the owner could answer, Kyle clarified the statement. "I believe my friend meant we are going to go hunting."

"There is a man putting together a hunt," Andre replied. "It is late in the season and the hides won't be worth as much, but if you want I will let them know you're interested. The boss comes in most every evening to drink coffee and have a smoke with me."

"What do you think we'd be doing?" Rene asked.

"He needs someone to drive one of his wagons and he needs skinners," the man replied.

Kyle thought about his saddle and other gear. He doubted that the buffalo hunters would let him drag that along. "I have a saddle and some bags that I'll need to keep someplace while we're with the hunters," the slim man told him.

"Do you plan to buy a horse soon?" Andre asked.

"No, but they are in good shape and someday I will get another horse," Kyle told him.

The man sat back, smiling. "Do they have any special meaning to you?"

"I liked the horse I used them on," the slim man said.

"And you sold the horse, I take it," Andre surmised.

Kyle didn't like the way the conversation was going. He feared that the owner was toying with him. "I will buy another horse."

"What I am getting at is you sold a horse that meant something to you, yet you are dragging the saddle and saddle bags around with you," Andre pointed out. "Why don't you sell the saddle and bags and get more once you buy another horse?"

Suddenly, Kyle realized that having the saddle and bags made him feel that he still had something of worth. When he had been forced to sell the horse to survive, to have done the same with his gear would have been admitting that he was broke. He'd have nothing but the clothes on his back and a little money to live on for a short while.

"I should sell the saddle," the slim man said.

"That and the saddle bags," Andre replied. "I could use them and will give you a fair price."

"Where would I carry my clothes and stuff?" Kyle asked.

"I am glad you asked that. A much more efficient way to carry your things would be in a knapsack. You should also trade in the small possibles bag and get a decent-size one," the owner told him.

The look on Kyle's face stopped the owner from making any other suggestions. The slim man told him, "The shooting bag is the only thing I have left from my father."

Without blinking an eye, Andre continued, "Then it is important to keep that. You called it a shooting bag. Use it for that," the owner said. "Keep your powder flask, oil, patches, balls, and any other tools for taking care of your rifle and pistol in it and use the possibles bag for the other many things you need."

Kyle had to admit that it was difficult to keep all the things he needed for the weapons in the shooting bag, much less anything else. It made sense, what Andre was saying. "What do you think my saddle and bags are worth?"

Grinning, the owner replied, "I never talk about what an item is worth. Only what I am willing to pay for it, leaving something for me to make when I sell it."

This was something Kyle had learned years ago when fishing in the channel. The market they brought the fish and never paid the fisherman what they eventually sold the fish for. He had just never thought about it the way Andre explained it.

The merchant had several knapsacks from the recent war. He had a wide variety of possible bags in stock. Trappers and hunters were always in need of them. Later that day Kyle brought the saddle, saddle bags, reins, and grooming items for the horse. He also brought the powder that Damas had given him to keep the mold off the leather.

Andre spent a lot of time going over the saddle. He would have to replace some of the strings. He liked that it was a western saddle. Kyle said he wanted to keep the scabbard for the rifle. The price on the saddle would run from $10 to $15. The reins, $2, and the blanket $1.

The saddle bags were well-worn, but in good condition. With a little stitching, and some work with saddle soap, Andre could get a fair price. Now the question was what he could buy them for and did he have something that would be useful to Kyle.

Then he thought of something he'd recently traded for. To begin the negotiations, Andre brought out a knapsack and three different types of possible bags.

Kyle first looked at the more ornate bags. Then he picked up a plain one much the same color as his shooting bag. "I like this," he told the owner.

A knapsack and the possible bag lay on his wooden counter. "How much do you owe me?" the slim man asked.

"What do you plan to wear while skinning the buffalo?" Andre asked.

Smiling, Kyle replied, "My old worn clothes. I almost got rid of them in Boston but am glad I didn't. They have come in handy more than once."

"There is lots of blood and fat when skinning. It is not easy to get out of wool clothing. It rots and gives off quite the smell. You're not always near a stream that you can scrub them, and when it rains you still skin, and the greasy, bloody wool pants get unbearable," the owner told him.

Rene sat back, not saying anything, just enjoying the dickering that was going on.

With some interest, he watched what Andre brought out. They were a set of buckskins. In fact, it was two sets.

"I just did some bartering with some Kickapoo braves and got these buckskins. These are what you want to wear when skinning buffalo. The fat just makes them softer," the owner told them.

When all was said and done, Kyle came out with some money in his flat pouch, a knapsack, possible bag, and a set of buckskins. It actually felt good not to have to drag the saddle around anymore.

CHAPTER ELEVEN

The men who Andre knew owned a company that went out for three weeks at a time and filled three wagons with hides. Ward Fifer was the boss. He wanted two men per wagon while he rode a roan. All the men had some type of smoothbore or rifled long gun. Kyle and Rene were assigned to third wagon which meant theirs would be the last one during the transit and the first wagon to be filled.

Clint was his shooter and drove wagon one. Like Kyle, the man carried a Harper's Ferry rifle. He had a determined look on his face as he looked out at the trail ahead.

Kyle drove the third wagon pulled by a team of horses. He could have almost laid the reins down. The two animals had been on several buffalo hunts and they knew their place at the end of the wagons.

He and Rene had on their new buckskins and got a little kidding about them even though half the other men had buckskins. The knapsack and possible bag worked out great, leaving room after everything was packed. His blanket roll covered by his ground tarp was tied to the bottom of the knapsack, and his M1803 rifle was in the scabbard, protecting it from weather and other things that could damage it.

He had put away the belt he'd gotten from Camille and was again using a broad belt. A skinning knife he'd bought from Andre and his pistol were carried in the belt.

The first night they camped on a small stream. Each wagon took care if their team. Rene led the horses to water while Kyle pulled their gear out of the wagon. The smell of the wagon reminded the slim man of the stacks of hides he'd seen ready for shipment near the levees.

The first time he had encountered the smell of hides was in France on the wharf when a man shot at him and it resulted in Kyle getting his pistol after killing the shooter.

Rene came back with the horses. They pulled the harnesses off and picketed them near the others to graze. In the morning, they would get grain before being harnessed and then again at the midday break.

Meals were a simple affair, most often something made in a pot. Once they start shooting buffalo, some of the meat would be boiled or roasted over the fire. Ralph did most of the cooking while others provided fuel for the fire.

The first night, Ralph boiled rice with some dried fruit. Each man was required to get a mess kit prior to leaving St. Louis. The sticky contents was scooped from the pot into a tin dish that could be a plate or bowl. The diet was very satisfactory to Kyle. He had grown up on soup in England.

Each wagon was provided a fly tarp to sleep under or keep their gear under. Most of the time the men just slept under the wagon. After supper, the long guns were fired. Most often there was a friendly competition at some chosen target. Then if needed they were cleaned before reloading.

This exercise was done to help prevent misfires. It was not to shoot at buffalo. Only Clint shot buffalo, but the hunting party was traveling through lands claimed by various tribes. Even though the Indians were mostly friendly and even traded with hunting parties, on occasion there could be hostilities and then a weapon that fired would be important.

Each day they saw small herds of buffalo and the slim man couldn't understand why they weren't shooting them.

George was on the second wagon and had heard the two friends talking about passing the buffalo. At the midday break he spat and scratched his white hair. "There's a good reason that we don't shoot buffalo on the way out."

At first Kyle didn't realize the old man was talking to him. George was sort of bent over and always seemed to be looking at the ground. Then the old man turned his head and looked at the two new hunters.

"If we were shooting buffalo this close to St. Louis, we'd have to haul the hides all the way to the big herds and back," he said. "It wouldn't make any sense." As he walked away they heard him mutter, "Green hands."

That was the second time an old-timer called him a green hand. *It must be after you learn everything you become an old codger,* the slim man thought.

Three days after leaving St. Louis they reached a large river. After crossing the men made camp. "What was the name of that river?" Kyle asked Clint.

"That was the Missouri River," he said. "It flows hell and gone all the way to the mountains I'm told."

Excited, Kyle hurried to tell his friend. "We just crossed the Missouri River, Rene. It is the same river that Lewis and Clark went up to reach the Pacific Ocean."

"They started just north of St. Louis," his friend said. "Why wouldn't they have cut across to here to start up the river?"

Frustrated at such a question the slim man replied, "Because they would have had to drag the boat for three damn days."

"Well, at the big falls they dragged the boat for over a month," Rene replied, defending his suggestion. Kyle didn't have a good response for that argument, so he just started pulling the harnesses off the horses.

After four more days of crossing endless plains, a large herd of buffalo was spotted. A more permanent camp was set up. Items such as the sledge, manila cord, lead and black powder were unloaded or moved to the other wagons so Kyles wagon could be loaded.

While having their meal that night, a young blond, skinner named Sonny was trying to talk the boss into letting him do some of the shooting. "Clint does the shooting," Ward said. "When you get your own outfit, you can do the shooting."

The next morning, while others were having breakfast, Clint rode away from the camp. Soon there was the sound of shots. As he ate his porridge, Kyle found himself counting. There were about 50 shots. The slim man wondered how many of the shots were kill shots.

Ward came over to the two friends and

told them, "You two will be hauling the hides to the camp today. Just fold the hides hair side out and stack them. We'll all flesh them before supper."

All the men climbed onto their horses and rode with the harnesses on in the direction of the shots. Ward led them on his roan.

The slim man was concerned. "Andre told us we would be paid so much for each hide we skinned. Today we're hauling and not skinning."

"Maybe everyone takes turns hauling hides to camp and today it is us," Rene replied.

The two friends hitched their team to the sledge and followed the others in the direction that they had disappeared. As they went over the rise, they could see the downed buffalo lying across the plain grass. The others had been only minutes ahead of them and Kyle saw that several buffalo had already been skinned.

The folded hides weighed from 50 to 150 pounds. When the two got to a large bull, both grabbed onto the hide to lift it onto the sledge. When they got 10 hides onto the sledge, they headed back towards camp to unload.

Those skinning used their horses to roll over larger buffalo, thus the need of the harnesses. The animals were skinned from the base of the neck down. The hide on the heads was difficult to skin and were covered with permanent hair. In some cases on the bulls it had grown quite long.

The skinners were finished well before the two friends were hauling the third load. All the tongues and some of the tenderloins had been taken from the kills. After loading the last of the hides onto the sledge, they headed for camp.

Kyle looked back at the white, bloating carcasses lying on the plain grass. It was something like catching gators. The value was in the skin, but with gators they'd take meat off all the gators. Out there on the grass was enough meat to feed 50 families for most of a winter and it was being left to rot.

By the time the sledge got to camp, the men were already scraping the hides. Ward call to them, "Park the sledge and start dragging the fleshed hides beyond the wagons and stake them to dry."

There were pails of stakes and some mallets in the first wagon. Kyle hurried and got them, while Rene went for the first hide. The two were kept busy dragging hides and staking them for the next several hours. Care was taken to put the stakes close to the edge of the hide.

While Ralph put most of a tender loin into a pot to boil, George and Sonny were salting down the tongues and packing them into a small barrel. Clint was cleaning his rifle for tomorrow's shoot.

The sun blazed down on the camp, helping the new grass push through last year's brown, knocked-down, grass. The horses grazed hungrily on the new sprouts. Kyle and Rene sat near their wagon wondering if there wasn't something they should be doing.

There was a copse of trees and brush near the stream they were using for water, and the two friends decided to collect wood for the fire. Using their short axes, the two cut and hauled wood for Ralph. The heavyset man nodded and thanked them.

With the day's work finished, the men led their horses to water and cleaned some of the blood and fat off themselves. The two friends had gotten plenty on themselves handling the hides.

While waiting for the boiling meat to get done, Ralph fried up the remaining meat and everyone got a chunk to chew on. Kyle found the buffalo very good. While enjoying the meat, he once again thought of all the meat left to rot a short distance away.

He had seen wolves and other varmint moving around the carcasses even before they'd finished bringing up hides. Each night they'd hear the wolves howling, calling to other packs.

Then the favorite part of Kyle's day

came when they'd fire their rifles and muskets. He and Sonny had set up a competition, and most often the slim man would win. Clint never fired with them. He'd be cleaning his rifle in preparation for the next day's shooting.

The next day was a repeat of the first. The two friends hauled the hides from the kill zone. This time they were instructed to leave them just beyond the hides, staked to dry so they wouldn't have to be dragged as far.

That night after supper, Kyle sat smoking his pipe. He looked at the other men lazing around. Ward and Clint were near the fire in some kind of discussion. From the bits and pieces, the slim man heard, it was about when to move the camp.

Rene was talking with George. Most everyone had a cup of coffee from the large coffee pot next to the fire. The slim man watched as his friend came walking back. "I think I found how we get paid," his lanky friend told him."

"Is it by the number of buffalo we skin?" Kyle asked.

"Nope, it is not," Rene replied. "It is based on how many buffalo hides we bring back to St. Louis and the time of year. When the hides are sorted by size and color and some other things that I did not understand. The hide buyers then pay different prices for the sorted stacks."

"That makes sense," the slim man said. "A gator skin with more damage was worth less per foot than one without damage. Also, bigger ones were worth more per foot."

"It is sort of like that," his lanky friend said. "Now what I did not understand was the seniority part of the company. Those that have been with the company longer get a bigger share of the sale."

"That doesn't work in our favor," Kyle replied. "We are what they call green hands and have just started with the company."

Shrugging his shoulders, Rene told him, "That's all of what I learned. The upside is we will get paid something."

Once the hides were dried, the two friends folded them hair side in and squeezed them with a makeshift press. They were then tied with cord and stacked into the wagon. The process and the jobs continued until two wagons were stacked high with buffalo hides.

The camp had moved three times following the buffalo and the stream. Buffalo chips were used for some of the fires while the white fat was taken off some of the kills and Ralph used it when cooking.

By this time all of the powder, lead, and other supplies were stored in the front of the first wagon. The other men were talking about heading back to St. Louis in another week. Then something happened that surprised Kyle. Another wagon came by and spent the night.

They carried an assortment of supplies, including things the hunters might need or want. George bought a knife and whetstone, Ralph bought some socks, and most who used it bought tobacco. The man also had whiskey, but Ward wouldn't have any drinking on his hunts.

Before the man left, he bought the salted barrels of buffalo tongues. Old George explained to the two friends, "Tongues bring in good money, but take up room and the difference that they'd sell for in St. Louis is more than made up by the extra hides it makes room for."

The night before they started filling the third wagon, Ward came over to the two friends. "I have heard about you two complaining about not being able to skin and flesh buffalo. Ralph and Sonny wouldn't mind a break from skinning, so you two take their place tomorrow. You can also do fleshing while they stake the hides."

Kyle wasn't sure if he should be happy or not. Evidently, he wouldn't be making any more money skinning and now he would be having to wrestle with the buggers.

The next morning, with their skinning knives sharpened, the two friends rode toward the buffalo kill. Old George told them, "You both start on the right."

Anxious to show the boss that he and

Rene could hold their own skinning, Kyle brought his horse to a trot. The harnessed horses could be trusted to remain nearby, so they were allowed to graze until needed.

The first buffalo Kyle tackled was a two year-old female. Cuts around the base of the head, around the front and back legs at the knees, and a quick slit up the stomach were quickly done as he rolled the buffalo back and forth. Frequent touch-up of the blade on the whetstone kept the blade razor-sharp.

Pulling and cutting, he quickly had the hide off. Leaving it near the carcass, he hurried to his next one, which was a calf, maybe three months old. Again, he had it skinned in short order.

Proudly, he touched up the blade and move to the next kill. It was a large bull. Taking his first cuts around the head, he found he could not work all the way around without rolling the animal. He next made cuts around two of the legs. Then grabbing the lower leg, he lifted to roll the animal. It hardly budged.

"Time to use the horse," Kyle muttered. When he looked for it, he saw that it had grazed a short distance way. Running to get it, the animal was startled and trotted a few steps away. Stopping the slim man walked while speaking softly to the animal and was able to get its lead rope.

Leading it to the buffalo, Kyle tied the

lower front leg using rope and then fastened it to the whippletree. Leading the animal, the big bull flopped over. Leaving the animal tied to the front leg, the slim man made the cuts on that side. After slitting it up the stomach, he began to take the hide off the exposed side.

The hide was thicker and heavier than the female or calf. The hump had thick fat under it and he tried not to leave too much on the hide. With the bull skinned as far around as possible, Kyle took the rope off the front leg and tied it to the one near the ground. Again, he rolled the animal over with the horse. Wasting no time, the slim man continued from the stomach, removing the hide. Once loose it slid down the back of the buffalo. Hurrying around, he attempted to spread the hide out and found much of it still under the carcass.

Leaving the leg tied to the horse, he tried to drag the buffalo off the hide. The horse pulled the rope tight and the 2,000-pound carcass did not move. As Kyle encouraged the horse it suddenly lurched forward as the rope slid off the leg.

Cussing with frustration, knowing he was losing time, the slim man brought the horse back around and retied it to the back leg. Playing out the reins so they draped over the carcass, Kyle got behind the buffalo and got the horse pulling. He then helped pushing and lifting on the buffalo. Slowly, it slid off the hide.

Covered with blood, fat, and sweat, Kyle untied the horse from the carcass, quickly coiled up the reins and hung them from the collar. The animal seemed nervous, and the slim man saw the reason. Wolves were already slinking towards the skinned carcasses.

He headed for the next buffalo and felt for his knife. It was gone. He couldn't remember putting it down after finishing skinning, but he also didn't remember putting it away.

He had a second knife and pulled it from the sheath. The next several buffaloes were small enough for him to handle without needing the horse to roll it. One was a couple year-old bull, and it was a challenge rolling it over the hump, but Kyle managed.

The slim man had lost track of the number of buffalo he'd skinned when the skinning was finished. He ached all over and was covered with blood and fat. George came over and told him, "You were a bit slow, but you did a good job. I saw you had trouble with the big bastard laying on its hide. I would have left it. A big bull hide like that ain't worth much anyway."

"I'll do better tomorrow," Kyle promised as he went to get his horse and head back to camp to start fleshing.

The comment George made about the

big bull and leaving the hide was no doubt to try and make the slim man feel less bad about the time lost. But Kyle knew that the old man would never have been in the situation of having the carcass lying on the hide.

Fleshing wasn't anything new to Kyle and Rene. The tool used was similar to the one they used on gators. The size of the hides to be fleshed was another thing. It was done on the ground, working from the edges towards the middle. Kyle found himself crawling in the meat, fat, and blood being scraped off the hide. He kept trying to wipe his hands on the grass because they would slip on the tool.

Ralph and Sonny had finished hauling the hides up and began to take the fleshed ones and stake them. With the last hide fleshed, Kyle sat next to it, feeling exhaustion in his muscles. He couldn't understand how an old man like George could do this day after day.

As he sat on the prairie grass, Sonny, with his blond hair sticking out from under his hat, came up to him. "We found your knife under the big bull hide. I put it on your wagon seat."

All the slim man could say was a weak, "Thank you."

Smiling, Sonny told him, "You'll get used to it. Starting out you make too many unnecessary moves and roll the animals at the wrong point, making them heavier."

The young man grabbed the hide that Kyle had just finished and dragged it to be staked. The slim man knew he should have gotten up and helped with the last hide, but his body wasn't ready to move yet.

That night, Kyle did his best to scrub the fat and blood from his hands, arms, and buckskins. They no longer had a new look to them. When Ralph was dishing out the beans and buffalo meat, he smiled and asked the slim man, "How was your day?"

"It gave me a lot of respect for you and the others skinning every day," Kyle told him.

That night, Sonny beat him when emptying the rifles. The slim man's arms were tired and his M1803 felt it weighed as much as the damn big bull. Taking his time, Kyle cleaned and lubricated the rifle. This task comforted him.

Rene had finished with his Baker and came over. "Do you think they'll put us back on hauling the hides tomorrow?"

Chuckling before he answered, he finally replied, "You can bet we get what we wished for the rest of the hunt. Old George promised me that skinning would get easier."

The two exhausted skinners fell asleep under the wagon to the sounds of wolves howling or fighting over a meal. There was thunder in the distance, giving a promise of a change in the weather.

The next morning Kyle found out that it wasn't thunder he'd heard, but rather the buffalo herd running. When the slim man asked why they stampeded, George told him, "No one knows why they suddenly begin to run, but when they do they'll run for a great distance. For us it means we'll be moving, looking for buffalo for the last shoots."

It took two days to find a herd big enough for the next shoot. Kyle was glad for the rest and getting away from the rotting fat and meat on the ground from fleshing. He couldn't get away from all the smell, though. In his wagon was a stack of smelly hides.

Finally, the last day of hunting came. They needed another forty hides to fill the first wagon. Kyle had found out that the old, white-haired man was right. Now, after a day of skinning, he wasn't nearly as tired.

Kyle had just rolled out from under the wagon when Ward came over. "Grab yourself whatever Ralph has to eat and then see Clint. You'll be helping with the shooting today."

The slim man felt his heart jump in his chest. He was going to shoot! Why he'd been asked he did not know, but he was not going to question it. Carrying enough balls, patches, and powder in his shooting bag, Kyle stopped by the fire.

Ralph already had a cup of coffee and some fried buffalo out for him. "The boss don't let just anybody shoot," the cook said. "You must have done something right."

Kyle had his broad belt around his waist with the pistol under it in the back. Often, he carried it like that in case a nosey wolf got too close. Putting it in the back kept the fat and blood off it.

As the slim man rode out of camp, he passed Sonny. The young man looked up smiling and said, "You lucky bastard."

Nodding at him, Kyle followed Clint. The buffalo were about a quarter-mile away over a small rise. The two men stopped short, and ground reined their horses. They crawled the rest of the way to the top of the rise. In front they could see the herd spread out about a mile. The nearest ones were about 100 to 150 yards away.

"There are many groups within the herd," Clint told him. "Each one has a leader and the others group around it."

He was quiet for a moment as they looked at the herd. Then he asked, "Have you picked one out yet?"

He had not and said so. "That is because you are looking at the whole herd. If you look hard enough, you'll see that it is made up of smaller groups led by a bull or a big female," the experienced shooter told him.

Then Kyle thought he saw one. When he pointed it out, Clint agreed with him. "You shoot at that group. Kill the leader first and the others will move around it. Then continue shooting until you have 10 buffalo down. Make every shot count. Aim behind the front shoulder for the lungs."

"Do we shoot prone?" Kyle asked.

"However, you are comfortable," the man told him. Then he asked, "What is the rifle sighted in for?"

Andre had told him it was sighted in at 50 yards and so far in target shooting it seemed to be accurate. Kyle told him, "50 yards."

"Your ball will drop, so you should aim figuring it will drop 8 to 10 inches. The wind is still, so you don't have to worry about that. We will alternate shots. I'll go first."

Clint fired and Kyle watched as one of the buffalo started to walk and then sank to the ground. The slim man had picked one he felt was the leader of his group and took aim at the animal standing broadside to him. He squeezed the trigger and smoke and fire belched from the rifle.

Smoke from the pan and muzzle blocked his target for a moment. Then he saw the animal still standing. *Have I missed?* He wondered. Then the buffalo rolled over to its side.

Taking his time, Kyle reloaded the M1803, his hands shaking with excitement. Clint fired again beside him. Adding powder to the pan, he was ready.

Other buffalo had gathered around the

downed leader. Sighting on one of them, he fired. It sunk to the ground. Loading and firing continued until 40 buffalo lay on the prairie grass.

From the camp, Kyle could see the men coming to skin the buffalo. He heard the sandy-haired man say, "Good shooting. Now bring your rifle to camp and go to skinning."

"Thank you," the slim man told him, and with his shoulder aching and ears ringing, he hurried to the camp and then rode down to do his share of skinning.

With the last of the buffalo skinned and the hides staked on the prairie grass, the wagons would remain for three more days in camp, allowing the hides to dry. Kyle couldn't help but wonder why he had been allowed to shoot.

Ward came by while the slim man was pouring hot water down the barrel of the rifle to clean out residual powder. "Clint said you did a good job shooting," the boss said. "All clean shots and no wounded ones."

"I appreciated the opportunity," Kyle told him. Then he couldn't help but ask. "Why did he let me shoot?"

"He liked the way you took care of your rifle," Ward replied and then headed back to the cookfire.

Kyle sat with mixed feelings. He took such good care because the M1803 was a new rifle to him. It was a good thing Clint hadn't seen him neglect the old Charleville. The compliment did make the slim man decide he would always take good care of the rifle.

The day before heading back a dozen braves came riding towards their camp. As instructed earlier, if such an occasion should occur the men sat with their rifles and muskets within easy reach.

Ward stood waiting for them to draw close. Kyle could see that they had travois loaded with buffalo hides. George happened to be sitting, having a chew with the slim man. In a low voice he said, "They're Osage and come to trade hides. We don't need any, but the boss will trade for them."

The tall leader of the Osage dismounted and spoke with the boss. The Osage leader towered over Ward as they walked to look at the hides. "What if they don't look good?" Kyle asked.

"The boss will buy them anyway," the old man said. "We are hunting in their territory."

After some discussion, the braves carried the hides near wagon one. Then at the boss' direction, Ralph got them flour, coffee, sugar, trade goods like mirrors, beads, and bells. Then to the slim man's surprise he saw Ralph take out a muzzle loader that looked like his Charleville, some powder, and lead. The muzzle loader he handed to the leader.

All the trade goods were packed onto

two of the travois' and the braves rode away. As the Indians disappeared over a rise, the men gathered around the boss. Ward looked at the concerned faces.

"I have delt with these braves before. They have been watching us for two weeks waiting for us to fill our wagons," the boss said. "The hides they traded are winter hides and worth twice what any one of ours are. If necessary, we will leave some of ours to fit these on the wagons."

As it turned out, it was not necessary to leave any of the hides. For the trip back the sledge was tied down on top of the third wagon's hides. On the way to St. Louis the wagons traveled slower, and the horses strained more. With enough grain left, the horse received small amounts three times a day.

When they got back to St. Louis the hunting party had been gone four weeks. After stopping near the warehouse, the boss traded his hides. They would be sorted and baled between two platforms compressed using a metal screw. Each bale would contain 10 to 12 adult hides, and the calves would have up to 20 in a bale.

Kyle and Rene watched for a short while. Ward came over and told them, "If you got someplace to go, you might as well go. Come by the Blue Goose tavern tomorrow morning and pick up your pay."

The two friends carried their knapsacks, bed rolls, and other gear as they walked toward Augie's Two Bits a Night boarding place. As they stepped in the heavy man in his stained shirt wrinkled his nose. "If you plan to stay here, go around back and take those smelly buckskins off and use the pump to wash up."

The two men walked around back. They knew where the pump was. It was only about 20 feet from the outhouse. The area was somewhat secluded. The two men stripped down, and then with one washing and the other working the pump handle, the two men cleaned up as best they could.

They then took long johns, wool pants, and shirts from the knapsacks. Once dressed they pulled on their smelly blood and fat-coated boots. They had been cleaned somewhat by using prairie grass at their last camp.

Leaving the buckskins near the pump, they went around front. The owner still wrinkled his nose but now the smell was somewhat less. "I should charge you extra," the man said. "You men will leave a stink on the bunk you sleep on."

Once they paid their two bits, Kyle told him, "Our buckskins are out back. You are welcome to keep them."

The man just cussed as the two men went back to put their gear on a bunk.

"Washing at the pump didn't do too much good," Kyle told his friend. "I think I'll go into town and get a shave and haircut along with a bath."

"It sounds like a plan," Rene replied. "We should have the clothes in our knapsacks laundered also. But first we pick up a bottle."

Soon the two men were sitting in a warm bath sipping from a bottle of whiskey. The barber chose to cut their hair and shave them after the bath. Their gear had laid on top of the folded hides during the trip back and had taken on the smell. The purchase of some replacement clothes might be in order.

That night the two men slept on the hard, wooden bunks and had to put up with complaints from other boarders. It did not bother them much because they had finished the bottle and quickly drifted off to sleep.

The Blue Goose was in the better part of St. Louis. The boss had on a suit with a white shirt and string tie. He also had on a pair of well-shined boots. He was finishing breakfast when the two friends walked in.

Ward smiled and said, "I am glad to see you two got some of the smell off. The others have been here already and still carried the smell and some hangovers."

Then he said, "Join me for coffee."

After the watered-down brew at the Two Bits, they looked forward to some coffee. Once seated with their steaming cups, Ward asked, "What did the two of you think about buffalo hunting?"

"You run a good camp," Kyle said. "We ate well and there wasn't a bad one in your crew."

"I pick them well," the boss replied. "Andre assured me that the two of you would be good men to hire." Then he asked, "How long have you known him?"

"Not long," Kyle replied. "I noticed he sold you the Charleville that you traded with the braves."

"He did," Ward told him. "He told me it was well taken care of and recommended that I hire the prior owner."

Rene was sitting listening and appeared to be anxious. He finally asked, "We were wondering what our pay would be?"

"You've got to realize I had to teach you near everything about hunting buffalo," the man said. "I must admit the two of you learned quickly and Kyle, you did a fine job of driving the wagon. I had no regrets hiring you."

He dug into his pouch and brought out some coins. He placed four $10 gold pieces in front of each man. He then placed another dollar in front of Kyle. "That's to pay for the lead and powder you used shooting the last day."

Both men were satisfied with the pay. They had kind of hoped for more, but then again it could have been less. $30 was considered fair pay for a month's work. They had just got $40.

As they got up to leave, Ward told them, "I will be going out again in September. You are both welcome to join me."

Thanking the man and telling him they'd let him know, the two men headed for Andre's to buy a few things.

CHAPTER TWELVE

Through the rest of the summer the two friends learned more about St. Louis and even found a better place to stay. Andre had a small shack behind his mercantile that he rented for a reasonable price. It had been the merchant's first home.

The shack wasn't more than eight-foot wide and ten-foot long, but it had a small stove for cooking and heating, a sideboard with a small window above it, a table with two stools near the door, and a single bunk.

There being only a single bunk and no room for another in the shack was solved by building an upper bunk. It was made to be easily taken out if Andre should ever want to remove it. There was also a small lean-to to hang smelly buckskins and store some firewood.

Rene took Kyle out for drinks to celebrate his birthday. The slim man wasn't sure what day in August it was, but he turned 24 several times that month. They had decided to hunt buffalo in September. Ward was pleased that they were coming back.

One hunt led to another. They found out how fast a buffalo hide could freeze on the animal when shot in the winter. Ward had purchased troop tents for the hunters to keep the cold wind off them. He suspended hunting during the coldest months of winter, and the two friends hung around the mercantile, keeping warm in front of Andre's potbelly stove.

Sometime during the idle winter days, the two friends decided what they would do come spring. Fascinated by what they'd read in the diary, the two friends began planning retracing the route that Lewis and Clark had taken on their expedition.

It would take lots of time plotting it out, and due to stormy weather they had the idle time being stuck in St. Louis. They went over the handwritten diary several times. They also had the book that Rene had to compare with the diary.

Lewis and Clark had used a 55-foot keelboat to travel up the Missouri River, but he'd had a crew of over 40 men and needed the size to carry supplies. There would only be the two of them and something much smaller would work.

"I am betting we can find a smaller keelboat that would work just fine," Rene told him.

"What we need is something like the yoal I had in England. It had a sail and still could be rowed," Kyle replied.

At one point the two questioned whether they even needed a boat. Maybe they'd buy a couple of horses and ride the route. They decided that riding wouldn't give them the experiences that those on the expedition had lived through.

In late February they were back hunting buffalo. Their pay had gone up from $40 a hunt to $50. The two friends figured it was because the cold winter temperatures created prime hides.

It was the end of March when they came back from their last buffalo hunt. Ward would be making one more spring hunt, but it would be without them. Their final pay was $60. Kyle felt he had given them a little extra for sticking with him through the winter hunts.

It was now time to start putting the trip together and they had the money to do it. Other than replacing buckskins, a few nights of drinking and an occasional lady of the night, the two hadn't spent that much of the hunting money. They also had some left from trapping in New Orleans and the keelboat trip up the Mississippi.

They had a month and a half to collect all the items they'd need for the trip to be able to leave by May 14th, the date Lewis and Clark had left. It had been 13 years ago, and much along the Mississippi River had changed since then.

St. Louis was the capital of the Missouri Territory. The buffalo hides they'd hunted were purchased by the Missouri Fur Company. The Missouri Gazette kept the area informed and Kyle enjoyed reading about the steamboats that were being developed in Pittsburgh. Little did he know that the first one would arrive in St. Louis later this year in August.

April was warm and Kyle would enjoy the sunshine by sitting on the levee and watching boats come and go. One day he saw Captain Jacob's boat and looked forward to seeing old friends. The only ones left were Wade the bosun and Claude. The others had moved on.

Various types of boats stopped along the levee at St. Louis. The slim man watched for any that might work for their trip. Whenever a smaller one pulled in, Kyle would go down to meet them. His first question was always if they were interested in selling.

One cloudy day that threatened rain, Kyle was watching and saw a man pull in with a canoe. The slim man had never seen one like that before.   When sailing to Martinique he'd seen dugouts used by locals. They had never seemed very stable.

This one reminded him of the dugouts, but definitely wasn't made from hacking out a log.   Kyle watched as an overweight man struggled to get out. The slim man decided to walk down and help him.

He immediately saw what his problem was. The craft was filled with beaver pelts. The man had left little room for himself to maneuver. Giving him a hand, the husky man stood up and stepped onto the shore. Grabbing the front, Kyle pulled it up on the sand.

"I thank you, lad," the man said.

"You caught yourself some nice beavers," Kyle told him.

"Caught them?" he replied. "I'm too old to wade in that freezing water to go after the buggers. I'm a voyageur and have taken what they owed me."

The slim man looked over the man. He was dressed in wool pants, a red wool coat, a tuque, and had a colorful sash around his waist. On his feet he had calf-high moccasins, and on his head he had a tuque.

"You are dressed rather warmly for the day," Kyle observed.

"I come all the way down the great Mississippi River to get here and am wearing all the clothes I own," the man replied. Then he said, "My name is Remy."

Reaching out his hand, the slim man told him, "I'm Kyle." Then he offered, "Can I help you with your packs?"

"You could, lad," he replied, "but my old bones aren't fit to carry packs anymore. I came all the way from Canada to live with my good brother. These beavers are my gift to him for his kindness."

"You'll want to take them to Missouri Fur Company. It's located in the warehouse on the edge of town," the slim man said. "I could find someone to haul the pelts there for you."

"If you could do that, my good friend, I'll be buying you a drink at the nearest tavern," Remy replied.

The fur company had men who would haul furs from incoming boats to the warehouse for a dollar. It wasn't long before the two men were at the Missouri Fur Company and the pelts were being graded and weighed.

Kyle thought about Remy's canoe sitting near the edge of the water. "I'll go down and pull the canoe further up the levee," he offered.

The stocky man just nodded and waved, being more interested in the grading of the pelts. As Kyle headed for the river, a slight rain had begun to fall. He pulled the brim of his hat down to keep the rain off his face.

Pulling it away from the river, he was surprised at how light the canoe was. He estimated that it was 20 feet-long, and by the looks it was made from birchbark. Near the top of the levee he started to turn it over and saw a leather money belt. *I bet you will miss this*, the slim man thought.

With the canoe turned over, he saw that the bottom was a little wider than the top opening. There was evidence of scrapes from going over rapids, but not tearing. Slinging the money belt over his shoulder, he headed back to the warehouse.

As he walked, he felt excitement rising. His mind was racing. All this time he'd been looking for a small keelboat or something like it, but why not a canoe? He began to wonder if the man would be willing to sell his canoe. When he got to the warehouse, he found that Remy was gone.

"After getting his money, he headed for the tavern," someone from the back called to him.

Thanking the man, Kyle hurried towards the nearest tavern at the head of the street. He heard Remy before he got there. Stepping in, he saw the stocky man regaling the patrons with stories of his trip down the mighty Mississippi River.

Sitting with him, the slim man ordered an ale. Remy continued with his stories, keeping everyone laughing. Finally, there was a pause as he downed his drink and motioned to the bartender for another.

Taking advantage of the pause, Kyle held up the money belt. "I found this in the canoe."

"That my friend is as empty as a poor man's poke," Remy told him. "I keep it to remind me of better days." Taking it, the stocky man set it on the table.

Anxious to know, Kyle asked him, "What do you plan to do with the canoe?"

Smiling as the next drink arrived, "I sure as hell plan to stay out of it. My arse couldn't take another two months."

"Would you be willing to sell it?" the slim man asked.

"Sell it," the man scoffed. "I would trade it for a bottle of whiskey."

"How about two bottles and we'll drink to the deal from one?" Kyle asked.

"You drive a hard bargain, lad," the stock man said. "I've got no choice but to say, the canoe is yours."

By late afternoon, Kyle had the canoe behind Andre's mercantile. The weather had cleared, and his spirits were high. Rene looked over the purchase. "How much did you say you paid for this . . . canoe?

"Two bottles of whiskey, which I got one drink out of," the slim man said, laughing. "At that I think I paid too much. I believe the old man had planned to leave it right where it landed."

"Maybe he knew what it was worth," his lanky friend said. "I can't see challenging the Missouri River in a birchbark boat."

"The man said he was a voyageur and he'd paddled it all the way down from Canada," Kyle replied, defending the craft. "And that was with the canoe filled with beaver pelts."

Andre finished up with what he was doing and came out to see the grand purchase. It was hard to tell what he thought as he looked it over. He pointed at things as he went, but didn't say if he found something good or bad.

The merchant said, "A voyageur is hired to carry other men's furs. A coureurs de bois trades for the furs and owns them. I believe your man didn't own the pelts or this canoe, and he just decided to take the south fork one day and paddled to here."

Frowning, Kyle asked, "Does that mean I can't keep the canoe?"

"I doubt anyone would come all the way from Canada to get the furs this canoe could carry. As far as the law would be concerned, this craft was abandoned here in St Louis," Andre told him.

Then Rene spoke up, "Do you think it will work for our trip and did you see anything wrong with it?"

Smiling at his two adventurers, the merchant replied, "It needs some repairs that can be done without too much cost, and I think it will be an excellent craft to use for your trip."

It turned out that Andre knew of an Ojibwe that could do any repairs that might be needed. To Kyle's surprise, the Ojibwe was an old woman. She smiled from the long-ago memories as she ran her hand along the cedar gunwale. Like Andre, she pointed out certain areas.

The woman spoke very little English, so between what Kyle had learned in Canada wintering with an Ojibwe woman and her limited English, they managed to communicate.

Every time she spoke the slim man felt a tug as he remembered that winter. It was good news after she finished looking it over. With help from Kyle and Rene, the canoe could be repaired.

First, a long piece of cedar was steamed and bent to replace a cracked rib. Next, the split-spruce root lacing was examined. A small area needed repair, and it was done with some cord Andre had.

One of the thwarts was cracked and replaced along with the cedar platform that supported the pack in the center of the canoe. Then, using spruce gum, she sealed the birchbark where necessary. Then, before she left, she painted something on each side of the bow of the canoe. When finished, she turned to the two friends. Kyle understood her to say, "This will bring you safely through your trip."

The Ojibwe woman had done a good job on the canoe and he nodded, agreeing that what she had done would make the craft safe and strong on the Missouri River. He paid her for her work, and she smiled and put her hand onto his chest and said, "Good man." Then she was gone.

Remy had only one paddle and it was splintered at the end from pushing the canoe away from rocks, so they had a wheel spoke maker carve them two new paddles. Andre recommended they purchase packs that laced up to seal them. They were fitted with straps so they could be carried on their backs during portages.

Andre gave them two leather cushions filled with horsehair to kneel or sit on while paddling. Should they need it, they could also help keep them afloat should they end up in the water.

Kyle didn't see Remy again before it was time to leave. He hoped the stocky man had found his brother and hadn't spent all the beaver money in the taverns. The canoe and their gear were ready.

A wagon rented from the livery carried everything to the levee. Andre came down to watch them off. The canoe and heavy packs were carried to the water's edge and everything was loaded. Rene had some doubtful looks as the canoe settled deeper into the water.

Rather than buckskins, they chose to wear woolen pants and shirts. In the packs were woolen coats and a second set of clothing. They each had their boots and calf-high moccasins. Kyle had his flat-brimmed leather hat while Rene had his felt one. They had tuques and choppers for the cold weather they'd encounter.

Everything they had was tightly rolled to save room for food supplies, which were kept simple. Beans, rice, dried peas, cold flour, and jerky made up much of their diet. They had the hand lines to catch fish and the rifles and pistol to shoot game.

The packs were covered with their fly tarp and the rifles were kept in scabbards tied to the top of the packs. Kyle kept the pistol in his broad belt along with the knife and scabbard. The both had short axes within reach.

Everything was packed in a six-foot section at the center of the canoe. Each of them would have five feet on each end. Both men had nervous stomachs and had hardly eaten anything for breakfast.

They were nervous about the scope of the trip, and neither had ever paddled a canoe before. Andre had given them pointers about the duties of the man in the front and those for the man in the back.

Kyle realized that they should have taken a short trip before setting off. It was too late now. Andre was wishing them well, and it was time to climb in and try not to look too foolish as they left the levee.

At first the canoe felt very unstable, and Kyle in front hardly dared to turn to wave goodbye. Taking their time, the two novices paddled away from the levee. They saw incoming flatboats coming at them and struggled to paddle closer to the shore to avoid them.

Something scraped along the bottom of the canoe and they were sure that the birch bark would tear open. After the first hour, they got the hang of things and had the craft moving upriver at about three miles an hour.

Rene reached for his water bag and drank to replace the nervous sweat that the launch had created. Kyle was surprised at the silence around the canoe as they progressed. On the keelboat where was always noise from the sweeps in the locks, men grunting and groaning, and the creaking of the keelboat.

Now, other than the dipping of the paddle, which became less as they learned to use them properly, there was nothing. They passed ducks and otters and hardly startled them. As far as Kyle was concerned, the day was perfect.

The point where Lewis and Clark had taken off was about 20 miles away. They had left right after breakfast and should be there within eight hours. They had managed to get a surveyor's map of the Missouri River to help keep them from turning up one of the larger tributaries flowing into it.

After eight hours of paddling, they turned into a small cove. Kyle had a chunk of iron tied to a rope that could be used as an anchor if needed. This cove had a perfect strip of beach to land.

Sliding onto the sand, Kyle tried to stand and found that it wasn't that easy. One stiffened up after so many hours of sitting. Both men walked around for a while before chewing on some jerky and drinking some water.

Then, after relieving themselves, it was time to push off. "I'll take the front this time," Rene said. "It looks easier than back here."

Kyle agreed but thought about the last four hours of travel and how often he wondered if his friend was just sitting there and letting him do all the work. Laughing to himself, he thought, *It probably always looks easier for the other person on a canoe.*

They reached the confluence of the two rivers about three hours before dark. Anxious to be able to say they were on their way, they paddled another hour up the Missouri before pulling in to make camp in a cove.

It was 10 May 1817, when the two men made a simple supper and some coffee. Andre had roasted and ground some beans so they wouldn't have to do so for a while. They realized that this would be the first night of many months before reaching their goal of the Pacific Ocean.

Kyle had his tobacco to smoke or chew and Rene had purchased a bag of hard candy to treat himself. Soon it would stick into a block, but that was okay. He could chip off a piece.

"What did you think about today?" the slim man asked his friend.

"I liked it," Rene replied. "I only wish we had taken the canoe out before leaving. I really enjoyed paddling upriver."

Then as they sat in silence listening to the sound of the night, they heard ducks coming in from the prairie and splashing down in the cove. That was the end of their quiet evening as the ducks chased each other and courted.

The next morning, Kyle got up, rubbing his whiskered face. Not far from shore some mallard ducks swam. He watched them for a few moments before going away from their camp to relieve himself. Then a thought came to him. Duck would make a fine supper.

He walked quietly back to the fly tarp,

not wanting to disturb the ducks nor the sleeping Rene. Picking up the M1803 from the edge of his blanket, Kyle sat and cocked the rifle. He aimed at a large mallard and squeezed the trigger. The fly tarp behind him flew up, followed by shouts of "What the hell!"

The black powder smoke drifted away, and lying alone on the water was one duck flapping its last and the rest of the flock flying way. His lanky friend came out from under the tarp with his Baker ready. "Where are they?" he hissed.

"I just shot a duck for our supper," the slim man said.

"What!" his friend snapped. "Warn me next time! I thought we were under attack," his voice fading as he started to laugh. "We have all the food we can carry and you decide to shoot a damn duck."

"It's right there waiting to be picked up," Kyle told him.

"Well. You shot it, so you can wade out and get it," Rene replied as he tried to push the rest of the fly tarp off his shoulder.

They ate the last of the peas boiled last night and made coffee using the grounds from the night before. The two men packed the canoe and pushed it off the grass-covered shore. The duck was scooped up and they were on their way.

The slim man took his first turn in the front and decided to kneel on the cushion.

They paddled toward the middle of the river so they wouldn't have to worry about snags along the shore. About an hour later, Kyle scrambled to sit to relieve the cramps that were starting in his legs.

Two days later, the two adventurers reached Washington Landing. It had been founded by families traveling with Daniel Boone. Three years before, some of the settlers had started a ferry across the Missouri River. There was a trading post near the ferry and both the canoers had a need. Boots in a canoe were very clumsy. They hoped to buy some regular moccasins that could slip on and off easily.

They spent time on the porch of the trading post learning about when Daniel Boon, came through the area and the need to build forts during the War of 1812 to defend against tribes that supported the British. The two men slept well that night near other folks

After a hot breakfast at the trading post, they departed from the landing, wearing the much more comfortable moccasins. Promises were made to stop again on their way back from seeing the Pacific Ocean. The weather continued to be fair, and the two men's spirits were high.

They had decided that they would travel for six days and then take a day off. Sunday was chosen to be the day of rest. Kyle kept a diary of the trip, to help keep track of the days and months.

As they left the trading post near the ferry, the river took a more northerly course, and the slim man finally felt they were on their way. Prior to that they had been going in a westerly direction, and according to the handwritten diary they had to take the river north.

The euphoria lasted only a day and they were again heading in a westerly direction. Three days later they reached a bend that would later be settled and named Westport. While not significant at the time, the river did turn to the north from there, and once again the two friends were on their way in the right direction.

For the past two weeks the river had been flowing past log homes and small forts. As they paddled by, the residents would wave to them, and it gave the two men the feeling that they still hadn't entered the wild frontier.

Once headed north there was nothing but the tree-lined river and prairie beyond. They stopped for a midday rest when they noticed wagon tracks coming down the back into the river. Little did they know that this sign would be the last of civilization they would see for some time.

The two men began to feel the isolation of being far from any town. The only company they had were the waterfowl, the occasional deer drinking at the river, or small herds of buffalo grazing above the banks that sloped to the river.

They had just started out after resting for a day when Kyle heard his friend whisper, "We have company."

The slim man looked around and spotted two men on horseback riding parallel to the river, watching them. They were Indians! They kept their canoe in the middle of the river and tried not to look at the riders. They hoped that the riders would become bored and go away.

They entered some higher cliffs to that side and the riders stopped. Kyle had been told that there were several tribes in Missouri, including Kickapoo, Shawnee, and Osage. The strongest were the Osage. Many had fought with the British in the War of 1812 and might not look kindly on the two men moving through what they considered their territory.

Both men were aware that most of the tribes traded furs and hides at trading posts around the territory. They had even witnessed it being done on their first buffalo hunt. They continued upriver until the sun was low in the western sky.

The two men pulled into a secluded cove and made a cold camp. They feared that a fire could bring in those watching them. If they were friendly, there were trade items in their packs. If they were not, it would only be the two of them against who knew how many.

The eastern sky was just getting light when they pushed the canoe into the river. Dipping their paddles into the water sounded loud this morning. The two men feared that any noise would bring attention to them.

They did not see any riders during the day and began to feel some relief. Maybe the two they'd seen had become bored or had decided that the canoe would be no threat to them. By afternoon much of the tension in Kyle had dissipated and he once again was able to enjoy the grand scenery along the river.

That night the two men used the handlines and caught four trout and two large channel catfish. This had been accomplished quickly and the excitement of fishing had to be quelled. They already had more than one meal of fish.

The fish were broiled over a small fire made with dry wood to prevent as much smoke as possible. The two friends couldn't help but talk in low tones, fearful that loud voices would carry too far.

The men had rigged a stringer to keep the two catfish alive in the river. That night they lay under the fly trap, listening to the sounds of the night. "It sounds peaceful out there," Rene said.

They hadn't fired their weapons in two days out of fear the sound would bring unwanted visitors. "I wonder if the damn rifles will even fire," Kyle worried.

Both adventurers knew that they had to come to grips with their fears. They would be on the river for a couple of months and couldn't worry constantly over that time. The coming day was their day of rest. Up until now they had only taken items necessary for camping out of the canoe. They decided to empty it and check all the items.

This activity kept their minds off the unknown riders. That night they fired their rifles. The Baker misfired, and after some fiddling with it, the rifle fired. Kyle's pistol fired without a problem. They heated water and cleaned all the weapons and rubbed them down with oil. Once loaded again, the two men felt confident that they'd fire if necessary.

The next morning, they got a late start, having to pack the canoe. They had now refreshed their memories of where everything was. Pushing out the canoe, they climbed in and paddled upriver.

They reached their first rapids the next day. It didn't look too bad, and they attempted to paddle through the rushing water. It was a foolish move and soon they were swept back down the rapids fighting to avoid any rocks.

Hearts pounding, they reached the bottom, the canoe floating crosswise as they tried to catch their breath. "That was stupid," Kyle muttered.

"It would have been a long walk back to St. Louis if we had crashed the canoe," Rene replied.

The rest of the day was spent carrying their gear and then the canoe around the rapids. While the slim man had dreaded the thought of doing so, it wasn't that bad. It took three trips with the packs and gear, and then one with the empty canoe, which was easily handled by the two men.

The two men ate their supper to the sound of the rolling water. "I imagine there are lots of these between the Pacific Ocean and here," Rene said.

"I believe so," Kyle agreed.

The next day there were more riders. This time four braves rode above the bank, watching their progress. Three had muskets and the fourth, a bow and lance. Rather than paddling and hoping they would go away, the slim man told his friend. "We may as well pull up to the shore and say hello."

"What if they are hostile?" Rene asked.

"Then we shoot three and hope we can kill that fourth before he kills one of us," Kyle replied.

"That's little comfort," his friend said. "That will leave me alone to make the trip."

The slim man couldn't help but laugh at his friend's comment.

They came to an area where the bank sloped lower and a small stream flowed in. Paddling the canoe to the shore, the two men climbed out carrying their rifles. Care was taken not to point them at the approaching rider.

Not knowing what to do next, Kyle held his hand up, palm out. Somewhere he had heard it was a sign that you come in peace. At least he hoped it was. The braves stopped and for what was only less than a minute, they stared at each other. To the slim man it felt much longer.

The brave with the lance dismounted and walked towards them. *Just our luck*, Kyle thought. *That will leave a brave with a musket if a fight breaks out.*

"We come in peace," Kyle said, hoping one of the four knew some English.

The brave facing them said something that neither understood. The slim man realized some of the words were French. Before he could respond, he heard Rene say, "We come in peace," in French.

The brave's French was somewhat broken, but they understood his next words to say, "You are crossing Osage territory."

The lanky friend replied, "We come as friends and bring gifts."

The brave did not reply, but continued to stare stonily at the two intruders.

"Get him some gifts," Rene said to his

friend.

Still carrying the M1803, Kyle turned and did the hardest thing he'd ever done. He walked to the canoe, anticipating the lance hitting him square in the back while those on the horses shot Rene with their muskets.

None of this happened. The slim man took four small mirrors, some beads, bells, and a knife from their packs. He returned to the brave. His lanky friend glanced over and said, "We give you these as a thank you for allowing us to cross Osage territory."

One of the other braves dismounted with a leather bag and put the gifts into it, then went back to his horse and leaped onto it. The brave in front of them nodded and walked back to his horse. After mounting, he held the lance high and cried out. Then the four turned and rode away at a gallop.

The two men stood there until they were out of sight. "I had no idea how much to give them," Kyle said.

"I guess it was enough," Rene replied.

"You did well in French," the slim man replied. "It took me a second to realize what he was speaking."

"It's actually my first language," his lanky friend replied. "The brave has lived among French trappers. He used some of their slang."

Wasting no time, the two men got underway. The next day they saw a group of about six braves riding off the river a ways and Kyle heard his friend say, "The word is out and now they'll come in bunches looking for trade goods."

They didn't come. As it turned out they were chasing down some buffalo. It was midday and the two paddled the canoe to the shore and took a break to have something to eat. They could hear muskets firing in the distance as the braves attempted to take down some buffalo.

Many lessons were learned while paddling the canoe upstream. Even the smallest rapid is best portaged rather than tackled by paddling. Most often close to shore had the slowest current to paddle against. They watched for eddies, which were always calm and gave them a short break. Naturally, they then had to dodge the snag, sandbar, or large rock that created the eddies.

With time, it became second nature to steer toward the calmest water. They also found that it was best to remain in either the bow or stern, so Kyle spent most of his time in the bow.

After a month of travel the two friends were out of jerky and had put a dent in their other supplies. They pulled up on a tree-lined shore where they had spotted some buffalo grazing. Their plan was to shoot a one or two-year-old and dry some jerky.

Using their short axes, the two cut

poles to make racks for drying the meat. They would cut strips of the hide to tie the poles together. They also cut wood to make a smoky fire to add flavor to the meat and assist in the drying.

When all was ready, they watched the buffalo graze as they worked their way around in wide circles. None came near, so they ate fish they'd caught for their supper.

The second day, a group led by a large bull was moving toward the river. The patient hunters watched from within the trees for most of the morning. There were plentiful berries to enjoy while waiting.

The two hunkered down as the sound of grunts and tearing of the prairie grass got closer. It was decided that Rene would shoot because Kyle had shot buffalo during the harvesting of hides.

A young female was chosen, and his lanky friend brought the Baker rifle to his shoulder and cocked it. The quiet of the copse of trees was broken by the explosion of black powder as it propelled the .625 caliber ball at the buffalo. The bovine sidestepped and went to the ground, its back legs thrashing momentarily.

The two men watched as the group closed around the downed female. It was almost an hour before the large bull moved off with the rest of the herd. With the Baker reloaded the two friends moved out to the downed animal.

Kyle heard his friend say, "If we were after the hide, we could be out of here in less than 15 minutes."

This was the first buffalo the two had gutted and one might say there were lots of intestines. The liver was set aside. Next, they skinned the buffalo keeping the carcass lying on the hide. They then quartered the animal. The tenderloins and tongue were taken for their meals, while much of the rest would be cut in strips and dried for jerky.

The hot summer sun would help hasten the making of jerky, but the temperature would also take its toll on the meat prior to being salted and hung on the racks.

The hide and quartered carcass was dragged into the shade and the racks were assembled in the sun. They used a bark-less windfall to cut the lean meat into strips which were then salted. The two men worked feverishly throughout the hot afternoon.

A smoky fire burned upwind from the racks. Close to the fire on some green sticks were pieces of the tenderloin broiling for their meal. Once the racks were full, the remaining meat could not be used. Even if it could be made into jerky, they wouldn't be able to fit it onto the canoe.

Grabbing the edge of the hide, the two men pulled it out well away from their camp. Wildlife on the prairie would have a good meal tonight. As they walked back the buzzards began to come in.

That night the fly tarp was put over the rack to protect the strips of meat. The jerky was for the most part ready, but they wanted a few more hours the next day to make sure.

The two men stuffed themselves on the tenderloin, liver, and tongue. Too much of it was left after they were full, but out in the wild there was no way to save it. They took turns that night watching the jerky rack to make sure something didn't come in and help themselves to the meat.

Throughout the night they could hear the sounds of wolves or coyotes fighting over what was left of the buffalo. By early afternoon the next day the jerky was ready, and it was put into a canvas bag.

As they continued up the river, the two enjoyed reliving the feast they'd had of the buffalo. The weather was changing, so they had been fortunate on the days they'd chosen to make the jerky.

Kyle decided to pull in early as they watched the dark sky to the west. The air was heavy and humid. They camped under a rock outcrop, bringing the boat and their packs nearby for protection.

From their vantage point, they could see the prairie to the west. The wind was picking up and suddenly there was hail. The two men tried to pull the canoe closer to the outcrop to give it more protection as bruising hail hit them.

Then in the distance they saw the funnel cloud come down. Dirt and grass swirled around it as it wound its way toward the herd of buffalo. In shock they watched as the funnel cloud overtook the herd and they saw the helpless animals being picked up and flung from the cloud, their lifeless corpses left behind as the funnel moved on. Then it was sucked back up into the clouds, leaving the havoc it had wreaked behind.

CHAPTER THIRTEEN

The monotony of paddling day after day hung over the two friends. They were into their third month and felt they hadn't made any progress. There was a sameness about the river as they paddled mile after mile.

The two friends' upper body strength now made it possible to travel 30 miles in a day, barring having to portage around rapids. They supplemented their food with wild berries and some edible greens that Rene recognized. There was plenty of small game to shoot, so they avoided killing the larger buffalo.

Their coffee and tobacco were gone. They would use red clover, birch leaves and even spruce needles to make a tea of sorts. As the summer wore on, the tender needles and leaves were less available.

They once camped for two days in a large grove of oaks and harvested acorns. They were boiled to help remove the shells. They then chopped and roasted the nutmeats to be used in place of coffee. Once finished they had enough to last several weeks.

The two men were not completely alone on the river. They met two trappers leading a flea bit mule. They wore dirty buckskins and carried one rifle and one musket. They also had knives in sheaths on their belts. They introduced themselves as Huck and Toby.

Toby was missing his front teeth and spoke little. Huck was the talker. While sitting around the two friends' fire, he told them about all the places the trappers had been. Both claimed to have Lakota wives.

Kyle did not feel comfortable around the two men. They asked too many questions about where the friends were going and if they had good trade goods in the canoe. As of yet they hadn't pulled the gear out of the canoe and had decided to try for fish and eat first.

Rene kept quiet. He was broiling some catfish over the fire. They had enough to share, and the two trappers accepted the offer to join them for an early supper. Kyle had the pistol in his belt, which they noted. Their rifles were within easy reach.

"If you want, I can make things go smooth for you with the Lakota," Huck told them. "My wife is a chief's daughter."

Ignoring the offer, the slim man said, "We can't offer you any coffee. We ran out some time back."

"I can do without coffee," Huck replied, "but I sure do miss my chew."

"I understand that," Kyle told him. "I ran out a couple of weeks ago. I'm hoping to run across a trading post where I can buy some."

Shaking his head, the trapper said, "Ain't no trading posts this far west."

With the meal finished, the slim man stood up, picked up his M1803 and smiled. "We got a couple more hours of daylight and want to get some more miles behind us. You are welcome to enjoy our fire."

Caught off guard, Rene stood, unsure why his friend had decided to move on. Then acting like it had been the plan, he picked up his Baker. He told them, "You two take care and say hello to your wives for us."

Kyle got into the canoe and placed his rifle on their packs. Rene got in and kept his Baker at the ready. As the slim man paddled away, Huck shouted, "You ain't very sociable bastards. We come in here friendly-like."

Once they were a safe distance from the trappers, they did some power paddling quickly, getting out of sight of the men. "Did you see something wrong with those two?" his lanky friend asked.

"Maybe I've been away from folks too

long, or maybe I am just getting skittish, but nothing about those two felt good," Kyle told him.

"Their packs on the mule looked kind of thin," Rene agreed. "They might have been planning on resupplying."

They tended to camp on the east bank, but after just over an hour, they pulled in on the west side. That put the river between them and the trappers. There was no reason to build a fire.

It was a cool, dry, moonlit night, so they didn't put up the fly tarp. The river at this point was about chest-deep, with a slow current. They had a sandbar above their camp that extended about one-third of the way across the Missouri.

Kyle was almost asleep when something in the still night brought him wide awake. There was something or someone across the river rooting around. It could be an animal coming down for a drink, or even some otters playing. Neither made too much sense after dark.

Then, as a stick cracked, there was muttering. The slim man didn't hear what was said, but it sounded like someone was being scolded. He and Rene were in the shadows of some trees, so he slowly sat up to get a better view of the river. He could see the canoe, its side lit up by the moonlight.

Straining his eyes at the water, he

finally caught a glimpse of moonlight on the barrel of a weapon being held above someone's head. Then there was a ripple of water next to the figure holding the weapon above his head, which would be the second intruder.

Cocking the pistol, Kyle called out, "Which one of you wants to die?"

Rene moved beside him grabbing his rifle. Then the slim man fired in the direction of the shadowy figures in the water. There was a yelp and one cried, "I'm hit!"

Picking up his M1803, Kyle shouted, "We got two loaded rifles here and we can see you in the water!"

The one with his weapon above his head turned it and fired in the direction of the western shore before scrambling toward the far shore. The ball flew wide. There was lots of splashing, and the slim man was sure that their musket and rifle had gotten wet.

The two friends moved deeper into the trees and watched the moonlit east bank. The river at this point was about 400 yards wide. The fact that Kyle had hit either of the two men with the pistol at the distance they were away from the west shore was a miracle. The ball might have even skipped off the water before hitting the man.

The two men sat in the trees until the moon went behind some western clouds, then they got into the canoe and began upstream. The starlight gave them just enough light to distinguish the shore.

By morning, the two exhausted men pulled into a cove on the west side. They dragged the canoe out of sight, into the trees. Kyle figured they'd paddled about ten miles in the dark, hopefully far enough to be rid of the two trappers.

Rolling out their blankets, they went to sleep. It was midafternoon before they started stirring. While Rene collected some wood for a fire, Kyle scanned the far bank. The only movement were some deer, a herd of buffalo in the distance, and three ducks diving for wild celery near the far shore.

Hoping that the trees would disperse the smoke from their fire, they brewed some acorn coffee. The slim man dumped the last of their cold flour into a pot of steaming water and made a gruel for their meal.

There were some wild plums near the shore and they picked a good quantity before striking camp and continuing up the river. The dark purple fruit was tart, with just enough sweetness to make them enjoyable.

Kyle could see that the current was slower on the east side of the river, but the two men stayed to the west, wanting to keep distance between them and the two trappers. Should they have gotten ahead of them, it would be unlikely that they could hit them at 400 yards, wider in some stretches.

It took several days before the two

friends felt secure enough to travel along the east side of the river. Two weeks after the trapper encounter, the two travelers saw teepees a short distance from the eastern shore. In the shallows of the river were children and young adults swimming and washing. Upon sighting the canoe, there were squeals and screams as they ran towards their village.

Unsure, the two men got their rifles ready and slowly paddled closer, staying near the middle of the river. They were dangerously low on supplies and the prospect of being able to trade for some made just passing by the village difficult.

Several braves brandishing bows and muskets came down to the shore. One shot an arrow well in front of the canoe and it skipped across the water. "They want us to know that they can hit us from the bank," Kyle said.

"Are we going in?" Rene asked. "We can turn around and go back downriver or head for the western shore."

"You paddle and I'll keep my rifle across my lap," the slim man said. "If they appear to be hostile, I'll fire at the meanest looking one and then we'll paddle like hell away from them."

Holding his hand up at the font of the boat, his friend slowly maneuvered it closer to shore. Unsure what language to speak, using French, Kyle said, "I come in peace."

He got no reaction. Now they were too close to try an escape from the bows and muskets. Then, slowly, one of the men raised his hand, palm out. Two of the braves stepped into the water and guided the canoe to shore.

Trying English this time, the slim man said, "I am Kyle. We come to trade with you." With this said, he handed some mirrors and beads to them that he'd dug out of the pack behind him.

The braves took them and then one said, "Come."

The canoe was pulled well up onto the shore and the two friends walked with the braves, still carrying their rifles. He had noticed some of the younger braves pointing at the Ojibwe woman's painting she'd done on the front of the canoe.

Kyle hoped that it indicated something friendly. The two men were seated near the fire and still had their rifles across their laps. An older man came from his teepee and looked at the two of them.

"We are Lakota," he said in French. "We are not enemies of your people. You can put your weapons away."

The braves had looked over the canoe and knew that the two men didn't have any trade muskets. Kyle set his aside and said, "We would like to trade for supplies."

"We have just finished a successful hunt and have much we can trade with you," the old brave replied.

"That is good," Rene told him. "We have traveled far from St. Louis."

"I have met men from St. Louis," the old brave said. "Black Buffalo was the chief then."

Kyle thought about the diary and what the man had written about the tension between the expedition and the Lakota. Black Buffalo was mentioned as the chief who had settled the problem between the two.

"I have read that Black Buffalo was a great chief with strong medicine," Kyle told him.

Things were moving painfully slow, and the two friends just wanted to trade and go. It was a good thing that the old brave spoke French. At least there wasn't a language barrier.

They ate and were talking of the hunt when a young brave came to the fire and said something to the old brave. He smiled and looked at the two men. "There is an elk, and the young men want to go get it."

The excitement of the young braves seemed to help lower the tension around the fire. The old brave nodded, and the braves were off. "They will practice their stalking and kill it with their bows," the man told them.

The ladies came with bowls filled with meat and berries. The two guests received theirs first and then the other braves. "This is from our last hunt," the old brave told them. "When my son gets the elk, we will have fresh meat."

The stewed meat was good with the berries. It was not a taste Kyle had had before, but it ate well. He worried about the canoe sitting near the water and hoped that other braves wouldn't help themselves to the trade items.

The hunt was successful and there was much celebrating around the fire that night. The two friends were able to move back away from the fire. The old brave told them that the stuff in their canoe would be put into a teepee where they would sleep. The trading would be done tomorrow.

The two friends were given some kind of fermented drink which left them slightly lightheaded. They drank it sparingly. It was well into the night when they finally went to the teepee to sleep. A quick survey of their packs told them that they had not been pilfered.

The inside of the tent had the strong odor of smoke, buffalo hides, and sweat. Realizing that the two of them hadn't bathed in a while, Kyle figured they would just add to the smell.

Sleep came slowly in the foreign environment. The two friends knew they would have little control over what happened the next day. They weren't sure what supplies the Lakota had to trade, but hoped they were good and would take them well up the river.

The next morning the flap was raised, waking the sleeping men as a young woman came into the teepee. She set down two sets of buckskins. Smiling, she said possibly the only word she knew: "Gift."

As she went away, the flap was left open, offering some light. "What did she mean by saying gift?" Rene asked.

"I don't know," Kyle replied. "Maybe we are supposed to put them on."

"It is doubtful they will fit," his lanky friend told him. "They didn't measure us or anything."

Kneeling in the teepee, the two men looked at the buckskins. "They have ties you can adjust them with," Rene said.

Figuring they were supposed to put on the gift, the two men removed their woolen clothing and put on the buckskins. They fit them well. Even being tall and slim, the britches were the right length.

Packing their dirty clothes into their packs and wearing the moccasins used in the canoe, the two men came out of the teepee. Four women were near the fire making something for breakfast. They looked at the men and smiled. Then turning back to the fire, they giggled and spoke rapidly. About what the two men did not know.

The old brave came over and said, "I see you got our gift. You traveled far to come here, and you brought good luck to my son during the hunt."

A buffalo robe had been placed on the ground a short distance from the fire. The three men sat. "What supplies do you need?" the old brave asked.

Everything, thought Kyle, but he waited for his friend to respond.

"We are low on food," Rene said. "We need salt, corn meal, and jerky."

"Our women have made wasná, and we have corn meal," the old brave replied.

"I don't know what wasná is," the lanky man replied.

"Some call it pemmican," the man told him. "It is made from buffalo, tallow, and berries. You can eat it like jerky or boil it for soup."

This conversation went on for a while, and with his limited knowledge of French, Kyle caught about half of it.

Suddenly the old brave called to one of the ladies near the fire. She replied and hurried away. The man asked, "Do you have powder or lead to trade?"

This Kyle understood. He waited for his friend to answer. "We have some," Rene replied. "We cannot spare much."

"That is good," the old brave told him.

"After the hunt we do have a need."

The young woman from the fire came back with a bowl. It contained the dried meat, tallow, and berries almost ground to a paste. She gave it to Rene. He took some and tasted it. He then handed the bowl to Kyle. The slim man found the stuff quite tasty. He thought about it as a soup or fried. He wondered how long it would last and asked the old brave.

"A year, maybe more," the man replied. "We eat it until we start hunting next spring."

Kyle thought that the wasná would be perfect for the trip. He wondered how much they could spare. The two men were hungry, not having eaten breakfast yet, and between the two of them they ate all the wasná.

Suddenly, Rene asked, "Do you know two trappers named Huck and Toby?"

The old brave's eyes turned cold. "I have met the men."

"They said they were friends of the Lakota and had married two of your women," the lanky man said.

"Are they your friends?" the man asked.

"They tried to steal from us and then made an attempt to kill us," Kyle answered.

"Where did you see these men?" the old brave asked.

Rene explained where they had met downriver. Then the man asked, "Did you see the women?"

"We did not," Rene said.

The old brave called to some braves and said something in Lakota. They hurried away and shortly the friends heard horses galloping away.

The old brave said something to the ladies, and they began to dish the breakfast. Before it came, he turned to the two friends and said, "They stole two of our young women that were picking berries along the river. They probably sold them to another tribe."

The food came. It was a cornmeal mush. The old brave scooped it up with his fingers and ate. The two friends did likewise, and the mush was also good. With the meal finished the man said, "It is time to trade."

Some powder, lead, and other trade goods got the two men two leather bags of wasná weighing a total of 80 pounds and 50 pounds of cornmeal. The old brave held up one of the knives. "This will be for my son."

Some young men carried the packs to the canoe. The two friends put them in. Once finished, the old brave smiled and said, "You were lucky. The two men are looking for supplies and a boat to leave the territory. They would have killed you. We will find them."

Looking at the cold eyes of the old brave, Kyle said, "God have mercy on their souls."

The man replied, "We will not."

The two friends left the Lakota feeling that they had made a friend of the old brave. Personally, Kyle hoped that the Lakota did find the two trappers. They were not good people.

The two adventurers continued north on the Missouri River. They were aware of the northern Lakota being more hostile towards those from outside their territory. They had enough supplies to take them to late fall. Rene started talking about having to winter someplace before they got to the mountains.

"The Mandan were a friendly tribe," Kyle told his friend. "According to the diary they made good neighbors near the fort they built. They did have trouble with the northern Lakota"

"We will have to build a cabin or some kind of shelter to withstand the cold," Rene told him.

The two friends also discussed staying farther south. The trouble was that all they had were the more hostile Lakota to trade with and they wouldn't have a defensible fort to hold them off.

They decided to continue as quickly as they could to reach the Mandan village and then build a log cabin with shooting notches to defend themselves if necessary. They also could consider the North West Fur Company run by the British. They would have a place where the two men could stay for the winter. Kyle was sure the Mandan could direct them to one of the posts.

They watched the shores as they paddled north. They managed to shoot a small deer feeding on the riverbank. With the days fair and the nights cool, they were able to keep the meat for several days. Having the fresh meat was a nice change from the wasná every day. They had scraped and dried the skin for future use.

It was mid-October and the leaves had started to turn. The two men had no real feel for how far they were from the Mandan village. They knew they should reach it within a few weeks. In the evenings Kyle pored over the diary, trying to find any landmark or description that might have been seen.

They had passed mounted braves who had sat and watched them go by. None of them tried to pursue them. Regardless, it didn't help the two men when they slept. Kyle would have dreams of being chased by an unknown attacker.

A cold, late October rain was falling on the two men as they paddled upriver, having no idea how far they still had to go. The ground cloths with a slit to stick their heads through kept most of the chilling water off them, but Kyle was beginning to see it collected in the bottom of the canoe.

"We should pull over and make a fire," Rene called to him. "I am getting damn cold."

They were going along the east bank and the river made a turn to the right ahead of them. The turbulence in the water warned of a rapids. "I think we have a portage coming," the slim man called back. "We'll get above the rapids and call it a day."

As they reached the bend, they saw two things. The turbulent water was almost an eighth of a mile long, and above it was a small boat with the sail furled!

"Do you see that?" his lanky friend shouted. "It's a damn boat coming down river and it has a sail!"

The small boat was a pirogue. It appeared to be under 25 feet-long. It was tied to some brush on shore and had swung around with the stern downriver. There were three men sitting above the bank under a fly tarp near a fire.

Pulling the canoe up onto the bank, the two friends loaded up with as much as they could carry and climbed to the top of the bank. There they found a trail made by wildlife and then followed by travelers who would be riding or walking along the river.

Kyle adjusted the pistol in his belt. They'd left their flintlock rifles for the second trip, when they'd try and carry the canoe with the remaining packs. When the men noticed them, two came and offered to help transport their packs.

Unsure of anyone they met on the river based on past encounters, Kyle let them take the packs and then hurried back to get the canoe. "I don't know if the rifles will fire," he told Rene, "but let's keep the scabbards positioned so we can get to them if they try anything."

Dragging the canoe to the top of the bank, and with each taking an end, they carried the canoe with the remaining packs. The rain made it a touch heavier, and normally they'd have carried the rest of the packs and then the canoe, but with the unknown men the two friends had to be careful.

Before they carried the canoe the eighth of a mile, the two men were back and offered to take the rest of the packs. The two men set the canoe down and picked up the rifles in their scabbards. One of the men smiled and said, "It's always a good idea to keep your weapons."

His comment gave the slim man some confidence that the men with the pirogue might be honest. Their fly tarp was just big enough for the five to sit out of the rain. A tarp and the deer skin were placed over the packs to keep the water off them.

"Where are you headed?" the apparent leader of the three asked.

Rene replied, "To the Pacific Ocean."

The man said, "I think you're a bit behind your party. They went through here 12 years ago."

Laughing at the response, Kyle told him, "We are sort of following Lewis and Clark's route, but right now we are heading for the Mandan village."

"We were just there two days ago," the leader replied.

A hot flash went through the slim man's chilled body. *Just two days from here*, he thought. Then he said, "That's good news. We weren't sure how far we still had to go."

Then Rene asked, "Coming upriver, how did you get your boat through the rapids?"

"With some difficulty," the leader replied. "We trade with the Mandan tribe and brought items they'd want or that they could trade with the Lakota's and others."

Kyle looked at the packs in the small boat and assumed it was furs and things made by the Mandan that would be profitable to sell in St. Louis.

The two friends learned that the three men made three trips a year up the river, the ones up taking the longest, but with the sail and the current, the trip back down was rather short. While it had taken them two days to get to this point, it would take the two friends a week to reach the Mandan village.

The leader asked, "Do you plan to

winter near the Mandan village?"

"I believe we will," Kyle told him. "We'll have to build a small cabin and hope to trade with the Mandan for food that we need."

"When you get there, tell them you are a friend of Walter and they will help you get ready for the winter," the leader told them.

The rain lasted two days, and the two parties shared information. Kyle warned them about the two trappers who were looking to steal a boat. Walter told them about the upcoming rapids they'd find the rest of the way to the Mandan village.

With the rain gone, the two parties went their own way. The slim man no longer felt so isolated. With their gear and the canoe dried out as best they could, the two friends continued north.

CHAPTER FOURTEEN

The two friends first caught sight of smoke on the west side of the river, alerting them that they had arrived at the Mandan village. It was the first of November, and they'd already dealt with some light snow.

They were wearing their woolen clothing under their buckskins. The prospect of having to build a shelter seemed overwhelming as they had thought about it the past couple of days.

Their original plan was to build one about the size of Andre's shack behind his mercantile, but as the days got shorter and colder, the size continued to get smaller and smaller. Kyle described the shelter he and Danny had built in Canada and how the snow and cold came right through their pole walls.

"We don't have horses or mules to

worry about, so as long as we make the walls tight somehow, we could make it through the winter," the slim man told him.

"How do we heat it?" Rene asked.

"It opens in the front, with a tarp to close it. When it's open we'll have a fire in front, which will give us heat."

Somewhat doubtful, his lanky friend did like the small size they'd have to build. The notes in the diary had said that Fort Mandan was on the east side of the river and a little farther north. The two friends knew that it had been burned but wanted to see the site.

As they paddled north towards the site of the fort, they noticed smoke from the Mandan village to the west. Kyle hoped that the riverbank was high enough to prevent being spotted by the residents. After looking over the fort would be soon enough to make contact with them.

Only a few charred remains and one chimney was all that remained. The river had cut into the bank during spring floods and was a short distance from where the front opening of the fort would have been. Pulling the canoe up onto the bank, the two friends walked around the fort.

"Do you think we could use the fireplace and chimney?" Kyle wondered.

"You mean that we build right here?" Rene asked.

"The original fort was 56 feet long on each side and had storerooms and a couple of sleeping quarters. They built it in a month. We should be able to build a small log shack and could use the existing chimney in much less time."

"They had over 40 men to do it," Rene reminded him.

"It is something we should think about," Kyle replied. "And we shouldn't spend too much time doing so."

Then his lanky friend said, "We have company."

Turning, the slim man saw three dugouts coming across the river with four Mandan braves in each one. Trying to wipe away the surprised look, he forced a smile. Kyle raised his hand palm out.

The braves were carrying both bows and muskets. Their dugouts scraped against the shore and the braves climbed out, keeping their weapons ready. Unable to think of anything else to say, the slim man blurted out, "We are friends of Walter."

Neither the expressions, nor the posture of the braves changed. One of them said something in their native tongue. Neither of the travelers understood. Then Rene spoke in French. "We are friends of Walter."

The brave, also speaking French, replied, "Walter has left."

While things might have seemed uncertain, both friends felt some relief. They had a common language they could communicate with.

Within a few minutes the two parties had an understanding that neither meant any harm. Speaking more fluent French, Rene explained that he and Kyle planned to build a winter shelter on the old fort site. He also told them that they planned to hunt for meat and wanted to trade for corn and other items the Mandan might have.

The lead brave told them, "Come." He and the other braves climbed back into the dugouts. As the two men headed back to their canoe, Kyle said in hushed tones, "We were stupid. In our hurry to look at the fort, we left our rifles in the canoe. All we had to defend ourselves was my pistol and our knives."

Settling into the canoe, Rene replied, "It's a damn good thing they didn't come to fight."

The village was on a high bluff across the river. The dwellings were domed, earthen lodges circling a center courtyard. Several additional circles of lodges were built spreading out from the river. The entryway of each dome was made of exposed logs extending out over six feet. Within it hung a windbreak to keep the weather out and provide privacy.

Carrying their flintlock rifles, the two

friends were escorted to the center of the village, where they were met by a man they learned was one of the chiefs. He looked at the two arrivals and said, speaking French, "My braves tell me that you come with a sign on your canoe that you are one with the great spirit."

This statement confused the two friends, but it sounded like it would be to their benefit, so the two of them kept quiet and acted like they agreed. Then Rene took a chance and said, "We follow the footsteps of other great men that came here in years past. They said the Mandan were friends and a people of honor."

They were unsure of the lack of reaction from the chief and stood wondering what to do or say next. Then the man said, "My braves have told me you want to build a new fort across the river. We would like to offer you one of our lodges for the winter."

Kyle remembered that the Ojibwe had offered the same in Canada when he and Danny had been trapping. The slim man wondered if this was a common offer of the various tribes. His friend seemed to hesitate to answer, so Kyle replied, "We would be honored to stay in your village."

The chief seemed satisfied with the meeting and left. An elderly woman came up to the two friends. She did not speak French, but made it clear that the two were to follow her.

They entered one of the lodges. The entryway went down, indicating that part of the lodge was below the ground level. While it had looked bigger from the outside, the inside was about 40 feet in diameter. The structure was held up by four sturdy poles in the center that were tied into a square frame that supported cottonwood logs that created the sloping dome shape. They learned that additional layers of logs were put on before the dirt and clay were piled on top to form the final dome.

Like the wigwam that Kyle had stayed in with the Ojibwe, that floor of the dome was covered with mats made of reeds or cattails. To make sitting more comfortable, there were buffalo robes and other hides or furs around the edges to sit on. The only light came from a square hole in the center at the top, and from the fire situated in the center of the dome.

The woman said something to some boys and they hurried out of the lodge. She then showed the two friends to an area with buffalo robes and made a sign that this would be their spot.

Soon the young braves were back with everything from the canoe, and they placed it near their new spot. The elderly woman moved away to do some other things and a brave about the same age as the two friends came over. "I speak English or French. Which would you like to use.?"

"English," both men replied.

"The woman you met owns this lodge. All around you are her family. I married one of her daughters and that's why I live here," the brave explained. "You can call me Red Deer."

The two friends introduced themselves and then confirmed that this was the place they should sleep. Then Red Deer told them, "We will be going on a hunt tomorrow and you are welcome to join us. We will have horses for you."

"Thank you," Kyle replied. "We will be pleased to go with you."

Rene was rather quiet while they arranged their gear and rolled out the blankets for later. Suddenly, he said, "I have never ridden a horse."

"How about when we were buffalo hunting?" the slim man asked.

"Climbing onto a horse with its harness on gave me lots of places to hang on and we just went a short way to where we needed to skin the buffalo," his lanky friend said. "I have seen the braves ride into a herd and shoot buffalo. I won't be able to do that."

"You know," Kyle told him. "I am not so sure I'll be able to shoot from a galloping horse and hit anything."

"Maybe we should tell them that we

can't go hunting tomorrow," Rene suggested. "I could have a cold or something."

Then, Red Deer was back, smiling. "Voices carry very well in the lodge, and I heard your concerns. We will be riding to the west and going after elk. Once we spot a herd, we will leave the horses and stalk them."

"I've done that before in Canada," Kyle replied. "You won't have any trouble," he assured his friend.

The evening meal was made with ground corn and was quite good. The large family ate in the lodge, sitting around the fire. Red Deer was very helpful in showing the two friends the proper place to relieve themselves, and a place where they could bathe.

When they went down to the river to move the canoe away from the river, Red Deer pointed to the markings that the Ojibwe woman had put on the front. "It says you are one with the great spirit. You are protected ones. If another kills you, they will face the fury of the great spirit."

When Red Deer went to get something, Kyle whispered to his friend. "When the old woman finished fixing the canoe and painted this on the front, she spoke Ojibwe and told me *this will bring you safely through your trip*. I thought she was talking about the canoe she fixed. She meant what she painted on the canoe."

"Can she do that by just making marks

on the canoe?" Rene asked.

"I guess so," Kyle replied.

When the three of them went back into the lodge, Kyle stopped and sniffed the air. "Is there tobacco here?" he asked.

"We do have tobacco," Red Deer replied. "Some we grow and some we trade for."

Then their new friend went away for a moment and returned with leaves braided into a rope. They were dried tobacco leaves. "I have a pipe you can use if you need it. Some of our people just chew the leaves."

Accepting the tobacco, Kyle said, "This is all I need."

The hunters left at first light. Red Deer brought a horse to Rene and said, "This one won't give you any trouble."

The saddles were grass-filled pads on the horses backs and the reins were a leather line tied to the lower jaw of the horse. The braves just leaped onto their mounts while the two friends used a log to get on. Kyle guessed that Red Deer had mentioned Rene's problem, because rather than galloping away from the village they rode out at an easy pace.

They rode through fields with stubble from harvested corn. Kyle also saw raised mounds that probably grown beans and other vegetables. He had been told that the women owned the lodges and grew the corn and vegetables while the men hunted and fished. It didn't sound quite fair to the slim man, but it was their way.

While paddling up the river, the two men had heard the bugling of elk on the prairies along the river. The rut was still going on and now the sound could be heard coming from the west. Kyle was looking forward to the hunt. Rene just worked at staying on his horse.

Near midday a herd of elk were spotted. The hunters left their horses and walked through the prairie grass, crouching low, attempting to stay below a rise. Once they couldn't get any closer the braves and the two friends lay in the grass and waited for the elk to work their way towards them.

Shouts from behind them made the hunting party forget about the game and turn as one to a startling sight. The young braves were galloping at top speed away from a band of Lakota's. It appeared that the attacking braves were after the horses, having already caught the reins of one.

Kyle swung his M1803 toward the attack. Red Deer warned him, "You might hit our young ones." The Lakota's chasing the young braves were about 200 yards away. With a smoothbore musket's accuracy of 50 yards there would be the chance of the ball hitting any one of the group coming at them.

Cocking the flintlock rifle, he aimed at a brave who was bringing up a musket to shoot at the fleeing young Mandans. Kyle fired and the Lakota twisted on his horse and went to the ground. The other Lakota braves pulled up. One fired as they turned to flee, pulling the wounded brave up behind another rider.

Rene was staring wide-eyed at the confrontation, holding his Baker Rifle with the barrel pointing up. "Shoot at the Lakota with our horse or give your Baker to me!" the slim man shouted.

Reaching over and grabbing Rene's rifle, Kyle aimed and fired at the retreating brave. The stolen horse ran free as the Lakota slumped over his horse's neck. The band of a half-dozen braves disappeared into the trees to the south. The young braves pulled up as their horses, churned in confusion.

Kyle handed the Baker back to his friend to load. "I couldn't shoot," Rene said.

"That's okay," the slim man replied. "We scored two hits and drove the Lakota away. We best reload our rifles."

Red Deer seemed upset. "You could have hit the young braves."

"The bores of our flintlocks are rifled, making them accurate up to 300 yards," Kyle told him. "There was no danger of hitting the young braves riding towards us."

"I should thank you then," the Mandan brave replied. "You saved one of our young men from being shot at and our horses."

Not only had the slim man saved their

horses, but the Mandan had also gained one from the wounded brave. The hunt was over for today. The elk were gone and it was unlikely they'd find another herd.

The young braves talked excitedly as the group rode back toward the village. The Lakota had come out of the trees from the south while the young Mandan braves were intent on watching the stalkers. Once they were noticed, the Lakota were too close to do anything but ride towards the hunting party.

Rene was quiet as they sat after their supper. Then he tried to explain, "I was back in the war. The redcoats were coming, and I couldn't see a target."

"Don't worry about it," his friend told him. "Along the trail, I am confident you'll be able to cover my back if it's needed."

That night, Kyle met the Mandan chief of war. The chief had heard about the slim man's turning the Lakota. The slim man knew that only smoothbore muskets were used for trade with the tribes. He did not want to have to explain to the chief the benefits of rifling.

From Red Deer they learned that the Mandan's built fish traps to put in the shallows during the spring and summer. They were baited with rotting meat. Catfish was one of the main types that was caught. They also caught flathead and bullhead. The fish would be dried for use year-round.

The next day the two friends went fishing with their handlines. Red Deer came out to watch them as they brought in three catfish. He commented that it was not a very good way to bring in fish needed to feed the tribe. Kyle tried to describe the excitement of hooking a big fish and bringing it in. Perhaps he didn't do a good job of explaining it because the Mandan didn't seem convinced.

While near the river they saw Mandan's in bowl-shaped bull boats made from bull buffalo hides stretched over willow frames. They would push them with poles and were used for crossing the river or checking traps. They wouldn't have been practical for going upriver, but could be used for transporting goods downriver.

With their packs in the earthen lodge and their canoe safely stored for the winter, more time was spent inside. The temperature had dropped and soon the hills and fields would be covered with snow.

Kyle would smoke his pipe and try to find enough light to make notes in his log. He knew that he'd already lost some days and hoped to correct that should he ever meet a man with a calendar.

The occasional hunt was a nice break in the routine. Another attempt to shoot elk was successful and the large horns were displayed in the center court. Twice they went after buffalo, taking sleds along to carry the meat back. Rene became comfortable riding but both men still used a log to get onto the horses.

The village experienced two days of cold wet snow and bull boats were dragged onto the dome lodges, then put over the square opening to keep it out. Smoke from cookfires was still able to get out around the loose-fitting boats.

In late November, the serious snow started. The two friends woke to a new, white landscape. The only snow Rene had experienced had been when buffalo hunting out of St. Louis. Kyle had wintered in Vermont and Canada. Both had faced freezing temperatures.

What came down from the northern plains, neither had seen before. Stepping out of the lodge into the frigid morning air caught their breath. Their intention had been to catch a few more fish before the river froze over. The biting-cold north wind would not even allow them to walk through the village to the river.

Stepping back into the lodge, the two men heard complaining from the elder woman about them letting cold air in. The fires in the center of the earthen lodge were not big. While they did give off some heat, the Mandan depended on the thick walls and sunken floor to provide protection against the winter temperatures.

In the dim interior of the lodge, along with the other families living in the lodge, Kyle and Rene would crowd around the fire for warmth. Stories were told by the elders, but neither knew Mandan so the two friends had to be satisfied with the heat.

Soon the courtyard was covered with ice. Winter games were played. One was with a flat stone that was pushed across the ice as men stood on the edges and threw spears at it in an attempt to stop it.

The outdoor activity that the two men looked forward to were the hunts to provide meat for the village. The river had frozen over and the horses were led to the east shore, then ridden across the snow-covered plains in search of buffalo. Being a practical people, they had Kyle shoot the number they wanted from a distance rather than chasing them down in the deep snow.

The two friends wore their tuques, wool coats, and buckskin pants over their woolen ones. The calf-high moccasins kept their feet warm and dry. The Mandan liked their choppers and made some for themselves.

The two friends found the long nights made more comfortable when two young women decided to join them. The warmth and comfort help the long winter pass more quickly.

The spring thaw began by the end of March with the ice breaking up in the river.

That was when the two friends learned about another way to get meat. While grazing, buffalo would move back and forth across the river. When the ice began to weaken, they would break through and drown. These carcasses would come down with the ice and the Mandan men would pull them to shore. The nearly freezing temperatures of the water would keep the meat from spoiling.

By early May, the time was coming close for the two travelers to leave. Trading was done with the families in the lodge, providing them with mirrors, beads, and bells. Red Deer was given a knife along with items for his wife.

The friends were given new moccasins and food to begin their trip. Kyle also got a good amount of tobacco. The Mandan had told the two friends a lot about the river as it turned to the west. They had been told about another great river that flowed into the Missouri River about a day's travel up the river. They were told to stay on the right fork to get to the Great Falls. They were warned of the long portage they'd have there.

All these things the men knew from the diary, but it was good to have them reconfirmed by the Mandan's. They knew that the next tribe they'd meet was the Shoshone. They hoped that they had enough trade goods to purchase horses.

The two friends paddled away from the

village knowing that the Great Falls was three weeks from the Mandan's by river. They had been told that there would be lots of game along the way to replenish their supplies.

The two young women they had spent their nights with did not come down to wish them goodbye. The two men knew that they were already in the fields tilling the dirt for planting. Much of it was done with a shoulder bone of a bison or deer horns fixed to poles.

The temperature was cool as they paddled up the river. It kept them comfortable while traveling. Kyle was surprised at how fast his arms fatigued, the result of lying around all winter. A few extra breaks were needed by both men.

Rene pointed out the entrance of the other large river on the second day. They continued to the right, trusting that that was the correct direction. They could see hills and mountains to the south and a wide valley to the north. The valley was covered with grazing buffalo, deer, and antelope. They had been told of the antelope by the Mandan's but these were the first that they'd seen.

At the end of the first week, Kyle shot an antelope and they roasted the whole animal over a large fire. The juicy, fresh meat was a satisfying change from the dried fish and corn meal they'd gotten at the village.

At the end of the second week, they met

some trappers who worked for the North West Fur Company. A small buffalo was shot and they spent two days with them. The slim man's English accent made him right at home with the men.

"Where are the two of you headed?" the burly one of the two asked him.

"We figure to do some trapping in the west," Kyle lied. "There are too many trappers in the east."

"You'll be selling to the Hudson's Bay Company," the stoop-shouldered trapper told them. "We've been back and forth with those rascals over the years."

Kyle shared his scarce tobacco with the men. Rene chose to speak only French around the two men. Early comments let them know that the trappers didn't think too much of the Americans.

They left the two trappers with a little more information about the portage around the Great Falls. The canoe glided easily through the muddy water. Their arms and upper bodies were beginning to strengthen to the rigors of paddling several hours a day.

The two reached a section of river that wound through many narrow valleys. Game was less plentiful and they depended more on their supplies for their meals. After three weeks and several portages, they reached the Great Falls.

It was an awe-inspiring sight to see the

churning water spray into the air. They now faced an 18-mile portage. They fished below the falls and caught enough trout to last a couple of days while they rested up for the portage. Their stiff leather boots were taken out of their packs.

There was a sort of a high plain beyond the crest of the falls. There were some deep valleys cut by small rivers flowing into the Missouri above the falls. The prickly pear cacti and short, scrubby brush mixed with rocks made travel slow and painful. The rocky ledges led to the river and a series of rapids above the falls extended for miles, explaining the need for the long portage.

Cottonwoods grew along the river and tributaries. About halfway around, they met some mounted braves. They slipped the packs off their backs and faced them, gripping their rifles across their fronts. The braves were Hidatsa who had come west from their territory to find spring hunting grounds.

The braves had heard about the guests of the Mandan's and didn't view the travelers as a threat. Rene spoke French and said, "We come in peace."

With a cry, the braves turned and rode down the trail east. Kyle realized that he was sweating. As they picked up their packs, the slim man wished he'd have been able to make a deal with the braves to transport the gear across the portage.

It had taken Lewis and Clark over a month to carry all their boats, supplies, and gear across the portage. That was with some boats being left behind and they cached some supplies to be retrieved on the way back.

It would take the two friends two days for each round trip. It would take three trips to bring supplies and the canoe. As they were walking back from the first trip, Rene asked, "What are we going to do if our canoe is gone when we get back?"

"We pulled it up into the brush and hid it the best we could," Kyle replied. "If it's gone, we have a long walk to the Shoshone."

The slim man also realized that if they lost their goods, they'd have nothing to trade for horses. Already he feared that they wouldn't have enough. When they got back to the foot of the falls, they found their canoe and other gear where they'd left them.

The two men tried lifting the canoe and remaining gear. While they were able to do so, and had done so on short portages, it would take days carrying it all in one trip. With the last of their gear on their backs, and the flintlock rifles cradled in their arms, they headed out on the second trip.

It was over a week before they put the canoe back into the river above all the rapids. The two friends didn't realize that they would reach the end of the Missouri River in just over a week.

They understood why the writer of the diary had been impressed with the rocky formations that rose above the river after the Great Falls. He said that they called it the gates of the rocky mountains.

When the two friends reached the end of the Missouri River they found that it was fed by three smaller rivers. They wondered if they should take one of the legs of the three rivers to continue. Camp was set up and Kyle roasted the leg of a deer they'd shot. Their fire had been made on the same spot as others from days gone by.

For a moment, the slim man had to wonder if it could have been one from the expedition. Then he realized that it wasn't that old. What he did see was that the same area they were in had been used by several other travelers over the years.

Rene was in good spirits. "We are over halfway to the Pacific Ocean," he crowed as he cut a piece of meat and speared it with his knife.

Kyle sat unable to eat. The handwritten diary just said that from here they had walked to the southwest, based on the memories of Sacagawea. She had led them to the Shoshone seasonal camp, where they'd found the tribe.

The writer said that when they found the Shoshone, he feared they would be killed. Sacagawea had been stolen as a child from the

Shoshone, and when this was realized the expedition was spared. Some Shoshone had then led them west over a pass and to a large river that flowed to the Pacific Ocean.

What if they did not find the Shoshone? Kyle worried. If they did, would they be helpful or just kill them?

CHAPTER FIFTEEN

In the fading light, Kyle read and reread the handwritten diary. He had become quite skilled at understanding the man's writing but was frustrated that the diary didn't reveal any hidden bits of information that would help guide them. It just told of some nameless pass somewhere to the southwest, and that there were too many mosquitoes.

The next morning the deer haunch was still hanging over the cold fire. Kyle put down some tinder and kindling, then striking the flint on steel, got the fire going. He filled the coffee pot and put the water heating next to the flames. They had no coffee, but the hot water would be better than nothing.

Rene continued to sleep, snoring softly while the slim man worried. He had already realized that they'd have to leave the canoe. The three branches flowing into the Missouri River appeared to come from the south. While collecting wood, Kyle noticed a trail leading towards the west. Whether made by man or animal, he did not know, but it was a direction to go.

Building up the fire, soon the deer was warm enough to eat. Having finally decided on the trail, worry left the slim man and he realized that he was really hungry. Cutting off big chunks of venison, he tore at it with his teeth.

Then he heard, "Save some for me." Rene was awake.

As the two men ate their meal and drank the hot water, his lanky friend asked. "So have you decided which way we're going?"

"The diary wasn't too much help, except for the mosquitoes," Kyle told him as he slapped one on his cheek. "I did see a trail leading to the west and thought that's the way to go."

The rest of the day the two men spent time sorting through their gear. They easily had 500 pounds, not counting their long guns and what they were wearing. They talked of putting some items into a cache which could be retrieved when they came back.

They also needed to find a place to store the canoe for use when they returned. They needed a place that was dry and not easily noticed. It took two days to choose an outcrop of rock partway up a hill. It was surrounded by evergreens and had no signs of anyone camping near it.

With the canoe taken care of, they spread their packs out. Kyle looked at the stuff with a feeling of distress. He could not see a thing that they could leave behind except some food and this he worried they wouldn't be able to replace as they traveled.

As they agonized over what to leave, some of the trade goods were put aside first. They had enough lead to fight a small battle, so some of that was set aside. Their mess kit and waterbags would have to be kept. The bags wouldn't have to be kept full when traveling near streams and rivers.

With regret the buckskins were left behind. They each weighed 10 pounds and they could survive without them. Kyle's worn shirt and pants were added to the discard pile. Making decisions became harder and harder.

Finally, after a lot of discussion, it was decided that if it didn't fit into their knapsack, it had to be left behind. One of the food packs would be kept and would be carried on a pole between the two of them.

What wasn't figured in the weight carried by each was their possible bags, Kyles shooting bag, the pistol, their short axes, and knives in sheaths. The slim man did realize there were some things in the possible bag that weren't necessary. Some were lifelong treasures and some reminded him of people he'd known.

Slowly, as the day progressed the discard pile grew. They still had nearly 400 pounds, too much to carry any distance. The wool coats were kept, while the extra change of clothing was left. They each had two blankets and ground cloths. There was a fly tarp, a couple of canvases and the deer skin which had been tanned by the Mandan women.

The canvases and deer skin were discarded. The discard pile grew. If an item was kept for purposes of comfort and not a necessity, it was discarded. By the end of the second day each man would be carrying about 150 pounds, some being shared by the pack carried between them on a pole.

The discarded items were cached near the canoe. Most would be useless when they returned on the way back, but it made them feel better than throwing them away. Over the fire that night, the two cast balls for their flintlock rifles and the pistol. Each rifle had enough for 20 shots while Kyle made 10 for the pistol.

At the end of the third day the two slept with their gear and supplies under the fly tarp. Tomorrow they would take the trail to the west. After eating a big breakfast of fresh caught fish, the two put on their packs and hefted the pole with the supplies to their shoulders. They headed away from the camp.

An hour later the two were sitting on the side of the trail, their bodies aching from the weight. "This won't work," Rene said, still breathless.

The first idea the two came up with was to split the gear and haul it in two trips. It would slow their progress, but at least they wouldn't end up injured from the excess weight. Kyle stared ahead, knowing they needed to start again.

Then the trees he was looking at gave him an idea. A travois! He had seen them when buffalo hunting. The Osage used them to carry the hides. They could build two and carry the gear and supplies that way.

Rene was doubtful when Kyle proposed making two. "They had a horse pull it. We aren't as strong as a horse."

"We'd make them smaller," the slim man replied.

Without waiting for his friend to come completely around, he took his short axe and began cutting down the saplings growing along the trail. Soon he had four poles, eight feet long. He cut an angle at the lower end so the bottom of the pole would slide like a sled runner.

Laying them onto the ground slightly tapered toward the top, he figured the cross poles should be cut just over three feet. He cut three for each travois to carry the load. Then each would have to have one at the top so they could hold it up and use their bodies to help pull the travois.

Meanwhile, Rene got line that was used to tie up packs. Two hours later, they had made the two travois. They still carried their knapsacks on their backs, but much of the gear in them was put onto the travois. Kyle picked up the narrow end and placed the cross pole against his waist. Lifting the hundred pounds of gear and supplies decreased to one third. Then he tried pulling it. It pulled well and the weight at the end of the poles was easily carried.

They were still moving the same mass plus the weight of the travois, but now they could travel for two hours before resting. Their bodies were much less fatigued. Kyle was wishing they'd done this at the beginning because they could have taken more of the supplies and gear.

That night they pulled off the ancient trail and camped in a grove of cottonwood. They made cornmeal mush and hot water for the meal. "Too bad we didn't save the rest of the deer," his lanky friend complained.

"I doubt if it would have been any good by now," the slim man told him. "In the next day or so I should get a shot at something with the pistol."

The two got an early start after eating

what was left of the mush. They reached a second stream two days later. They filled their water bags. With the travois they could carry all the water they wanted.

Kyle noticed horse tracks near the stream. Someone had stopped here to water their animals. "We better keep our eyes open," he warned Rene. "We are not alone anymore."

The words were barely out of his mouth when they heard running horses. In a desperate attempt to flee, the two friends headed upstream along the bank, dragging their travois.

The was the sound of branches breaking as the horses swept around them and stopped directly in front. The brave on the paint horse began to laugh and point at the two men. They had found it easier to leave the flintlock rifles on the packs and all Kyle had was the pistol.

He dropped the travois and put his hand onto the grip. "I wouldn't do that, friend. You'll be dead before you get that little shooter out."

Turning, he saw an old, white-haired man sitting on a dun. It took him a second to realize that the man had spoken English. "We come in peace," Rene, who was right behind him, replied.

"The chief here says you two are dogs pulling your travois," the old man laughed.

"We feel like dogs and have been pulling these damn things for almost a week," Kyle replied. "We would like to talk to the chief about getting some horses."

"Well, pick up your travois and follow us," the white-haired man replied, still chuckling.

They were just a mile from the Shoshone village. When the two friends saw the valley with the mountains behind it, the scene was almost breathtaking. The only drawback was they were surrounded by Shoshone and an old codger, all holding bows or muskets while they held their travois.

In the center near a river was the village. They walked the quarter-mile across the valley and stopped near the river. The old man got off his horse and looked the two friends over.

"The chief was thinking of making a game of you two, but I convinced him that you meant no harm to the village," the man told them

Stepping away from the travois, the slim man told him, "We thank you for that. How did you know we spoke English?"

"Hell, we been listening to the two of you come along the trail for two days," the white-haired man told them. "The way you two kept talking let me know you had no bad intentions."

"I am Kyle," the slim man told him.

"My friend is Rene."

"They call me Cappy around here," the man replied. "When I came to be with the Shoshone, I told them I was Captain Bolgart. They had a problem with the name, so we settled on Cappy."

The man was a little over five feet and had a wiry frame. His bearded face gave him the look of a leprechaun that Kyle had heard about back in England.

"Leave your stuff here," the old man told them. "Someone will come and get it for you."

"We'll be taking our rifles," the slim man replied.

The old man squinted, looking at him. "Just remember, you only got one shot. Don't be foolish and waste them."

I got two, Kyle thought as he touched the pistol.

That evening they sat around a fire. The two friends found out that the chief spoke some French, when he asked them where they were heading.

"The Pacific Ocean," Kyle replied.

"Years back we had men dressed like you that brought Sacagawea back to us," the chief told him in French. "They were going to the great waters."

"We follow their trail," the slim man told him.

That night, after a supper of boiled

meat, the two were escorted to Cappy's teepee. There they found their gear. The old man had an elderly Shoshone woman who took care of the place for him and kept him warm on winter nights.

The Shoshone wintered in this valley. It offered good hunting for bison and elk. There were a variety of wild plants that were good for food, including Jerusalem artichokes. During the meal, the two friends had been given some kind of tea with a pungent smell, yet a mild flavor.

Sitting in the teepee and going through their gear, the old man sat and watched them. "You carry a lot of stuff considering you are walking to the Pacific," the wiry old man observed.

"Up until two weeks ago we were traveling by canoe," Rene told him.

"Why the hell did you stop?" Cappy asked.

Thinking it should be obvious, Kyle replied, "It doesn't work well on land."

"Where you're going, you'll need it on the Columbia," the man told them.

"What we'll need before that are horses," the slim man said.

"Horses could be a problem," Cappy replied. "It don't look like you got much to trade, unless you figured your travois were worth something." The old codger laughed at his own joke.

Not appreciating his humor, Rene told him, "We would have had more to trade, but we had to leave it with the canoe."

"Why don't you go get it?" Cappy asked.

"We don't have time," the lanky man replied. "We got to get started west to beat winter."

"When do you figure winter starts in the mountains?" the old man asked.

"We've spent a winter this far north already, and snow didn't come until November," Rene told him.

"You'll be crossing the Bitterroot Mountains along the Lolo trail," Cappy pointed out. "Winter starts in September in those mountains. I figure if you left tomorrow, you'd be pushing through waist-deep snow in about three weeks and come spring we'd find your bodies."

Both men were shocked at that revelation. They had been sure that they'd be through the mountains mentioned in the diary well before winter.

Kyle's mind was racing at that information. "If we were walking and carrying our gear, we might be in trouble, but what if we had horses?" he asked.

"That would be with horses," Cappy replied.

Maybe the old man was less than truthful, but the two friends had no way to counter what he was saying. Then the slim man suggested, "If we start now and find a valley to winter in, at least we would have some of the miles behind us come spring."

The old man reached into his possible bag and pulled out something and stuffed it into his cheek. Kyle watched the man and was no longer thinking about the trail west. He was thinking about tobacco.

Rene still thinking about what Kyle had proposed, asked, "Don't you agree that we could still make some miles before winter?"

"When you came into the valley, what did you see?" the man asked.

"The river and the village," the lanky man replied.

"And beyond the village?" the man pressed.

"Mountains?" Rene asked, uncertain of where the man was going.

"That's where they start," the old man said. "Any valleys and passes fill with snow."

The old man shook his head and left the teepee. The Shoshone woman remained on the other side of the teepee working on something. "He's kind of grumpy," Rene muttered.

"He is probably right," Kyle replied. "In the diary the writer talked of being stuck in the snow and having to eat their horses."

"But they left in September," the lanky man argued.

"In a couple weeks it will be

September," Kyle reminded him. "We have to make a deal to get horses and hunt to make jerky. We could easily lose a week or more."

"Well, I don't want to spend the winter with that cranky old man," Rene replied.

Laughing at his friend, the slim man said, "You just don't like him because he is making sense. We have to face it. We will be staying with the Shoshones for the winter. I say we go back and get the rest of our supplies."

Then Rene looked concerned. "What if they won't let us stay?"

"Chances are they will," Kyle replied. "I would recommend you don't argue with Cappy anymore. I think he's our ally with the Shoshones."

Having nowhere to go, the two men spread out their blankets and tried to go to sleep. Sometime later Cappy came back in and joined the older woman. The slim man spent some hours thinking about the next leg of their journey. Finally sleep came and for some reason he dreamt of the village in England.

The air was cool when the two friends emerged from the teepce. Cappy was sitting near the fire. He looked up and asked, "Have you decided when you're leaving?"

"If the Shoshone will have us, we would like to winter here," Kyle told him.

"Fair enough," the old man replied. "I

don't like a messy teepee, and I don't want the two of you making more work for Eve."

After agreeing to the rules, Rene then said, "We would like to go and retrieve our gear we left at the river."

"You going to use your travois, or did you want horses to do it?" Cappy asked.

"Horses would be nice," Kyle replied.

The old man arranged for the two friends to take two pack horses to get their gear. The pack saddle was a simple affair, with leather straps to tie the gear to a padded saddle. They were able to ride the animals to the river, which made the trip much faster.

The cached gear had already been visited by rodents, but other than a couple of holes chewed through, it was in good condition. Both were glad to get their buckskins back. They camped that night and roasted a rabbit Kyle had shot with the pistol.

Walking back toward the village, the two horses were lightly loaded, but the two friends didn't want to take advantage of the loan of horses and ride them with the gear. It was the last week of August by the time they forded the river near the village.

Cappy seemed happy to see them. Both men were wearing their buckskins. "You two look like a couple of mountain men," the old man told them.

The two friends had gotten back in time to join in a hunt the next day. They had a chance to watch some braves stalk a small herd of buffalo. From their vantage point on a low bluff, they watched the young men crawl close to the herd and then rise as one with bows drawn. The arrows flew true, bringing down two buffalo.

There was great excitement with the young braves. They danced and cried as they went around the downed animals. In the meantime several women from the tribe moved in to butcher the buffalo.

Cappy said, "They want two more. That will be our job."

Riding down from the bluff, they headed toward another herd about a half-mile away. They left the horses tied to some cottonwoods and continued on foot, using a wash to remain concealed.

"I'll save my powder today," Cappy told them. "You two can shoot."

There was always a degree of excitement when hunting such a large animal. They moved up the wash to within 150 yards. Then cocking their rifles, each chose a buffalo. Sighting on the animals, Kyle whispered, "Now."

Fire and smoke belched from both flintlock and seconds later two buffalo lay on the prairie grass. There were no cries of joy or dancing. The two men just walked to the downed animals while the remaining buffalo moved away.

The slim man stared at the buffalo and thought that there was a big difference between harvesting meat using a rifled flintlock and hunting a buffalo by crawling up close and bringing it down with a bow. He had a great respect for the young braves.

He watched as women came up to butcher the buffalo. "We are done here," Cappy told them. "You did a good job with them fancy rifles."

Kyle looked at the old man's Kentucky flintlock. "I believe yours is rifled also."

"Yep, it is," the man said, "but at my age, I don't like to waste powder."

One of the buffalo hides was given to Eve, and with the help of a younger woman they worked tanning it. By mid-September, the old man pointed at the white caps on the mountains. "It would be cold and rough traveling through them now."

Life was easy for the men in the village. They participated in some of the games with the braves, listened to stories around the fire, and hunted for meat to make it through the winter.

Some of the games were throwing a spear, short axe, and a knife. Kyle had spent many of his young years throwing at a board leaning against the stone cottage in England. He had not lost the ability and won some of those contests.

Shooting at targets was not done

because it would waste powder and lead. To keep their flintlocks in shape, the two friends would shoot once each evening. It had become kind of a contest, and they would choose a target about 100 yards away to fire at.

It wasn't long before they'd go to the edge of the village and look out on the prairie, where there would be something a little farther to shoot at. The young braves and few of the older ones would come to watch each day.

One evening there was a group of antelope coming for water at the river about 200 yards away. It was obvious that the young braves wanted them to try and knock a couple down.

Knowing the meat would be useful, Kyle looked at this friend. "Let's do it."

The two men took careful aim and fired as one. For just a moment nothing happened, and then the antelope were off at a full sprint, except for two which lagged and then went down. The young braves were off like a flash, wanting to pretend to count coup on one of the animals.

When Eve finished with the buffalo robe, she brought it over to the two friends. Behind her they heard Cappy say, "She worried about you getting cold come winter." The young woman who had helped her smiled broadly when the robe was presented.

Kyle noticed that she watched Rene

when he was anywhere within sight. The slim man kidded his friend that the girl liked him. The lanky man would blush and tell Kyle he was wrong.

The leaves changed color and fell, leaving the naked branches reaching out. Each day many of the women would go out with weaved baskets and collect things for food, decorations, or medicine.

One of the cloudy days threatened rain. Kyle had just finished cleaning and reloading the M1803. The women had just gone out, gathering whatever they could find. The slim man caught some movement out of the corner of his eye. From the trees came riders with intentions of hauling away some of the women.

The women screamed and dropped their baskets, running for the village. Kyle had the flintlock rifle up and took aim at the leader's horse and fired. The .54 caliber ball streaked across the 300 yards and struck the front shoulder of the attacker's animal dumping the rider.

It broke the attack as riders from the village rode hard after the intruders. With their plan foiled, the attackers turned and rode back towards the trees with the Shoshones in hot pursuit. The wounded horse had managed to get back onto its feet and stood with its head down near the brave who had been riding it.

Rene was still cleaning his Baker and said, "You shoot pretty fast, Kyle."

Feeling no remorse for the brave lying on the prairie grass, the slim man replied, "They were after the women."

It was nearly dark when the Shoshone who'd gone after the attackers returned to the village. The women had already gone out, killed the horse and butchered it. The brave was left were he'd fallen. When the braves returned, they did gruesome things to the dead man's body so he wouldn't be a danger in the afterlife.

Cappy sat near the fire when Kyle joined him. "You made some friends today. The chief's daughter was out there with the other women."

"I wasn't aware of that," the slim man said. "I couldn't let them get to the women."

"Would you like a chew?" the old man asked.

"I would," Kyle told him, tearing a chunk of the twist.

"I figured so," Cappy replied. "I always saw you watching when I'd take a chew."

The tension of the attack drained from the slim man's body as he laughed at the crusty old man.

Winter came without any more attacks. Rene finally admitted to Kyle that he liked the smiling young girl. He had found out her name was Nita, which meant strong. His lanky friend seemed to be disappearing more often. The slim man had a good idea where he'd gone and out of courtesy wouldn't go looking for him.

She moved into the teepee in January. The wedding had been a simple ceremony with Kyle standing with his friend. The newlyweds got the buffalo robe. Kyle slept in his own part of the teepee, declining the offer from Cappy to get him a woman.

The slim man began to wonder about the two friends' plan to follow Lewis and Clark's route to the Pacific Ocean. They used to talk about it every day, but now not so much. He worried that Rene had found happiness right here and would stay with the Shoshones. He didn't ask his friend about this. He just hoped it would come up before spring.

It did not and the snow was melting. The tribe was on lean times, with their food mostly gone. Kyle went out with some braves to hunt buffalo, elk, or anything that could be added to the pot.

Rene chose to stay in the village. His wife was making him some new buckskins. Cappy was riding the dun and Kyle was using a gray. They rode a couple hours away from the village before they spotted a herd of elk. They were grazing about 400 yards away.

"You think you can hit one at this

distance?" Cappy kidded him.

"That I could," Kyle replied, "but the meat would be spoiled before we could get to it."

Three of the braves got off their horses, and holding their bows, they started to stalk the elk. The two men watched the horses as the Shoshone worked their way closer. Suddenly, something spooked the elk, and they began to run towards them. Kyle could see wolves close behind the elk.

"If we stay still, the damn things will run right by us," Cappy told him. "They won't see us standing behind the horses."

The elk went by the braves, out of range of their bows but some of the wolves did not and arrows flew, bringing two of them down. The horses were getting nervous as the elk and remaining wolves got closer. The two men held the reins and spoke softly to the animals, trying to prevent them from taking flight.

The old man said, "We might have to chase down our stock, but you and I can bring two of the elk down."

Stepping out from the horses, the two men brought up their flintlocks and fired. The sound sent the wolves fleeing along with the horses. The wolves ran for the bluffs and again within range of the braves coming back with their first kills. The arrows flew, taking another wolf down.

The two elk that the men shot were lying on the grass. Cappy turned and whistled. The dun and gray stopped, looking back. The man whistled again, and the horses trotted toward them. The other Shoshone ponies were still running for the village.

Cappy handed the reins of his horse to one of the braves. "Go get the other horses."

The Shoshone was off as Kyle offered his to a brave who did the same. The old man watched them go and said, "the horses will stop in a couple miles. We best check on the elk that we shot."

It was nearly dark when the hunting party reached the village. There was great excitement at getting two elk, and along with that there were the wolves. "We'll be eating wolf tonight," Cappy told him.

The women wasted no time and started to gut the elk. Most everything would be used in one way or another. Rene came running to meet them. "You got some meat!" he shouted.

"Two elk and three wolves," Kyle told him.

"I was getting tired of soup made from roots," his friend replied.

"You could tell that to your wife if she spoke English," Kyle kidded him.

"If you took a minute to talk to her, you'd be surprised how much English she has learned," Rene proudly told him. "I've also learned some Shoshone."

The slim man had to admit that he had been avoiding his friend's wife. He was glad the two of them could communicate.

The three men sat around the fire that night. Rene seemed kind of thoughtful. Cappy had shared a chew with Kyle and the slim man was rolling it in his cheek and spat at the fire. Then out of the blue, his lanky friend said, "The snow should be melting in the mountains."

The old man piped up, "The passes should open in another month."

Kyle looked at Rene, his face serious. "Are you planning on leaving Nita and go?"

"I am not," Rene replied. "I am taking her with me. She is going to have my baby."

The slim man's jaw dropped. "Does she know that she is going? And what's this about a baby?"

The lanky man looked at his friend and said, "It is rather common that married folks have babies."

"And is she okay with going?" Kyle repeated.

Laughing at his confused friend, Rene told him, "We have already talked to her folks. They understand about me taking her. She is only two months along and the trip shouldn't be a hardship on her. Her father is giving us two horses."

"We'll have to wait until the baby is born to come back then," Kyle replied.

His friend just smiled and said, "Me a father."

CHAPTER SIXTEEN

Kyle had never seen a happier expectant father than Rene. It was difficult to get him to discuss the trip west. One night, sitting at the fire, Cappy came by and offered the slim man a chew. "You have been wandering around like you lost your best friend," he said.

"I believe I have," Kyle replied. "Rene and I always planned every step of this trip, and now I get the feeling he doesn't care when we see the Pacific Ocean."

"The newly married will do that," the old man said. "He has found himself a new best friend and it is hard for him to think about anything else."

The slim man found it hard to speak as he said, "I can't plan the trip alone. I need his ideas, and he's supposed to have my back."

Cappy spat at a bug crawling by. "I guess you forced me to make a big decision. I will guide you on the Lolo trail to the Columbia River."

"Have you talked to Eve about the trip?" Kyle asked.

"She won't go," the old man replied. "We ain't married or anything. We just like each other's company. I got needs and she likes to spend time with me."

The slim man must have had a confused look on his face, because Cappy suddenly added, "She has three brothers to take care of once I'm gone. They'll be happy to have the teepee back."

It turned out that not only was Cappy willing to guide, but he also owned three horses. The old man not having money for the past few years, was happy to sell a buckskin to Kyle.

Rene came by while the slim man was making a deal on the horse. "When do we leave?" he asked.

"I was beginning to wonder if you'd be going with me," Kyle told him.

"Not go?" his surprised friend replied. "You know I got your back."

It was the end of May when they left the Shoshone village. There were not long goodbyes that morning. Anything that had to be said was done the day before. The four of them just rode away toward Lemhi Pass.

The horses were saddled with pillow like pads filled with buffalo wool. They all had stirrups to make mounting easier. A single rein made of braided horse hair was tied to the lower jaw and the horses were controlled using this and pressure of the riders knees. Cappy's extra horse was used as a pack animal carrying supplies needed for the trip.

When they crested the continental divide at the pass and saw all the mountains to the west, Kyle was thankful that they hadn't attempted to cross them last fall. Some of the trek over the Bitterroot Mountains they were able to ride, but much of it they had to lead the horses. It took them two days to travel 12 miles to a valley that went north and south. They turned north, with the highest mountains to their west.

Kyle was surprised at how the trail had improved. It was as good as many that he had ridden on in the east. That night they camped at a place where many others had done so in the past. There was a fire pit and logs to sit on. Nita went right to work putting a meal together.

They had plenty of pungent tea with them to drink. Rene's wife began to dig up small tubers from the roots of a blue flower. These were washed and roasted. They had a sweet flavor, but she cautioned them about eating too many.

Another evening was spent near some hot springs. Everyone shed their clothes and bathed. Kyle found it awkward being naked with his friend's wife present. The four of them soaked in the soothing waters. Due to being pregnant, Nita didn't stay in too long, and the slim man averted his eyes as she climbed out.

Upon reaching the Lemhi River valley, Kyle was surprised to see that the Lemhi River flowed north. On the second day in the valley he saw the salmon. Kyle wasn't aware that they had come all the way from the Pacific Ocean, but what he did know was they were going to eat well.

Their hand lines were not needed to catch them. One could just stand in the shallows and scoop them up, tossing them onto the bank. They spent three days catching and drying fish for future meals.

Three days later they saw the bears! They were large, with golden-colored fur. "Grizzlies," Cappy said.

There were six large bears and a few cubs near a rapids, catching salmon. When they caught one, they'd sit on their haunches and tear the meat from the flapping fish. They stood for several minutes watching the cubs chase and splash in their attempts to catch one of the slippery fish.

The valley floor on their side narrowed at the rapids and Rene asked, "Should we go back a way and wait until they leave?"

"Won't do no good," Cappy said. "They stay here and eat for days. When one leaves others will come. We'll pass them on the other side."

The group went to the south about a mile and crossed the river. "Have your rifles ready," the old man said. "They should be too busy eating to bother us, but there might be a cranky one that thinks it has to protect the rapids."

Single file, they started north. Cappy led the group and Kyle took his place at the rear. Nita led the pack horse, riding behind her husband. In confidence, the old man had cautioned the slim man that the possibility of the horses being spooked by the bears was their biggest danger.

The horses began to snort as they got closer, not only seeing the grizzlies but also smelling them. The riders attempted to calm the horses. As they passed the bears, the horses suddenly broke into a run, jumping over windfalls and dodging boulders. It was all the riders could do to hang onto their flintlocks and stay seated on the animals.

Once well past the feeding grizzlies, they managed to pull the horses back to a walk. Kyle figured the danger was now behind them as they rode through the lush foliage. It was not. Each day they passed more bears. Neither the riders nor the horses ever got comfortable during the encounters.

After another 10 days of riding up the valley, Cappy stopped and swung off his horse. While the animal drank, he looked towards the west. "It is time to go back into the mountains."

They camped for two days to rest the stock. Cappy made a rough sketch in the dirt describing the route through the Lolo Pass and along a tributary that led to the Salmon River. While he did not tell them, he did this in case something should happen to him so they'd have an idea of the route west.

Breaking camp early on the third day they rode west. The party wound through the craggy peaks and valleys to the Lolo Pass. Beyond the pass the mountains weren't as severe as the first ones they'd crossed. They travelled along the Clearwater River. The valley it flowed through wasn't nearly as wide and lush as the Lemhi River. Where the river cut through the jagged rocks, they had to find a route around it.

Kyle couldn't help but think of the canoe they had abandoned and how much faster this part of the trip would have been. The slim man had to admit that the rushing waters coming down from the mountains would have been more of a challenge.

Bears were still an issue as they fed on the salmon swimming upstream. They gave the gold behemoths as much space as possible and the well-fed animals paid little attention to them.

Rene and Cappy began to complain of the diet of fish every night. Kyle had lived on fish from the channel for years in England and found it satisfying. What Nita thought about it the slim man did not know. She never complained about anything.

When the party reached the confluence of the Clearwater and Snake Rivers they found a village of the Nez Perce. Cappy warned Rene, "Don't let your wife speak. The Nez Perce don't get along with the Shoshone."

The warning wasn't necessary. Nita recognized the longtime enemy of the Shoshone, and she sat quietly while a white-haired old man spoke with them. Her dress and look could not be hidden, and when one of the Nez Perce chiefs asked about her, Cappy simply told them that they had captured her while she picked berries and thought she would be useful on the trip.

When the chief wanted to trade for her, Cappy laughed, shaking his head. "The man with her has gotten her with child and put a claim on her."

This did not seem to deter the chief. He even offered to trade one of his daughters to Rene for the pregnant woman. The negotiations were becoming somewhat strained when Kyle reached into his shooting bag and took out the watch Lisa had given him. Due to being in the wilds and having no church bellS to go by, the watch could no longer be set, but the hands still moved when it was wound, and its shiny cover was attractive.

In desperation the slim man held it up with its silver fob. "Offer him this for a horse," Kyle told Cappy, hoping to take the conversation away from trading Nita.

The sun shining off its silver case caught the chief's eye. Cappy told him, "This watch is strong medicine. It catches time as its hands move around its face."

The chief took it and held the timepiece. When he opened the front, he saw the hands and numbers on the face of the watch. He closed it again, held it up and the braves around him murmured in awe.

With the watch, some mirrors, and bells, a deal was made with the Nez Perce chief for one horse. Thanks to the salmon run they didn't lack supplies. The horse would be Kyle's. It was a tall sorrel about five years-old.

Before the group left the Nez Perce, the slim man got to display his shooting ability. A bull elk with felt-covered horns came into the valley south of the village. There was much talk among the braves of how to get close enough to the animal for a kill.

The flat river valley offered no cover, and the grass was too short for stalking. It was 300 yards from the camp. The elk's head came up as it sniffed the air nervously. "Ask the chief if he wants me to shoot the elk," Kyle told the old man.

Cappy looked at the slim man. "We've done alright here. Let's leave well enough alone and move on."

"Maybe they'll share some of the meat with us," Kyle replied.

Shaking his head, the old man turned to the chief and spoke briefly. The chief smiled and replied in Nez Perce to Cappy.

"He thinks you are being boastful and would like to see you shoot. If you miss, he might go after Nita again," the old man told him.

Suddenly, the slim man wished he'd left well enough alone. He looked down the valley and wished that the elk would decide to run south, making taking a shot impossible. It did not. The damn thing kept cropping grass, standing broadside to him.

Lying prone and balancing the M1803 with the forward arm, Kyle cocked the flintlock. He knew he'd done this many times before when hunting buffalo. The wind was calm in his favor.

As he squeezed the trigger, the rifle recoiled against his shoulder. Smoke and sparks burst out of the barrel, sending the .54 caliber ball across the valley floor. Kyle rose up to look and saw the bull elk begin to run across the valley, its head tilted to the left, and then it went down.

The slim man gasped, not realizing he had been holding his breath after the shot. There were cheers from the braves as several leaped onto their horses and rode towards the elk.

"Well done," Kyle heard Cappy say.

They left the Nez Perce the next morning after a supper of elk meat. The slim man had chosen pieces of the liver. The trail along the Snake River was well-worn but filled with narrow ridges and steep valleys to navigate.

The water beside them was ferocious, tumbling over rapids and small falls. Kyle couldn't believe that Lewis and Clark had traveled the Snake River by dugouts. There were stretches where the old man moved away from the river, following animal trails miles off from the winding river.

Ten days later they reached the Columbia River. Coming down the last stretch of the Snake River, the landscape had turned drier, almost arid. The tall forests had disappeared and were replaced by shrubs and grass. The only trees were along the waterways.

Kyle felt excitement run through his body. They were now getting close to their goal. It had been just over two months since they had left the Shoshone village, and they had successfully gotten over the mountains.

Camping at the confluence, Cappy said that the Nez Perce chief had told him that the North West Company had built a fort just south of them. "We should make it there sometime tomorrow," the old man said.

The fort meant that there would be a trading post and tobacco, which was music to Kyle's ears. That night Cappy talked of enjoying some whiskey. Nita told her husband she would like some ribbon and a comb. The moods of the camp were high as they ate the steelheads caught with handlines.

By midafternoon they reached the Walla Walla River and Fort Nez Perce, built by the NWC just a year before. It was established to purchase pelts from the Nez Perce, Walla Walla, and other tribes in the area. At this time, the number of British or American trappers were few. The hope was that having the trading post would draw more British trappers and settlers to the area, helping to claim this area for Britain.

The politics made little difference to the group. After months they could finally purchase scarce items. They found several Nez Perce teepees set up outside the fort and a Walla Walla village nearby.

Being stared at by all of the braves gave the group an uncomfortable feeling. Their looks at the arrivals were more curiosity than threatening. In the fort they met their first Kanakas, who came from Hawaii under contract to be boatmen, builders, or working with cattle or horses.

After buying some supplies from the fort, they set up camp near the Columbia River away from the teepees and the Walla Walla village. Cappy recommended they keep an eye on their horses and rifles. Two fly tarps were set up facing each other. Their fire was built on the fort side of the camp, leaving the river to protect them on the other.

The horses were picketed near the river on some sparse grass. It was decided that someone would stand watch throughout the night. All these requirements made enjoying the purchase from the fort difficult. Cappy had a couple of bottles of whiskey and tobacco. Kyle and Rene had also gotten a bottle and drank sparingly of it that evening.

Nita was thrilled with the ribbon she'd gotten and was working it into her hair. The slim man watched her and realized she was going to be a good wife for his friend. Much of Rene's time was taken up with her, but Kyle had accepted it and spent more time talking to Cappy.

Kyle took the first watch. Due to a couple of drinks after supper the slim man had to fight the urge to doze off. To fight it he brushed his sorrel and buckskin. Rene and Nita took the next watch. The plan was to have Cappy do so, but he'd had too many drinks to be ready to wake up.

The hung-over old man managed to take the final watch. He didn't make sleeping easy for the others with his cussing and stomping around the camp. It did help keep him awake and alert.

Rene and Nita visited with some of the Kanakas the next day. Working for the British had taught them enough English to have an enjoyable visit. The Kanakas talked of the ocean voyage from their island in the Pacific Ocean to work, and when their contracts were finished, they could stay in the northwest or go back to Hawaii.

The group stayed for three days which was about how long it took Cappy to finish his whiskey, then they continued to follow the Columbia River west. The trail was good and the horses were rested. They passed camps of various tribes as they traveled. They steered clear of them, having nothing to offer or trade.

Five days later, as they approached the Dalles, they camped near some braves who were constructing rafts for travelers to use going down the Columbia. Lewis and Clark had used dugouts and other boats to traverse the rivers they'd already passed and then did the same on the Columbia River. Cappy was familiar with the challenging rapids of the Columbia and sat quietly while Kyle and Rene discussed purchasing a raft or boats from local tribes.

Finally, he spoke. "You are talking about going down the Columbia River. Who is going to bring your horses?"

"The brave I was talking to said they would drive them over the mountain for us," Rene replied.

"If they can drive them over the Cascades, then we can do so," the old man said. "The Columbia from here on has dangerous rapids. I say we avoid them."

"Lewis and Clark took the Columbia River to the ocean," Kyle told him.

"If you want to experience what they did, I'll take the horses over the mountain," Cappy told them. "But remember, the expedition also took boats down the Snake River, and you saw those rapids. The mountain will be difficult but less dangerous."

Nita began to talk softly to Rene. Kyle stared at the river. The two of them turned to the old man and Nita said, "Go over the mountain."

They spent two nights at The Dalles and then started what would be up to a two-week trip around the north side of Mount Hood. There was an ancient trail used by the various tribes, which tended to fork off and then go nowhere. Due to the rugged terrain, most of the time they were leading their horses.

Rene worried about Nita, who was now

showing. The group had to rest more often for her or lead a horse with her riding. This was all done to her objections. The Shoshone woman felt she could keep up.

Barring the beautiful views that they had from the side of the mountain, the crossing was rigorous. They reached several places with plentiful grass and let the horses graze, and there was plenty of wood for their fires and cooking. Runoff from Mount Hood offered water. But seldom did they find a level spot big enough to set up camp.

It was almost three weeks before they reached the Willamette Valley. They were exhausted and bruised from the ordeal, so the group had to stop and heal for a few days. Two of the horses had gone lame from bruised hooves. Cappy looked them over and felt they would heal with the rest.

Other than knowing they weren't too far from their destination, they had no idea of how much longer it would take. It was early August according to the trading post in Fort Nez Perce. Kyle figured it would be near September by the time they saw Fort Clatsop.

They were able to shoot a deer near the camp, and Nita found the familiar blue camas flower and dug roots to add to their meal. There were majestic oak trees as far as Kyle could see and the valley floor was carpeted with thick grass for the horses.

After a good rest, they continued

following the Columbia River to the west. It was no longer the raging torrent that they'd seen near the Dalles. It spread out some, creating islands as it worked its way towards the Ocean.

An unexpected surprise was coming onto Fort Astoria on the south bank of the river. The brackish bay that it was built on opened to the Pacific Ocean. Kyle's heart raced as he learned that. For all purposes they had reached the Pacific Ocean.

The trading post was well-stocked, so the group took advantage of it and bought items they had originally avoided because of the distance in front of them. Now they found out that Fort Clatsop was only five miles south.

They learned that Fort Astoria, which was founded by the Pacific Fur Company, was named after John Jacob Astor. That made the fort American. It had been supplied by an American ship named *Tonquin.* There was another ship coming in soon bringing supplies, settlers, and equipment.

Rene and Nita spent time talking with people living at the fort. When they left, he told the slim man, "Passage will be available to Boston on the next ship."

It was the latter part of September when they reached the Pacific Ocean and the fort. Kyle knelt and splashed his face with the salty water. He could close his eyes and the sound of the waves and smell of the ocean brought him back to the channel. It seemed so long since he'd been there.

Fighting back the tears of joy, the slim man told his friend, "We made it. By God, we made it."

Rene and Nita walked into the water and let the waves wash over their legs. Rene was not a stranger to saltwater, but for his wife this was the first time. She thought of all the trips her people had made to gather salt from the licks. Here you could just dip it out with a bucket.

While seeing the Pacific Ocean had been Kyle's first goal, the second one had been to retrace the route taken by Lewis and Clark. Fort Clatsop marked the end of it and was a disappointment. The fort was in bad shape due to rotting timbers and the locals hauling others away.

Kyle walked around what was left of the rooms and tried to envision spending the winter with his men. He had pictured it being bigger, but it would have made no sense to build something bigger than they needed.

Notes toward the end of the handwritten diary talked of the crew hoping to find a ship near here to take them back by water. Kyle was unsure if that had been the writer's wish, or the expedition's leaders. Much had been learned on the trip back overland.

They set up camp on the shore not for from the crashing waves as the tide would come in and reflected on the journey they'd taken. The slim man had a chew and remained on the beach until the sun set beyond the horizon of the ocean. He ached inside as he felt the loss of his home land and the life he'd had in England.

Kyle knew they would have to stay on the coast until next spring. What few timbers that remained at the fort could be used to start a shelter for everyone to live in. From the diary he knew the winter would be raw, rainy, and long.

He was making a list of tools in his mind that they'd need to build a two-room cabin. Rene and his family could sleep in the back room and he and Cappy could sleep in the front room. Suddenly, he wondered if Cappy would be staying. He could help guide them back over the mountain. If not, the slim man was sure he could retrace the route.

He heard Rene walking behind him. "Are you going to spend all night on this beach?" his friend asked.

"Was it worth it?" Kyle asked his friend.

"I met Nita," Rene replied. "It was definitely worth it."

Then his friend said something that the slim man had not expected. "We won't be going back."

"You and I?" Kyle asked, wondering why.

"No. I'll be staying here with Nita," his friend told him. "If you want, you can go back by ship and if you get to New Orleans, you can have the shack."

Kyle almost asked, how about the canoe? But then he realized that it was a stupid question. The slim man heard his friend walk away from the beach. He was feeling pretty alone. His friend just told him it was time to go their separate ways.

In the dark, he asked himself: What would he be going back to? Everyone he knew back east had their own lives. Kyle heard footsteps behind him. This time it was Cappy. Sometimes it was hard to be alone with one's thoughts.

"Rene just told me that he and Nita are settling down around here," the old man told him.

"That's what I understand," the slim man replied. "Tomorrow, they have to get axes and stuff to build a cabin to winter in. Maybe come spring, after the baby is born, they will change their minds."

"A ship is coming if you wanted to go back east," the old man said.

"I can't think about that now," Kyle told him. "There is a cabin to build so the baby will have a home to be born in."

With renewed purpose, Kyle got up. "I

best get some sleep. I have work to do tomorrow."

* * *

The next morning Rene and Nita went to find a place to build the cabin while Kyle went to buy tools. The Olson family were running the trading post. Mr. Olson had all the tools Kyle would need. He suggested they hire a couple of Kanakas to help with the building.

When they all met at the camp that afternoon, Rene told his friend that they'd found a spot. It was near another family that had a farm. Kyle told him that the man at the trading post had suggested hiring some Kanakas and that they were experienced builders.

Cappy stuck around and helped with the building of the cabin. One of the Kanakas was good with stone and built an impressive fireplace. A sledge was used to haul the rocks.

The floor was packed dirt, with plans of making a plank floor in the future. Soon the cabin was finished enough to move in. Rene and Nita got along well with the neighbors and plans to work together on other projects had been discussed.

Kyle purchased a saddle and reins for his sorrel. The animal took to them without too much problem. The slim man enjoyed riding around the area after the day's work was finished. Most often he'd end up at the ocean and think of his life back in England. Rebecca was often part of this memory.

He still had the letters from her and Karen Green. While both had told him any life with them was over, he still felt a comfort knowing that they had put their hand to pen and paper to write him.

There was great excitement when the ship came in. The ten-mile trip to Fort Astoria was made and they had a chance to greet many of the newcomers. Some were from Boston, and one even knew of Christopher, his longtime friend.

The man said that Christopher was a big deal in Boston. There was talk of him getting into politics. Kyle walked away from the man, smiling. His friend had always had a way about him when it came to talking. He'd make a good politician.

Cappy came out of the trading post with a flour bag full of supplies. "Did you make arrangements for taking the ship back east?" the old man asked. "I saw you talking to the captain."

"I was just talking sea talk with him," Kyle replied. "The ship will be here for two weeks taking on furs and salted salmon, so I got plenty of time to decide."

"The cabin is done and I got my supplies," Cappy told him. "After a good drunk tonight, I'll be leaving."

"Are you going on the ship?" the slim man inquired.

The old man shook his head no. "They got some trees south of here that it would take six men hand-to-hand to reach around them," Cappy told him. "I am going south to see them. Then I might ride down to Yerba Buena and keep out of the winter weather."

The two men rode back to the cabin and found a housewarming party going on. There was even a man with a fiddle and some folks were dancing. Kyle saw his friend and went over. "What's happening here?"

"Word got out that the cabin was finished, and folks came out to welcome us home," Rene replied.

That night, enjoying the music, Cappy and Kyle drank whiskey. While not making a fool of himself, the slim man even danced some. The next morning glass windows for the cabin came, and despite the hangovers the two drinkers helped put them in.

"Now that the cabin is complete," Rene asked, "Have you decided if you're going east on the ship?"

Looking toward Cappy, Kyle replied, "I think I'd like to go see some big trees that it would take six men hand-to-hand to reach around."